Developing Churn Models Using Data Mining Techniques and Social Network Analysis

Goran Klepac
Raiffeisenbank Austria Zagreb, Croatia

Robert Kopal
University College for Law and Finance Effectus Zagreb, Croatia & University College for Applied Computer Engineering Algebra Zagreb, Croatia

Leo Mršić
University College for Law and Finance Effectus Zagreb, Croatia & University College for Applied Computer Engineering Algebra Zagreb, Croatia

T0320728

Information Science
REFERENCE
An Imprint of IGI Global

Managing Director:	Lindsay Johnston
Production Editor:	Jennifer Yoder
Development Editor:	Allison McGinniss
Acquisitions Editor:	Kayla Wolfe
Typesetter:	John Crodian
Cover Design:	Jason Mull

Published in the United States of America by
    Information Science Reference (an imprint of IGI Global)
    701 E. Chocolate Avenue
    Hershey PA 17033
    Tel: 717-533-8845
    Fax: 717-533-8661
    E-mail: cust@igi-global.com
    Web site: http://www.igi-global.com

Library of Congress Cataloging-in-Publication Data

Klepac, Goran, 1972- Developing churn models using data mining techniques and social network analysis / by Goran Klepac, Robert Kopal and Leo Mrsic.
    p. cm.
  Includes bibliographical references and index. ISBN 978-1-4666-6288-9 (hardcover) -- ISBN 978-1-4666-6289-6 (ebook) -- ISBN 978-1-4666-6291-9 (print & perpetual access) 1. Customer loyalty. 2. Consumer satisfaction. 3. Data mining. I. Kopal, Robert, 1964- II. Mrsic, Leo, 1973- III. Title.
  HF5415.525.K56 2015
  658.8'342--dc23
              2014017276

British Cataloguing in Publication Data
A Cataloguing in Publication record for this book is available from the British Library.

All work contributed to this book is new, previously-unpublished material. The views expressed in this book are those of the authors, but not necessarily of the publisher.

To our families, friends, and colleagues. To all researchers and students out there ready to accept new directions.

Table of Contents

Chapter 8

Chapter 9

Chapter 10

Chapter 11

Foreword by Gino Yu

In 2011, I was invited to give a talk in Ljubljana about my work related to under-standing the relationship between mind and body. It was my first trip to Croatia/Slovenia region and the innovation and start-up community that was emerging there surprised me. It was during that trip and at my talk that I met the authors of this book.

My talk centered on the new opportunities arising from the convergence between science and the humanities. How we process our past experiences has a direct impact on our worldview, how we interrelate, and the conscious decisions that we make. This book represents a commercial application of these ideas.

Interactive media and the Internet enable new methods for understanding human behavior. Understanding the target audience's behavior is essential to creating suc-cessful online services. By observing how users respond to media stimuli delivered through the Internet, the delivery of more effective, personalized experiences may become automated and dynamically optimized based upon specific metrics. There are tremendous implications for online services such as e-commerce, education, and relationship management as more of these services go digital and engagements are quantified and collected in real-time. The authors apply these techniques toward reducing churn and thereby improving effectiveness and customer retention.

This well researched book provides a theory-to-practice primer to this exciting new field written by three PhD researchers with strong commercial experience and expertise. I am both delighted and honored to be asked to write this foreward and wish the authors and you, the reader, every success in your endeavors. I would per-sonally recommend this book to all researches and practitioners, but also students dealing with market and especially churn management.

Gino Yu
PolyU, China

Gino Yu *received his BS and PhD at the University of California at Berkeley in 1987 and 1993 respectively. After receiving his PhD, he taught at the University of Southern California and worked to establish multimedia initiatives including the Integrated Media Systems Center. From 1995 to 1997, he taught at the Hong Kong University of Science and Technology where he helped to establish the Center for Enhanced Learning Technologies. In 1999, he established the Multimedia Innovation Centre (http://www.mic.polyu.edu.hk) at the Hong Kong Polytechnic University (PolyU), a leading edge think tank and research center on digital entertainment. He is currently an Associate Professor and Director of Digital Entertainment and Game Development in the School of Design at PolyU where he founded M-Lab (http://www.m-lab.hk), a commercial digital entertainment entity that provides consulting, research, instruction and new ideas for the industry. His main research interests involve the application of media technologies to cultivate creativity and promote enlightened consciousness. Gino Yu also founded the Hong Kong Digital Entertainment Association, and Asia Consciousness Festival. He also curates TEDxHongKong.*

Foreword by Sachit Murthy

In retail, a significant amount of effort and money is spent in attracting new customers to their stores. With the passage of time, these customers may stop buying from the retailer for various reasons. It is well known and established that the cost of acquiring new customers is far higher than the cost of retaining existing ones. Moreover, the lifetime value of existing customers is higher than that of new ones. It then becomes critical for retailers to know in advance which of those shoppers are likely to stop buying from their stores. This process of customers who stop engaging with the retailer is called "Churn." And knowing which customers are likely to churn is called "Churn Prediction."

In general, Churn Prediction is a data mining methodology used to predict if current customers or consumers are likely to stop engaging or transacting with the business entity that they have transacted with in the past. The churn model analyzes the purchase behavior and demographic profiles of customers and identifies trends that lead to churn. If the retailer is able to predict the customers who are likely to churn, the retailer may be able to prevent some of them from churning by reiterating or emphasizing the value proposition of the retailer's store and assortment to them and improve or increase the level of engagement.

The analysis allows retailers to detect changes in customers' spend patterns such as drop in basket value, or in trip frequency that may be precursors to future churn. To further improve accuracy, the churn model recognizes that each customer is unique and analyzes their behavior at an individual level and not as a group.

This book titled *Churn Modeling Using Data Mining Techniques and Social Network Analysis* written by the authors Klepac G., Kopal R. and Mršić L., provides a wonderful window into the world of churn modeling. I am sure the material put forth in the book will be enlightening to readers and encourage them to experiment with churn analysis in their own environments. I am deeply grateful to Dr. Mršić and IGI Global for giving me the opportunity to write the foreword for this book.

Sachit Murthy
Manthan Systems, India

Sachit Murthy *is a key player in the space of retail analytics having helped leading retailers across the world embrace and adopt analytics to solve critical business issues across areas like customer engagement, pricing, assortment, and store operations. Sachit is currently part of the leadership group at Manthan Systems, Bangalore, India, a leading provider of analytical solutions for the retail and consumer goods industries.*

Preface

Churn detection and mitigation in everyday business is always interesting, but it is also a very important topic for companies. Data mining as a discipline increases productivity and efficiency in churn detection and mitigation.

The existing literature is mainly concentrated on data mining techniques, and churn is mentioned as an accompanying topic, often as an illustration for specific method usage. Data mining books with case studies in churn detection are more detailed about churn, but they do not provide a systematic, holistic approach to churn where churn is the central topic of the book.

This book is a reference book for solving churn problematic with data mining techniques and SNA. The main aim of the book is the integration of data mining techniques with business requirements, taking into consideration market conditions, existing data sources, information extraction from existing data sources for knowledge extraction, and reducing uncertainty for making right decisions, churn monitoring, churn mitigation, and reduction. The book provides answers to how to plan churn projects regarding different industries, market conditions, disposable data, changes in market, and how to prepare data for building churn detection/mitigation models. The book also gives information on how to apply this knowledge for business decision purposes. The presented methodology is a synthesis of 20 years of experience in data mining and churn development models in different industries.

The systematic approach to churn problematic is the main characteristic of this book. It makes a step-by-step connection between business needs, data sources, data mining techniques, and decision making. Regarding all those facts, the target audience includes managers, business analysts, data mining analysts, practitioners, students, and in short, any audience that wants to understand churn problematic from a business perspective or from the perspective of how to solve specific churn situations with data mining methods or how to manage/struggle with churn in different industries.

Churn observation within the company should not be obvious, because in this situation, it is often too late to change negative trends. It should be always present as a part of the early warning system. This book is about to demolish several myths connected with data mining and churn modeling.

Contrary to the belief that churn modeling is mainly concentrated on using data mining models, this book gives proof that churn modeling is not only about data mining methods. Using data mining techniques in churn modeling covers 20% of the whole process. The remaining 80% includes aim definition, data extrapolation, derived variable construction, data sampling, attribute relevance analysis, hypothesis testing, choosing adequate analytical strategies, and many other activities that are the basis for data mining technique usage.

Another myth the book demolishes is the assurance that usage of one data mining method for churn-modeling purposes is enough. Churn modeling is like a building edifice with bricks. It implies using different data mining techniques by chaining it or using it parallel, depending on the current problem. There is no cookbook for churn solutions. It depends on industry, current situation in the market, the internal situation of the company, and many other factors. Most of the situations in this book are covered with proposed strategies and solutions, depending on enumerated factors.

Building predictive churn models is often synonymous with churn modeling, which is wrong. It is in line with the proverb, "If all you have is a hammer, everything looks like a nail." Predictive churn models are important and a common piece of churn solutions, but there are a variety of other approaches and methods that give insight into other churn aspects. Finding out who will probably churn in the next period is a valuable piece of information, but this information does not tell us anything about churner profiles (except maybe through attribute relevance analysis); it does not give us information about churner value for the company, preferences, or other important staff.

That information uncovered with predictive models is important for making churn mitigation and reduction. Strategies like discount prices for all clients with high churn probability are not a good idea because some of them are unprofitable for the company and some of them—even profitable—will not react to the discount because discounted prices could be offered for the items or services for which customers do not care. On the other hand, churn intensity related to the time variable could be important information, as well as its influence. It could be seasonal influence or it could also be caused by competitors' activities.

These facts show the complexity of churn projects where predictive churn models do not provide all-important information for making good churn reduction strategies.

Involving businesses in modeling stages is a must in churn modeling. Business people have information and experience, which is often neglected during modeling stages, which is not the right approach. They can help in the aim definition phase of churn modeling, derived variable construction phase, data sampling, model testing, and use test. No one data mining analyst or churn modeler could be a better expert in the industry for which it develops churn solution than experts who work in the industry and live with the problems every day. Even two companies that are in the same business, like retail, regarding company size, market conditions, and buyer structure, could be the benchmarks to each other regarding churn solution. The myth that a data mining analyst is sufficient for churn solution development will be demolished in this book.

With churn problematic as a central piece of the book, data mining methods, sampling, derived variable construction, prospective customer value calculation, and attribute relevance analyses are described from the perspective of churn reduction/detection/mitigation service.

It is a different approach in comparison to other books dedicated to data mining that put churn as an illustration for using data mining techniques.

CHAPTER DESCRIPTIONS

Divided into 11 chapters with a conclusion at the end, our journey starts with an introduction about churn. Using simple language to explain churn and the corresponding environment, the first chapter introduces the reader to the overall churn perspective, giving several samples through real world situations.

Once we know what churn analysis is, it is important to understand what really can or cannot be done. In addition, it is important to understand common errors analysts have to be aware of when planning and conducting churn analyses. It is advisable for the reader to move back to the introduction and Chapter 1 after finishing reading in order to once again understand the full potential and restrictions of the proposed methods and techniques.

The next chapter overviews data mining starting with an explanation of the data mining methods used the most. Data mining methods are explained together with recommendations of when and how to use them and how to iteratively combine different methods. The methods are explained briefly to understand their role in projects.

Social network analysis is intentionally covered in a separate chapter for two reasons. First, the importance of this method has rapidly increased in past few years, and second, there are very few useable studies that cover social network analysis concepts in churn management. By understanding the methods explained in Chapter 3 and combining them with knowledge of SNA concepts, the analysts (readers) can unlock the full potential of advanced analytics in one of the most important fields of research today, customer relationship and especially churn analysis.

The next chapter describes data preparation techniques for different churn models. The central topic is data sampling as preparation for building churn models, especially for predictive models. The chapter shows how to construct a data sample that will reflect business reality and show good performance regarding building predictive models. A significant part of the chapter is dedicated to construction of derived variables, which are a direct reflection of expert knowledge used within churn models. Beside data preparation for predictive models, the chapter also describes data preparation techniques for other methods usable for churn modeling like survival models, fuzzy expert systems, K-mean clustering, etc. The attribute relevance analysis chapter described different techniques for attribute importance detection usable in churn modeling. It gave descriptions with examples of how to make an attribute relevance analysis for predictive churn models in case of binomial target variables, as well in case of multinomial target variables. This chapter covers dummy variable construction and profiling techniques based on attribute relevance analysis, as well as logic checks from the perspective of business users.

After explaining how to prepare data, an introduction to structured analytic techniques is covered in this chapter. The importance of structured techniques comes from their simplicity and wide usage, making them fast to use and efficient to structure in even complex environments.

Structured problems need to be quantified by relevance, as covered in Chapter 7. By completing this chapter, the reader is ready to start with examples in the next chapters.

The next chapter explains churn model classification, describes techniques for developing predictive churn models, and describes how to build churn segmentation models, churn time-dependent models, and expert models for churn reduction. Analysts (readers) are shown a holistic picture for churn modeling and presented an analytical method with techniques described as elements that could be used for building a final churn solution depending on current business problems and expected outputs.

Once evaluate model is chosen, its power needs to be evaluated. Simple but efficient methods for evaluating predictive power are explained in Chapter 9.

The next chapter chapter is based on the fact that the finalization of the model building stage is the beginning of the periodic monitoring and redesigning stage. The churn solution should be adopted by market changes, internal company policy changes, portfolio structure changes, and other factors. The chapter gives answers about monitoring frequency and techniques with which the company could realize when to change into the existing churn solution. Another important topic covered in this chapter is "what if" analysis techniques, how to make scenarios for future churn trends regarding planned changes while taking in consideration the current state of the existing portfolio. The chapter ends with business strategy creation based on revealed knowledge from the churn solution and explains the importance of cooperation between business sectors and analysts in all stages of churn solution development from planning and realization to usage.

The case study chapter brings two business cases in the domain of churn, both unique in many ways, combining almost all the topics covered inside book.

The first business case presents a retail company facing new competitors and consequently preparing a customer-retention strategy. The case introduces the business environment in which the company was operating prior to the arrival of new competitors while the model is being devised for the purpose of preventing or at least buffering the churn trend as a reaction to the new competition. Development of an early warning indicator system based on data mining methods is also described as a support to the management in the early detection of both market opportunities and threats.

Second business case describes the situation in a telecommunication company called Veza in the domain of churn prediction and churn mitigation. The churn project was divided into a few stages. Due to a limited budget and cost optimization, the first stage concentrated on the prospective customer value calculation model based on fuzzy expert systems. This stage helps Veza to find the most valuable telecom subscribers. It also helped the company better understand subscriber portfolio structure. Developed fuzzy expert systems also helped Veza detect soft churn (subscriber did not cancel contract, but he decreased usage of services). Profiling and customer segmentation based on time series analysis was the next important part of the project, and it provided potential predictors for predictive churn models. The central stage concentrated on developing a traditional predictive churn model based on logistic regression. This model calculated the probability that the subscriber will make churn in the next few months. The final stage was dedicated to SNA (Social Network Analysis) model development. The SNA model find out the most valuable customers from the perspective of the existing subscriber network. In other words, this model gave us the answer to which subscribers have the greatest influence on other subscribers. If they leave Veza, they will motivate other subscribers to do the same thing. All three steps made a complete churn detection/mitigation solution that took into consideration past behavior of subscribers, their prospective value, and their strength of influence on other subscribers. This project on the one hand helped Veza to decrease its churn rate, and on the other hand, it gave directions for better understanding of customer needs and behavior, which were a basis for new product development.

Goran Klepac
Raiffeisenbank Austria Zagreb, Croatia

Robert Kopal
University College for Applied Computer Engineering Algebra Zagreb, Croatia
& University College for Law and Finance Effectus Zagreb, Croatia

Leo Mršić
University College for Applied Computer Engineering Algebra Zagreb, Croatia
& University College for Law and Finance Effectus Zagreb, Croatia

April 2014, City of Zagreb, Croatia, Europe

Introduction

The motivation for this book stems from fact that there is no complete reference book on the market which is focused on churn modeling as a discipline. Looking especially in the way of a detailed approach in which all aspects of churn modeling are covered, existing books with some references on churn modeling by using data mining methods, presents churn area only through illustrative examples of using data mining methods.

This book aims to be a reference book for all the aspects of churn predictive modeling using data mining techniques but also modern SNA concepts for different industry areas, from the project planning stage to the decision process aimed at churn reduction and mitigation.

The target audience for this book will vary from business practitioner, analyst, and manager, through marketing and IT students to wide area researchers interested in churn problems.

For managers, this book can be valuable source of information about the general nature of predictive churn modeling, how to set up churn projects right, what they can expect for the output from the models, and how this information can help them for making business decisions.

Analysts can find systematically described data preparation techniques, analytical techniques, different analytical strategies based on different industries, data sources, and types of problems as well as proposed holistic solutions for some specific problems in the domain of churn modeling for different industries, which can be used as a starting point for a similar type of problems.

IT students can find systematically described data preparation techniques, analytical techniques, different analytical strategies based on different industries, data sources, and types of problems as well as proposed analytical techniques and software tools for solving described problems.

For marketing students, this book can be a valuable source of information about deep understanding of churn nature, as well as an introduction to available analytical techniques, their outputs, and usage of their outputs for different churn mitigation and reduction strategies for portfolio management.

Researchers will find a complete reference book covering all aspects of churn management that can be used as a guideline in their work or as reference to expand their views.

We as authors look forward for a wide audience, and we will be grateful for feedback which will help us in our future works.

Goran Klepac
Raiffeisenbank Austria Zagreb, Croatia

Robert Kopal
University College for Applied Computer Engineering Algebra Zagreb, Croatia
& University College for Law and Finance Effectus Zagreb, Croatia

Leo Mršić
University College for Applied Computer Engineering Algebra Zagreb, Croatia
& University College for Law and Finance Effectus Zagreb, Croatia

Chapter 1
Churn Problem in Everyday Business

ABSTRACT

This chapter is an introduction into customer relationship management, explaining the modern business environment and techniques to monitor it. As part of that process, churn management is introduced and explained across industries. Throughout the chapter, a wider churn perspective is explained together with several examples from real cases. As the chapter comes to its end, the business approach become more and more involved, and the reader starts to realize the importance of churn management and its complexity. At the same time, the idea of techniques and methodologies as to how it can be managed start to shape key book points.

1.1 INTRODUCTION

While looking for more effective and profitable business, can we afford to lose some customers from time to time? Is it possible to create service (or product) that will be perfect match for every customer? Even to lose some customers over time period in highly competitive environment? Customer churn, also known as customer attrition, customer turnover, or customer defection is a business term used to describe loss of clients or customers. Usually for a business, churn is bad news although it can be good news as well, under specific circumstances. In this book we will focus on techniques used to understand, analyze and manage churn. Although mostly recognizable as negative in terms of business impact, this book will explain many useable

DOI: 10.4018/978-1-4666-6288-9.ch001

and efficient ways how to manage churn and, in best case scenarios, turn it through deep understanding and quality management into additional value for company.

Many businesses with large customer bases, particularly subscriber-based businesses (like telecommunication companies, cable television companies but also banks and retail companies) monitor and manage their churn numbers very closely. The metric tracked is typically known as the „churn rate" and is expressed as a percentage. Basic calculation to express churn rate is relatively straightforward: number of customers that defected divided total number of customers (Ants Analytics, 2013).

Customer attrition is an important issue for any company, and it is especially important in mature industries where the initial period of exponential growth has been left behind. Churn (or retention, if we look at it from the other side) is a one of the most important application of data mining. Industry uses term churn for example, in telephone industry to refer to all types of customer attrition whether voluntary or involuntary. Churn is a useful word because it is one syllable and easily used as both a noun and a verb (Berry & Linoff, 2004).

For introduction example, let us follow telco[1] companies. Telecommunication industry is volatile and rapidly growing, in terms of the market dynamicity and competition. To be aligned with modern market and life needs, it creates new technologies and products on regular basis, which open a series of options and offers to customers. However, one crucial problem that commercial companies in general and telecommunication companies in specific suffer from is a loss of valuable customers. To predict that kind of changes, companies are investing into predictive and advanced analytics models like ones called customer-churn prediction models or widely applicable loyalty analysis models. Researches so far shows that customer who leaves a carrier in favor of competitor costs a carrier more than if they gained a new customer. It is similar in many industries. Therefore, customer-churn prediction can be marked as one of the most important problems that (telecom or other) companies face in general. To be able to manage this problem company needs to understand the behavior of customers, classify performance indicators and look for churn and non-churn customers so that the necessary decisions can be made before churn happens or while it is happening. In more words, the goal is to build up an adaptive and dynamic data-mining model in order to efficiently understand customer behavior and allow time to make the right decisions. By understanding complex environment in structured way company can be more efficient comparing to traditional available techniques, which are generally more expensive and time consuming. As will be shown, advanced analytic methods provide space for different approaches using different methods like Bayesian networks, association rules, decision trees and neural networks (Rashid, 2010) (see Figure 1).

Figure 1. Dimensions of loyalty (Kumar, 2005)

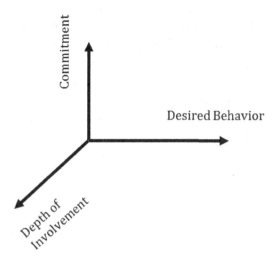

At the same time company needs to identify and recognize, follow, understand and manage their most loyal followers. Most loyal, from the company perspective, can be also known as most valuable. Questions which pop-up:

- If company is rewarding its loyal customers, where it earns value to be able to reward?
- Are loyal customers and most valuable customers, same group?
- Does loyal customers and most valuable customers deserve same treatment if different one from each other?

We can better explain loyalty through three dimensions: level of customer commitment, depth of customer involvement and desired customer behavior. By analyzing those dimensions we can create customer base overview and forecast expectations for future.

All kind of additional benefits, membership cards for specific offers, all kind of social networking activities provide special feeling of acceptance, "members" belong and feel like part of special group. In new researches term "loyalty" is more and more substituted with term "affiliation" or "identity". Secret message is more than commitment, it says: "you belong here". To be able to efficiently manage this "belonging" situation we need to be very careful between new and old customers both in terms of cost, value and satisfaction. What is probability that customer attracted with some special benefit will have "strength" or potential to become "loyal"?

Shall that customer returns to our product/service over time or we lost current ones because of over aggressive campaign for acquiring new customers? Although modern concepts of group coupons are in raising trend of popularity, their success is generally on short term basis. With exception of service oriented businesses like hotels od travelling packages, many of acquired customers who went for special discounts are looking for same and better deals in future and are not likely to look for premium packages in future (idea is to attract new customers with special deal since they otherwise won't be looking for similar service) (Noize, 2015).

Although this book is not about loyalty programs we can't skip behavioral economy issues. Just to complete problem overview for introductory part, elementary guidelines for customer management will be noted as follows (Cooper, 2011). Efficient customer management should:

- Provide long term positive feeling about service and customer care,
- Manage proactive relationship with client,
- Constantly reward value/loyalty,
- Deeply understand customer needs,
- Look for feedback from customer on quality of product/service,
- Keep relationship personal as much as customer allows,
- Provide continuity in quality of relationship (let 50th customer visit be same exciting as first one),
- Provide permanent education of company's employees,
- Deeply understand competition,
- Be able to surprise client with something completely new from time to time.

Due to intensive competition, complex and saturated markets, companies in all industries realize that their existing client database is their most valuable asset. Also, it is widely known fact that "if you want to be effective in any industry you need to know more about (at least) three main competitors than you know about yourself". After acquiring, retaining existing clients is the best marketing strategy to survive in industry. Lots of studies showed that it is more profitable to keep and satisfy existing clients than to constantly attract new ones. However, to be efficient, company has to find way to balance between these two activities. Churn management, as the general concept of identifying those clients most prone to switching to another company, led to development of variety of techniques and models for churn prediction. Efficient models has to concentrate on the highest possible accuracy, robustness and low implementation costs, as every delay in understanding and reaction means increased costs for the company (Popović, Bašić, 2009).

As conclusion, we can express as common knowledge within companies that their most valuable assets are their customers, especially existing ones. As markets have become increasingly saturated, companies have attempted to identify ways in which to improve customer loyalty, satisfaction, and retention. The marketing approach within many organizations has gradually evolved from product-centric to customer-centric. This approach is supported by modern database technologies, which enable companies to obtain the knowledge of who their customers are, what they have purchased, when they purchased it and predict their behavior of estimate their "next step" in advance. An environment has emerged where customers are offered a huge choice of service providers to choose from, making acquiring new customers difficult, costly and very complex. Traditional methods of predicting customer churn mostly use predictive analysis. Several studies are available today provided by major CRM software vendors which are covering this field looking for way to find most effective analysis model. We can define predictive analytics as the process of identifying trends in data using mathematical algorithms. However, churn management incorporates a lot of imprecision, due to the fact that an organization will never know for certain if a customer is considering moving to a competitor until it is too late. The best a company can expect is a formulated prediction, based on a customer's behavior. Another field, known as soft computing, explores this in detail and is dealing with this ambiguity because its aim is to utilize the tolerance for imprecision, uncertainty, approximate reasoning and partial truth in order to achieve tractability, robustness and low cost solutions. Although most research was focused on using demographical data for the purpose of churn prediction, modern approaches are following contract detail rather than only on a customer. Moreover, we can conclude that for every project researchers have to investigate and create different approach. Best variables has to be identified and neural networks, classification trees, regression and other methods has to be combined and compared for their suitability for churn prediction using certain type of data.

Figure 2. Starting with basic churn groups

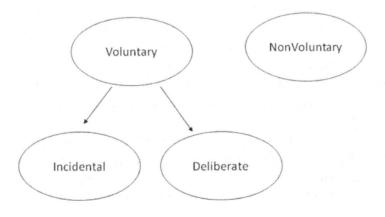

Churning customers can be divided into two main groups, voluntary and non-voluntary churners. Non-voluntary churners are the easiest to identify, as these are the customers who have had their service withdrawn by the company. There are several reasons why a company could revoke a customer's service, most often abuse of service and non-payment of service. Voluntary churn is more difficult to determine, because this type of churn occurs when a customer makes a conscious decision to terminate his service with the provider. Voluntary churn can be sub-divided into two main categories, incidental churn and deliberate churn. Incidental churn happens when changes in circumstances prevent the customer from further requiring the provided service. Examples of incidental churn include changes in the customer's financial circumstances, so that the customer can no longer afford the service, or a move to a different geographical location where the company's service is unavailable. Incidental churn usually only explains a small percentage of a company's voluntary churn.

Deliberate churn is the problems that most churn management solutions try to battle. This type of churn occurs when a customer decides to move his/her custom to a competing company. Reasons that could lead to a customer's deliberate churn include technology-based reasons, when a customer discovers that a competitor is offering the latest products, while their existing supplier cannot provide them same product/service. Economic reasons include finding the product at a better price from a competing company. Examples of other reasons for deliberate churn include quality factors such as poor coverage (in telecom), bad service (in banks or retail) or possibly bad experiences with call centers etc. Companies have realized that they need to understand the needs of their customers in order to be able to respond in quality way. Intense competition is forcing organizations to develop novel marketing strategies to capture customer needs, and improve customer satisfaction and retention. Selling more to everyone is no longer a profitable sales strategy and a market place that continually grows more competitive requires an approach that focuses on the most efficient use of sales resources. Much work has been done in the area of CRM and predicting customer behavior, although it appears that to-date customer churn management has not received the attention that it requires (Hadden et al, 2006). Why is that so? General problem is that company has to follow two approaches at the same time: strategic (top-down) and operational or customer-centric (bottom-up). If, because of competitive advantage, company focus only on its strategic level (most common "we are the best and no one can deliver in similar way") things could change on customer level very fast and dramatically change overall company market position (like for example today's telecom operating systems competitive battle between Nokia, Google, Microsoft and Apple). By changing market paradigm, companies with different approach can be very successful in changing market environment in their favor while "old" ones cannot adopt in available time frame.

1.2 WHAT IS CHURN AND HOW TO RECOGNIZE IT?

Modern market especially after late 2000's crisis mostly changed from growing (or even rapidly growing) into a state of saturation and hard competitiveness. That shift moved company focus from expansion to large customer base into keeping customers in the company. For that reason it is very important to analyze customer behavior, to be able to understand customer preferences and to be able to proactive react on significant influences which can lead towards customer change to a competitor in (near) future. Customers with intention to change to a competitor are called churned customers while phrase churn is based on English verb meaning "to agitate or produce violent motion".

One of the first challenges in modeling churn is deciding what it is and recognizing when it has occurred (Berry, Linhoff, 2004). It is followed with who did it, why it happens and how it happens. How hard it is to manage this depends from industry to industry. This is harder in some industries than in others. At one side are businesses that deal with anonymous transactions like textile retailers. At the other side are businesses that deal with strong commitment to relationship often including customer value factor like banks. When a once loyal customer deserts his regular provider for another, someone who knew habits of exact customer may notice something is changed but that fact will not be recorded in any database. Even in cases where the customer is identified by name, it may be hard to tell the difference between a customer who has churned and one who just hasn't been around for a while. If a loyal laptop brand customer who buys a new model every 5 years hasn't bought one for 6 years, can we conclude that he has defected to another brand? Or, if someone close its banking account can that be 100% sign for churn?

Churn is a bit easier to spot when there is a monthly billing relationship, like with credit cards in banking or service in telecommunication industry. Even there, however, attrition might be silent. A customer may reduce usage of credit card, but

Figure 3. Churn analysis breakdown

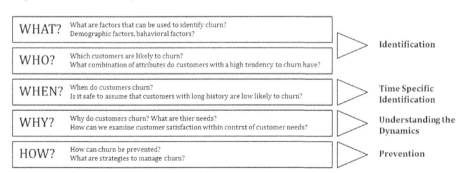

doesn't actually cancel it. Churn is easiest to define in subscription-based businesses, and partly for that reason, churn modeling is most popular in these businesses. Long-distance companies, mobile phone service providers, insurance companies, cable companies, financial services companies, internet service providers, newspapers, magazines, and some retailers all share a subscription model where customers have a formal, contractual relationship which must be explicitly ended (Berry, Linhoff, 2004).

With intention to measure and analyze churn factors, measure called churn rate was introduced and it is widely used in modeling marketing projects or any sub-scriber-based service model like mobile telephone networks or pay TV operators. Churn rate (sometimes called attrition rate), in its broadest sense represents a mea-sure of the number of individuals or items moving out of a collective over a spe-cific period of time. The term is also used to refer to participant turnover in peer-to-peer networks but is more known as important input into customer lifetime value modeling.

Raising demand for understanding and predicting complex market environment invoke several measures to determine and manage value of customers over time. Most common measures are cost of customer acquisition (COCA), customer lifetime value (CLV) and customer equity (CE).

While COCA and CLV combines acquisition costs and past behavior to determine customer value, CE if focused on future revenue measuring value equity (value of

Figure 4. Summary of core CRM processes (Filip, 2012)

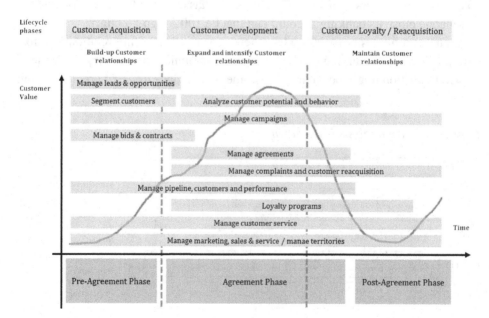

product or service used by customer and provided by the company), brand equity (how it improves brand value) and retention equity (tendency of customer to stick to brand).

Churn analysis is traditionally relevant subject in data mining and has been applied in field of banking, mobile telecommunication, insurance etc. Generally all companies who are dealing with long term customers can take advantage of churn models. Models like neural networks, logistic regression, decision trees are common methodologies in analyzing churn prediction problem with goal to distinguish churners from non-churners. With every new offer to customers or with every new customer offered, model attempts to predict customer classes and to predict behavior change (positive or negative) in order to manage it. Depending on way you look at the target group, model can be focused on individual customer, group or class of customers but also can indentify peers and peer-to-peer network for analysis.

Churn is usually distinguished as voluntary and involuntary. Clearly, voluntary churn refers to churn due to the customer's choice while involuntary churn concerns customers whose relationship is cancelled by a company (due to payment delay or fraud). Involuntary churn can also be possible if customer does not have any activity for long period of time. While analyzing churn most important thing is to be able to determine environment and target groups in best possible way and with clear

Figure 5. Customer lifecycle (Retention Science, n.d.)

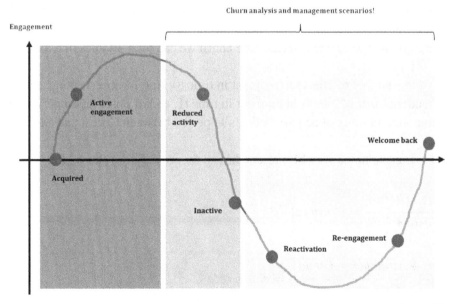

Figure 6. Customer value over time

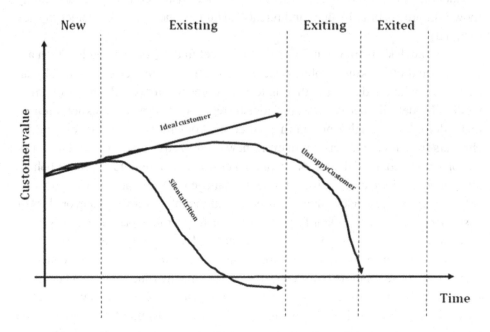

definitions in order to have base for comparison and results tracking (for example problem of analyzing pre-paid customer churn in telecommunications since customer data is limited). Past researches show that, for example in telecommunication industry, even loyalty club members and heavy users are like to churn (Ahn et al, 2006).

For simple way to define and calculate churn we can use variables like follows:

- Ctstart; number of clients in moment in time t0, start of observation period
- Ctend; number of clients in moment in time t1, end of observation period
- Anumber; number of acquired clients in period between Ctstart and Ctend

Following explained variables researches so far are defining churn like:

$$\frac{\left(Ctstart + Ctend\right)}{Ctstart} = churn\,rate \tag{1}$$

$$\frac{\left(Ctstart + Anumber - Ctend\right)}{Ctstart} = churn\,rate \tag{2}$$

Figure 7. Conceptual model for customer churn

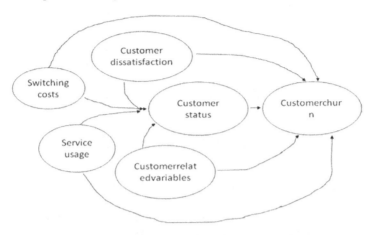

As we can realize looking at the equitation, churn can be calculated in many ways. Formula (1) is commonly used in direct reporting while formula (2) can commonly be found in date warehouse built for specific purpose.

By analyzing different approaches, we can generally conclude that every customer will someday terminate its relationship, question is only when will he do that. To explain this in more words, in 200 years from now we can agree that 100% of current customers will churn at rate of 100% (all of them). If we know today specific target group of customers today have 20% churn probability rate this month, we can estimate that in 5 months from now they will all terminate their relationships. During that period we have to be aware of their behavior and we need to create activity plan including motivating current but also new customers who can substitute current ones. However, our primary goal is to extend or maximize relationship duration and increase customer lifetime value.

Efficient churn analysis project should have churn reduction and/or churn prevention policies as one of the most important outcomes. As we can realize, there are many ways to improve our perception and understanding of behavior of our customers. Therefore there are many ways how we can (re)activate current or attract new ones. This book will help you to find (at least) one of those ways.

To explain term "churn" in more details we can use simple visual analysis: "churn" is a word derived from "change" and "turn". It means the discontinuation (of a contract/service). We can generally classify three types of churn however with some additions to those basic types.

First, active or deliberate or voluntary churn when customer decides to quit his contract and to switch to another provider. Reasons for this may include: dissatisfac-

Figure 8. Different types of churn

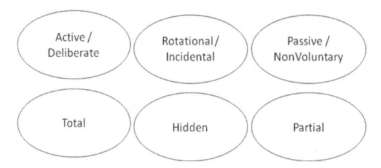

tion with the quality of service (like not fulfilling service level agreements), too high costs, not competitive price plans, no rewards for customer loyalty, no understanding of the service scheme, bad support, no information about reasons and predicted resolution time for service problems, no continuity or fault resolution, privacy concerns, etc.

Second, rotational or incidental churn when customer quits contract without the aim of switching to a competitor. Reasons for this are changes in the circumstances that prevent the customer from further requiring the service, like financial problems, leading to impossibility of payment; or change of the geographical location of the customer to a place where the company is not present or the service is unavailable.

Third, passive or non-voluntary churn when the company discontinues the contract itself.

Voluntary churn (active, rotational) is hard to predict. And while incidental churn only explains a small fraction of overall churn it is particularly interesting to predict and react taking appropriate action to prevent deliberate churn. In order to prevent customers' voluntary contract discontinuation, however, the company needs to know and identify possible churners with low probability of error in the prediction and why this specific customer has decided to leave the company for the benefit of a competitor.

Furthermore, churning can be divided also in three other groups: total (the agreement is officially cancelled), hidden (the contract is not cancelled, but the customer is not actively using the service since a long period of time) and partial (the agreement is not cancelled, but the customer is not using the services to a full extent and is using only parts of it, and is instead using constantly a service of a competitor).

Depending on the company, the contract type and the business model that is being applied hidden or partial churning can lead to considerable money loss (like in telecommunications: the customer only pays the monthly subscription fee, but does not place a single call) and also needs to be identified and action should be

Figure 9. Segmentation and predictive modeling (Tsiptsis & Chorianopoulos, 2010)

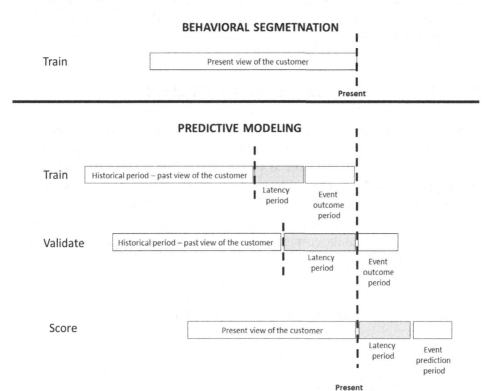

taken in order not to lose completely the customer. Moreover, it is important to classify which of the possible churners are of further interest for the company, like which customers are likely to generate more profit (these are typically customers who generated substantial revenues and then found a better offer with a good loyalty program at a competitor), and which customers are not interesting, because, for instance, they are identified as risky. Then the company marketing department can consider direct marketing strategies in order to retain important customers. Although churn in general is an unavoidable phenomenon, it can be managed and the potential losses to the business can be minimized. The timely detection of possible churners, together with effective retention reports support this goal (Lazarov, Capota, 2010)

As will be described in more detail in next chapters, simple churn analysis process explanation include data training as part of behavioral segmentation and data training, validation and scoring process as part of predictive modeling. Structured that way, we can easily understand basic idea. Analyze past and find attractive segments, move further with deeper analysis of defined segments, create scenarios, validate data sample and scenarios and we are ready for "real action" – predictive model execution. As shown, process is multi layered and iterative so ability to have overall perspective and ability to fast adopt scenario are crucial for final success.

1.3 SOFT CHURN, SILENT BUSINESS KILLER

Managing customer churn is one of the great concerns of modern market especially in telecommunications and insurance but also banking and retail. The annual churn rates are increasing for highly 20% to 40% in middle 2000's (Berson, 1999) (Kim, 2004) (Madden, 1999). Customer churn adversely affects these companies because they are risking great deal of price, profit levels and possible loss or referrals from continuing service customers. Furthermore, the cost of acquiring a new customer can substantially exceed the cost of retaining an existing customer (Silber, 1997).

Modern approach follows customer through lifecycle creating value called customer experience (CE or CX) as more appropriate measure for today's environment. By managing customer experience companies should turn themselves into position of customer with focus on questions like (Peppers, Rogers, 2008):

- What's it really like to be our customer?
- What is the day-in, day-out "customer experience" our company is delivering?
- How does it feel to wait on hold on the phone?
- To open a package and not be certain how to follow the poorly translated instructions?
- To stand in line, be charged a fee, wait for a service call that was promised two hours ago, come back to an online shopping cart that's no longer there an hour later?
- What's it like to be remembered?
- What's it like to receive helpful suggestions?
- What's it like to get everything exactly as it was promised?
- What's it like to be confident that the answers you get are the best ones for you?

Using those questions we can define customer experience like customer journey which makes the customer feel happy, satisfied, justified, with a sense of being respected, served and cared, according to its expectation or standard, start from first contact and through the whole relationship with company products and/or service.

By managing customer experience (often called Customer Experience Management or CEM) company should value its ability to understand, define, predict, execute, control and manage, to go beyond and influence environment creating new

Table 1. Lifetime value of triple play customer, example (Pitney Bowes Business Insight, 2011)

LTC Calculator	Year 1 value	Explanation
Customers	500,000	Total customers on file (within segment)
Churn rate	12%	Annual Churn of Customers
Retention rate	88%	(1.00 – Churn rate)
ARPU	$ 141	Total Annual Revenue per Customer
Total Revenue	$ 846,000,000	Total Customers * ARPU
Costs		
CPGA	$ 600,000,000	Total Customers * CPGA
Landline CCPU	$ 156,000,000	Total Customers * Landline CCPU
Broadband CCPU	$ 120,000,000	Total Customers * Broadband CCPU
TV CCPU	$ 210,000,000	Total Customers * TV CCPU
Marketing Expenditure	$ 5,000,000	Total Expenditure on Marketing
Total Cost	$ 1,091,550,000	Summary (All Expenses)
Gross Profit	($ 245,550,000)	Total Revenue – Total Cost
Discount Rate	1.00	In Year 1, this is always 1.00 as it is the present value
Net Present Value Profit	($ 245,550,000)	Gross Profit / NPV
Cumulative NPV Profit	($ 245,550,000)	Cumulative NPV
Lifetime Value	($ 122.78)	Cumulative Gross Profit / Total Customers

standards. Customer experience management should be executed cross-channel (contact center, Internet, self-service, mobile devices, brick and mortar stores), cross-touch point (phone, chat, email, web, in-person) and cross-lifecycle (ordering, fulfillment, billing, support etc.) affecting nature of the customer experience process.

Every successful business relationship with clients is similar one to another however every churn has it own way why it ends without success. Managing modern global market environment sometimes is very hard to acquire new clients to use our product or to follow or brand having so many products and brands available. To achieve targeted goals companies mostly execute intense campaigns which, beside regular campaign costs, include product or service price decrease (in order to be more competitive) and quality improvement (again, in order to be more recognizable in competitive market). Once when we reach targeted sales plan, when we justified our campaign costs, we start a new battle, battle to keep our customers satisfied and loyal. There are multiple reasons for customer churn like successful campaign made by competitor who is aggressively fighting for market growth or churn caused by product or service dissatisfaction. High initial costs for new product development

Table 2. Full three year LTV calculation, example (Pitney Bowes Business Insight, 2011)

Lifetime Value Framework		Acquisition Year 1	Year 2	Year 3
Customers		500,000	440,000	387,200
Churn Rate		1.0%	0.98%	0.95%
Retention Rate		88%	88%	89%
ARPU		$ 141	$ 151	$ 161
Revenue		$ 846,000,000	$ 797,000,000	$ 748,070,400
CPGA	$ 1,200	$ 600,000,000		
Landline CCPU	$ 26.00	$ 156,000,000	$ 137,280,000	$ 120,806,400
Broadband CCPU	$ 20.00	$ 120,000,000	$ 105,600,000	$ 92,928,000
TV CCPU	$ 35.00	$ 210,000,000	$ 184,800,000	$ 162,624,000
Database Marketing	$ 1.10	$ 550,000	$ 484,000	$ 425,920
Total Marketing	$ 10.00	$ 5,000,000	$ 4,400,000	$ 3,872,000
Total Cost		$ 1,091,550,000	$ 432,564,000	$ 380,656,320
Gross Profit		($ 245,550,000)	$ 364,716,000	$ 367,414,080
Discount Rate		1.00	1.16	1.35
Net present Value		($ 245,550,000)	$ 314,410,345	$ 272,158,578
Cumulative NPV		($ 245,550,000)	$ 68,860.345	$ 341,018,923
Lifetime Value		($ 122.78)	$ 34.43	$ 170.51

together with campaign costs companies treat as investment into market share increase. Success in that way can be measured as time through specific customer is using product or service because during that time company does not need to invest into new product development and is taking advantage of its market position.

Let us imagine hypothetic company dealing with spare parts for automotive industry. Company core business is to sell products to B2B segment. With large numbers of business partners, company's relationship is long term and stable. In past 6 months they achieved 10% more new customers while 0.03% of customers cancelled relationships. Those facts without doubt indicates successful business while mentioned 0.03% are in most cases uninteresting for any further analysis because of their small impact to overall business result especially since company have very large customer base. Is this assumption always the right one?

Awareness of business environment is very often crucial to determine important from fad or to understand what is really happening. Therefore we have to introduce term known as soft churn. While hard churn represent relationship termination without any doubts, soft churn can be explained like latency period in which customer is not active but he also did not determine itself like churned.

Soft churn has to be analyzed separately from hard churn. Very careful segmentation and behavior analysis is needed in preparation phase for soft churn analysis. At the same time, activities which will take place have to be defined, executed tracked and adjusted very precise in time with constant focus on outcomes. Sometimes our customers can have a bad day while at the same time they can be teased from our competitors or they can simply wait to be contacted from our customer service to regain its confidence. How it will be explained later in text, for simple model we can define three groups of key indicators: profitability, loyalty and future perspective. While all three groups should be combined in order to have efficient analysis and customer score, soft churn analysis is mostly linked to loyalty. Once we re-activate our customer we can use used knowledge for future similar customer re-activation while activated customer became part of overall sample.

One raising trend needs to be pointed out here, strong raising trend of M2M connections especially in mature markets like Europe. M2M stands for "machine 2 machine" connection or relationship and is used to describe different products which can use mobile communication like bikes, pacemakers or cars. Forecast expects that many objects that we use will communicate in future for many purposes: tracking (pets, family), fun (cars, bikes) or business (remote access to data) etc. This kind of relationship includes strong commitment and value factor and with strong raising trend pretends to be very important for every service and product provider in (near) future.

M2M communication market in 2011 was worth \$44.0 billion, and is expected to grow \$290.0 billion by 2017. It is expected to have an increasing CAGR of 30.1% from 2012 to 2017. Europe, APAC, and North America regions are emerging market, whereas in Latin America and Middle East & Africa regions considered a high growth in the markets. In 2011, Europe accounted for about 30.0% of the global

Figure 10. Churn analysis scenario sample

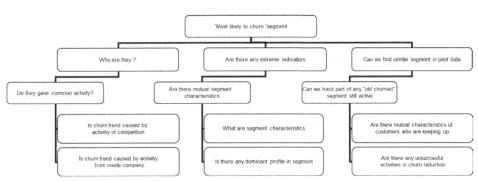

Figure 11. Total M2M connections forecast (Masse, 2010)

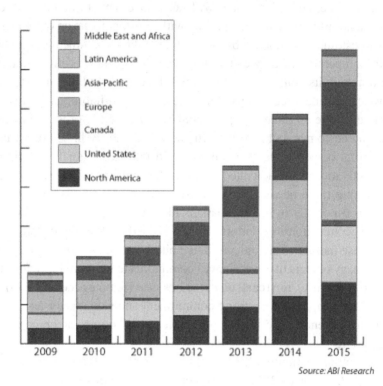

revenue, and is expected to grow at a CAGR of 27.4% from 2012 to 2017. APAC and North America are estimated to contribute $92.8 billion and $56.3 billion, respectively, by 2017; at a CAGR of 33.2% and 28.3%, from 2012 to 2017 (Markets and Markets, 2014).

1.4 WHEN NUMBERS CAMOUFLAGE REAL BUSINESS PICTURE

Let us imagine what if those 0.03% of clients who churned have some similar characteristic, like for example, related to same product or service or provider. If we found any similarity between clients who churned, that is almost always out of randomness and often related to more complex problem and it have to be treated as early warning signal for market risk.

If, for example, majority of those 0.03% customers were ordering spare parts made by same manufacturer or all those customers are located in similar part of the city/region than we have to analyze those indicators in more detailed way because they implicate certain trends which could lead to significant churn in (near) future. Once those trends became transparent, without proper reaction and treatment, it is often too late or even impossible to regain market position and to re-establish business relationship with customers who churned.

For efficient analysis, early diagnostics of churn trends and to calculate length of customer relationship data mining methods are used for analysis often called survival analysis while related models are called survival models. Those models were firstly used in medicine to determine success factor of treatments through certain time frame. Business practice recognized enormous potential of those methods in order to diagnose and analyze churn since those models can very efficiently and very early warn that something is gone wrong together with correlation factor (if any) between customers who churned. Going back to example, if we determine that similar characteristic of all churned customers is that they bought spare parts of same manufacturer we can look for reasons in competition who offers similar parts with lower prices or with additional benefits. On the other hand, if all churned customers are coming from similar area we should look for competition in that area or we can analyze economic situation in that area.

Some of mentioned models for analysis allow possibility to weight attributes so we can define most attractive influences having very detailed report of clients who churned. Why is so important to find similarities? Because based on those similarities we can analyze and estimate future churn candidates and, more important, we can affect or manage those trends Experience in researches so far shows that identification of links leads to increase of like hood for future churn in comparison with samples in which we cannot find similarities between churners.

As early as we are able to identify trends and similarities/links we can be earlier prepared to create strategy to fight those trends before it negatively affect our business result. Lost clients who churned are very hard to regain while not completely impossible. Moreover, it is easier to affect potential churning customers in early stage of their churning trend in comparison to final churn stage while they are more likely to made final decision. Mentioned survival models, beside its primary function to identify interesting trends, links and correlation, churn prediction, relationship length analysis are only small part of analytical methods available for churn analysis. Further analytic tasks should be aimed to provide answers to questions like "how we can affect and stop negative trends and churn"? We can find answers using probability modeling based on raw data for market environment simulation and decision support with focus on impact on negative trends. For that purpose, newest methodologies use Bayesian networks.

Looking back on churn topic, we can conclude that it is kind of artistic work in how to find early trend indicators for churn. Looking forward, it is more of the art to determine events which can lead to negative trend in the future. To be able to be efficient in determine right signals, beside survival based analytic methods, we have to also build systems based on expert knowledge for every specific business segment.

To go further into details we can create two hypothetic environments. Let us imagine dynamic market segment and company COM1 having 6.000 clients with monthly churn rate 0.6% while they are able to acquire new customers with 0.9% monthly rate. Total rate of terminated relationships in past 4 years is 2.5% while up to date data are showing increasing churn trend in past three months. Company COM2 is working in another, more conservative, market segment. They have 7.000 clients, monthly churn rate 0.3%, acquired customer rate 3.5% and termination rate in past 4 years at 8.5%.

Simple churn rate comparison should lead us to wrong conclusion that company COM1 is worse situation when compared to company COM2. However, by working in emerging market segment it is normal to expect high volatility while their numbers over years show that they are able to be competitive. They have to focus on last three months of negative trend and first guess will be that competition is active and they should focus on that fact. At the same time, by working in more conservative environment, company COM2 is much less effective over years. They are more easily attracting new customers but they are losing them with high rates and they should be focused on internal quality of products and service while their marketing and sales should be awarded for contribution in overall results. We can realize that by providing careful analysis we can realize important indicators. We need to learn how to use this knowledge to estimate environment conditions even before important indicators are starting to show that crisis is starting to happen.

1.5 HOW TO RECOGNIZE SPARKLE WHICH HAS POTENTIAL TO BECOME A FLAME?

As example we can imagine company specialized in sales custom merchandize to B2B segment which uses call center to communicate with customers. After taking orders into call center, deliveries were packed and delivered through proprietary, own, logistic channel. Call center operators were committing every order but they were also writing down all other types of calls like suggestions, claims etc. with short description regarding customer response.

In observed timeframe (several months) company recognized significant but not worrisome number of orders cancellation to raise churn alert (0.03% syndrome or "how small is big enough"). Since company did not want to ignore those those events no matter how small they were, they provide deeper analysis with goal to better understand reasons of cancellation and with intention to create damage control methodology if similar events occur in future. Deeper analysis came up with interesting results. Analysis showed that all churners have similarity in 3+ calls to call center with significant remarks to quality of service. Analysis also shows that all churn clients are running business that can be describes as "urgent or emergency services". Sample data analysis of remarks came up with fact that all reasons can be described as delivery delay for more than 1 day comparing to usual delivery schedule.

Detailed analysis shows several important business facts like fact that different customers from different business segments experience delay differently and that feature was not something that our company was paying much attention on. With raising demand for business optimization and with raising logistic operational costs, decision was made to sometimes sacrifice delivery tome for optimized total cost. It was clear that majority of targeted customers were not significantly influenced by that rule however specific target group was very sensitive in delivery schedule.

This kind of example illustrates usability of systems based on expert knowledge being able to notice early signs of potentially problematic events from business perspective. Our company should develop system based on set of rules which will activate certain alerts and activities every time when system will notice specific event or set of events without on-demand analysis like in our example. That kind of rule based system will independently, without additional initiative from analyst, start survival analysis process. In complex business environment, when we are working with large number of customers, it is relative to discuss frequency, however understating of environment is really a trigger for making 0.03% from our example enough important to proceed with analysis. By managing expert rules relative frequency can be set into efficient framework able to identify potential for dangerous trends in future.

By looking back at our example we can ask ourselves a question: how it came that no one was able to see or predict this kind of trend? If we take in consideration that our company was not specialized in very specific, observed market segment this came up randomly through time executing regular daily operations, further questions are coming up like: are there more specific interesting segments in our customer base and what are their main drivers for being loyal to our service? This kind of questions and problems can show us our strengths and mistakes from past and give us opportunity to learn from past. But real power of survival models is coming from fact that they can provide much important information using which we will be able to manage and prevent future problems, to avoid crisis situations and to provide stable and successful relationship with clients and partners.

So far it is obvious that churn can be found in different ways in different businesses. Moreover, companies can manage churn in ways to optimize their business models by reducing churn generally (less present in practice) or by reducing or even encourage churn in specific segments (most profitable clients/clients with low perspective) through industries. For example, although economy of scale will improve income in telecommunications company, strong increase of customers can heavily affect performance in conditions where networks have its capacity limitations. Therefore large number of general customers, can increase turnover but can at the same time affect performance for most profitable customers who can consequently churn over time. Telecom companies are using intelligent agents for past decade to manage network workflow and to manage client experience sometimes with questionable approaches like slowing down less profitable and bandwidth demanding customers. Some of today's tariffs include for example prearranged data plan with guaranteed performance/speed for download up to some amount while after exceeding that limit customer will experience significant slowdown in performance.

With raising trend of importance to focus on so called, Customer Centric business, companies should look for technology and process solutions helpful for better understanding what and when customer needs to be able to react proactive and in most efficient way.

Although churn can be calculated using similar criteria but with different approaches (customer churn, revenue churn etc.) and using different perspectives (churn customer age, churn by customer behavior etc.) to-do list includes data and

Figure 12. Customer centric metrics (transforming from product-centric to customer-centric) (Pitney Bowes Business Insight, 2011)

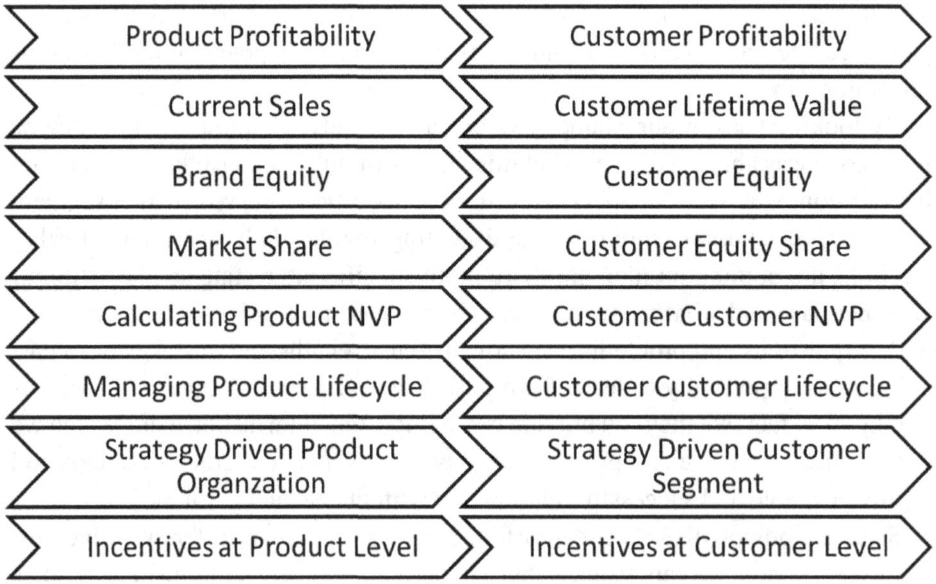

Product Profitability	Customer Profitability
Current Sales	Customer Lifetime Value
Brand Equity	Customer Equity
Market Share	Customer Equity Share
Calculating Product NVP	Customer Customer NVP
Managing Product Lifecycle	Customer Customer Lifecycle
Strategy Driven Product Organzation	Strategy Driven Customer Segment
Incentives at Product Level	Incentives at Customer Level

environment understanding, definition of strategy and action plan and, maybe most important, activity impact measuring and management. Although it is possible to find related works that are indicating that almost 50% customer churn is likely caused by internal factors (Corr, 2008) which are under our control (interaction with our organization) in modern market environment and global influences every industry and almost every situation should be treated as separate occasion before we start. Also, researches so far are showing that even with few activities but with right understanding of problem area companies can do major improvement in reducing churn. For example, with carefully targeted apology to specific customer we can regain its confidence in our service.

REFERENCES

Ahn, J. H., Han, S. P., & Lee, Y. S. (2006). Customer churn analysis: Churn determinants and mediation effects of partial defection in the Korean mobile telecommunications service industry, Science direct. *Telecommunications Policy, 30*(10-11), 552–568. doi:10.1016/j.telpol.2006.09.006

Ants Analytics. (2013) *The Executive's Guide to Reducing Customer Churn with Predictive Analytics.* Retrieved from www.11antsanalytics.com

Berry, M., & Linoff, G. (2004). *Data Mining Technique for marketing Sales and CRM.* Wiley.

Carpenter, H. (2009). *Foursquare + Square = Killer Small Business CRM.* Retrieved from http://bhc3.com/2009/12/14/

Cooper, C. (2011). *10 Tips for Retaining Loyal Guests.* Retrieved from http://www.hotelnewsnow.com/Articles.aspx/6068/10-tips-for-retaining-loyal-guests

Corr, J. (2008). *Why could 'frustration churn' be costing you over 15% of the potential value of your business?* London, UK: Close Quarter Limited.

Filip, A. (2012). *Best Practice: Requirements of CRM Processes.* Retrieved from http://www.ec4u.de/en/2012-09-24/best-practice-requirements-of-crm-processes

Hadden, J., Ashtoush, T., Rajkumar, R., & Ruta, D. (2006). Churn Prediction: Does Technology Matter? *International Journal of Electrical and Computer Engineering, 1,* 6.

Kumar, S. (2005). *Understanding the Relationship Between Loyalty and Churn.* Retrieved from http://www.information-management.com/specialreports/20051018/1039409-1.html

Lazarov, V., & Capota, M. (2010). *Churn Prediction*. Retrieved from http://home. in.tum.de/~lazarov/files/research/papers/churn-prediction.pdf

Markets and Markets. (2014). *Internet of Things (IoT) & Machine-To-Machine (M2M) Communication Market by Technologies & Platforms (RFID, Sensor Nodes, Gateways, Cloud Management, NFC, CEP, SCADA, ZigBee), M2M Connections, IoT Components - Worldwide Market Forecasts (2014 - 2019)*. Retrieved from http:// www.marketsandmarkets.com/Market-Reports/internet-of-things-market-573.html

Masse, D. (2010). Cellular M2M Connections Will Show Steady. *Growth*. Retrieved from http://www.microwavejournal.com/articles/10376-cellular-m2m-connections-will-show-steady-growth-to-2015

Noize, V. (2015). *Financial. The Pro & Con of Groupon*. Retrieved from http://www. evancarmichael.com/Marketing/3973/The-Pro--Con-of-Groupon.html

Peppers, R. (2008). *Rules to Break and Laws to Follow* example taken from *"Customer centricity in the telecommunications industry"*. Pitney Bowes Business Insight.

Pitney Bowes Business Insight. (2011). *Customer centricity in the telecommunications industry*. Author.

Popović, D. (2009). Churn Prediction Model in Retail Banking Using Fuzzy C-Means Algorithm. *Faculty of Electrical Engineering and Computing, 33*, 243–247.

Rashid, T. (2010). Classification of Churn and non-Churn Customers for Telecommunication Companies. *International Journal of Biometrics and Bioinformatics, 3*(5).

Retention Science. (n.d.). Retrieved from http://retentionscience.com/products/ Pitney Bowes Business Insight. (2011). *Customer centricity in the telecommunications industry*. Author.

Tsiptsis, K., & Chorianopoulos, A. (2010). *Data Mining Techniquies in CRM: Inside Customer Segmentation*. Wiley. doi:10.1002/9780470685815

KEY TERMS AND DEFINITIONS

Customer Churn (Customer Attrition, Customer Turnover, Customer Defection): Business term used to describe loss of clients or customers, basic calculation to express churn rate: number of customers that defected divided total number of customer

Cost of Customer Acquisition (COCA): Cost which needs to be invested in acquiring new customer

Customer Lifetime Value (CLV): Prediction of the net profit attributed to the entire future relationship with a customercustomer equity (CE) – total combined customer lifetime values of all of a company's customers.

Customer Experience Management (CEM): Customers' perceptions – both conscious and subconscious – of their relationship with your company resulting from all their interactions with your brand during the customer life cycle

ENDNOTES

[1]   "Telco" as short from telecommunication

Chapter 2
Setting (Realistic) Business Aims

ABSTRACT

This chapter explains different perspective of churn analysis and points out the importance of understanding what really can or cannot be done. In addition, it is important to understand common errors analysts (readers) have, so that one can be aware of them when planning and conducting churn analyses. It is advisable for the reader to move back to the introduction and Chapter 1 after finishing reading in order to once again understand the full potential and restrictions of the proposed methods and techniques. Although this chapter covers churn topics on a conceptual level, it is very important for the reader to be able to understand and express key points on this level. By using industry-related cases and by combining churn with early warning systems, the complete scope is covered, and the reader can move to the next level, techniques, explained in next chapter.

2.1 INTRODUCTION

Often while exploring all powers of analytical methods ideas what else we may analyze just pop on one after another. Being able to control obviously large potential we need to be able to manage business aims in realistic way, both in time and resources. Looking from the churn perspective, churn is important because lost customers have to be replaced with new ones, and new ones are expensive to acquire and generally generate less revenue in the near term than established customers (Berry, Linhoff,

DOI: 10.4018/978-1-4666-6288-9.ch002

Figure 1. Understanding business aims

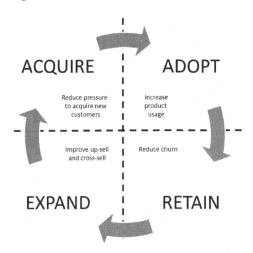

2004). This is more present in mature industries where the market is saturated, anyone likely to want the product or service probably already has it from somewhere so the main source of new customers is people leaving a competitor (Figure 1).

Market saturation leads to decrease in response rate from acquisition campaigns while cost for acquiring new customer goes up. Looking for efficient business balance, company has to be always faced to choice is it more efficient to invest into retaining current customers of focus on acquiring new ones.

Retention campaigns can be very effective but also very expensive. A mobile phone company might offer an expensive new phone to customers who renew a contract. A credit card company might lower the interest rate. The problem with these offers is that any customer who is made the offer will accept it. Who wouldn't want a free phone or a lower interest rate? That means that many of the people accepting the offer would have remained customers even without it. The motivation for building churn models is to figure out who is most at risk for attrition so as to make the retention offers to high-value customers who might leave without the extra incentive (Berry, Linhoff, 2004) (see Table 1).

2.2 WHEN CHURN BECAME OBVIOUS IT IS TOO LATE FOR DATA MINING

As we define, churn can be voluntary or involuntary. However there is a third choice, expected churn (Berry, Linhoff, 2004). Involuntary churn, also known as forced attrition, occurs when the company, terminates the relationship most commonly

Table 1. Business aims, scenario analysis

Profitability	Loyalty	Perspective
Total gross margin over 6 months	In-store traffic over 6 months	Sales trend over last 6 months
Total marketing costs for loyalty program over 6 moths	Loyalty card holders campaign response over 6 months	New product adoption over last 12 months
Total overall marketing costs over 6 months	Loyalty card membership points	Cross sell trend in last 6 months

due to unpaid bills. Expected churn occurs when the customer is no longer in the target market for a product.

Babies get teeth and no longer need baby food. Workers retire and no longer need retirement savings accounts. Families move away and no longer need their old local newspaper delivered to their door. It is important not to confuse the different types of churn, but easy to do so. Consider two mobile phone customers in identical financial circumstances. Due to some misfortune, neither can afford the mobile phone service any more. Both call up to cancel. One reaches a customer service agent and is recorded as voluntary churn. The other hangs up after ten minutes on hold and continues to use the phone without paying the bill. The second customer is recorded as forced churn. The underlying problem, lack of money, is the same for both customers, so it is likely that they will both get similar scores. The model cannot predict the difference in hold times experienced by the two subscribers (Berry, Linhoff, 2004).

Companies that mistake forced churn for voluntary churn lose twice, once when they spend money trying to retain customers who later go bad and again in increased write-offs. Predicting forced churn can also be dangerous. Because the treatment given to customers who are not likely to pay their bills tends to be nasty, phone service is suspended, late fees are increased, and dunning letters are sent more quickly. These remedies may alienate otherwise good customers and increase the chance that they will churn voluntarily.

In many companies, voluntary churn and involuntary churn are the responsibilities of different groups. Marketing is concerned with holding on to good customers and finance is concerned with reducing exposure to bad customers. From a data mining point of view, it is better to address both voluntary and involuntary churn together since all customers are at risk for both kinds of churn to varying degrees.

Having types of churn in perspective we also need to consider churn from business point of view. For example, public service companies like public transportation are scaled for specific optimal number of client who will use their service. Normally, if number of clients increase, more money will be collected from tickets. However,

Figure 2. Churn potential

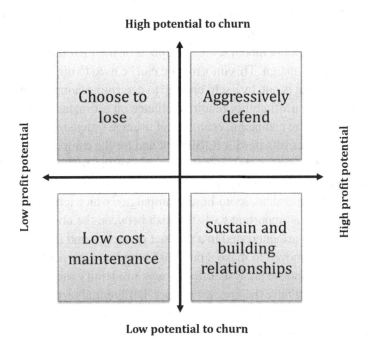

by increase of clients who are using service without control profit can decrease because it will require significant cost to serve on bigger level. Same thing can happen with telecom companies when too many clients can reduce quality of service if capacity was not planned in right way. Although this examples are also in area of data mining, they are not related to churn analysis but with business performance capacity planning and optimization measures. When we are talking about churn as well as while talking about acquiring new customers, we need to be aware about internal and external environment. Furthermore, besides fact of understanding what is going on (why we are losing or acquiring customers) we need to always assure that our strategy is in line with activities and results. Churn analysis is essential to performance improvement but it takes time and resources for company to be able to use it efficiently in custom environment.

2.3 100% CHURN REDUCTION IS IMPOSSIBLE TO ACHIEVE

Data mining is used in support of both advertising and direct marketing to identify the right audience, choose the best communications channels, and pick the most appropriate messages. Prospective customers can be compared to a profile of the intended audience and given a fitness score. Should information on individual prospects not be available, the same method can be used to assign fitness scores to geographic neighborhoods using appropriate.

For example, a response model scores prospects on their likelihood to respond to a direct marketing campaign. This information can be used to improve the response rate of a campaign, but is not, by itself, enough to determine campaign profitability. Estimating campaign profitability requires reliance on estimates of the underlying response rate to a future campaign, estimates of average order sizes associated with the response, and cost estimates for fulfillment and for the campaign itself. A more customer-centric use of response scores is to choose the best campaign for each customer from among a number of competing campaigns. This approach avoids the usual problem of independent, score-based campaigns, which tend to pick the same people every time. It is important to distinguish between the ability of a model to recognizepeople who are interested in a product or service and its ability to recognize people who are moved to make a purchase based on a particular campaign or offer. Differential response analysis offers a way to identify the market segments where a campaign will have the greatest impact. Differential response models seek to maximize the difference in response between a treated group and a control group rather than trying to maximize the response itself.

Information about current customers can be used to identify likely prospects by finding predictors of desired outcomes in the information that was known about current customers before they became customers. This sort of analysis is valuable for selecting acquisition channels and contact strategies as well as for screening prospect lists. Companies can increase the value of their customer data by beginning to track customers from their first response, even before they become customers, and gathering and storing additional information when customers are acquired.

Once customers have been acquired, the focus shifts to customer relationship management. The data available for active customers is richer than that available for prospects and, because it is behavioral in nature rather than simply geographic and demographic, it is more predictive. Data mining is used to identify additional products and services that should be offered to customers based on their current usage patterns. It can also suggest the best time to make a cross-sell or up-sell offer.

One of the goals of a customer relationship management program is to retain valuable customers. Data mining can help identify which customers are the most valuable and evaluate the risk of voluntary or involuntary churn associated with each customer. Armed with this information, companies can target retention offers at customers who are both valuable and at risk, and take steps to protect themselves from customers who are likely to default.

From a data mining perspective, churn modeling can be approached as either a binary-outcome prediction problem or through survival analysis. There are advantages and disadvantages to both approaches. The binary outcome approach works well for a short horizon, while the survival analysis approach can be used to make forecasts far into the future and provides insight into customer loyalty and customer value as well.

We need to be aware that 100% churn reduction is impossible to achieve. However, churn management can help us to have more customers at the end of time period than we had in start even with some of our customers churned. Important fact is ability to adopt and to be able to do that we need to deeply understand all components of our business, from partners through added value provided by our company, to our customers.

2.4 WHEN IS THE APPROPRIATE TIME FOR APPLYING DATA MINING METHODS?

Main focus of this chapter is to explain when and how different methods can be use in practice (for any additional information on methods theories please address to other authors publications (Panian, Klepac, 2005)). By following simple characteristic of every method, focusing on how to select and preprocess data, going through examples of different problems that can be solved with specific method and how to interpret analysis data following each method appliance this chapter will introduce reader to powerful world of advanced analytics. Selected methods will be explained from the perspective of everyday business practice.

The starting point is to quantify the type and level of churn and its impact on the business. Given the existence of a churn issue, the next phase is to understand the key factors driving churn. Depending on the nature of the factors influencing churn, a predictive churn model may be required. Armed with the capability to identify who is likely to churn, retention initiatives can be developed and designed to manage this. The final phase is to measure the effectiveness and refine as needed.

Figure 3. Phases of analytical process

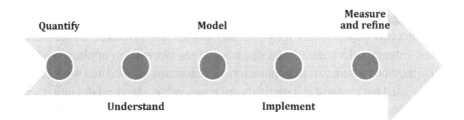

Generally, elementary statistical methods, OLAP analysis and visualization are covering very wide area and are hard to fit all of those in one chapter. From technical point of view, it is not recommended to try to do so. However, from business point of view all-in-one approach has every right to be used. Common characteristic of mentioned methods is that knowledge discovery based on them mostly relies on person, analyst, who is performing analysis. That method does not have out-of-the-box created algorithms able to recognize similarities in data samples but are based on analyst capability to find knowledge and correlation using wide range of available attributes while trying to find information useful from business perspective. Overall success of those methods usage mostly relies on analyst intuition and expertise. In other words, that means that in wide number of combinations available for creating report using OLAP analytic tool, analyst choose which of attributes will use for specific report. Not only is that he selecting attributes but also its aggregation level and way of sampling. Final report can provide useful information and discover knowledge hidden in data but also can be a dead end. It is similar with visualization or with usage of basic statistic methods. This approach is mostly based on heuristics while in this case expert knowledge and specific business experience are important in order for usage of those methods should bring us to quality business information. It is important to understand that this approach should be recognized by researcher without doubt in power of methodology but to express different character caused by business usage. It is also important to point out that in order to unlock full potential of explained methods researcher should combine methods with other advanced analytics methods.

Talking about starting to apply advanced methods first we need to mention data selection and preprocessing. From the preprocessing point of view, difference between methods became more visible. Readiness for OLAP analysis include data quality and structure, preferable data warehouse storage, which implicates that ETL phase was conducted and we have metrics for data quality. Data prepared in that way can also be entry sample for visualization phase or entry sample for analysis based on basic statistic methods. Instead of OLAP tools, visualization and basic statistic methods can be successfully applied even on data sample which is not completely structured and cleaned. It is possible to apply visualization and basic statistic methods can be applied directly on raw and not processed data with intention to discover basic data population characteristics which will be used for further analysis. In specific situation usage of explained methods is introduction into ETL phase. For example visualization can, depending of approach and tool used to visualize, use continuous variables, categorical variables and discrete values likewise in appliance of basic statistical methods where variable characteristic determine method that we plan to use.

Mostly used basic statistical methods are mean value, standard deviation, curve coefficient, mod, median, correlation and frequency. Every of mentioned methods use specific attribute type so we need to preprocess variables for specific statistical method application. For example, if we would like to discover average age of specific product user, we are looking for continuous attribute value to calculate mean. If we would like to calculate frequencies based on age groups, we need to name every case by age group and then calculate frequency using those categories. As example we can use table as follows:

Taking in consideration large variety of methods it is not possible to suggest universal approach for preprocessing. It depends on method to be used. As mentioned before, OLAP analysis is focused on analyst as primary subject who is not characteristic of traditional statistic methods. Therefore analyst is in this case supervised to algorithm used in traditional approach to data mining. In simplified words, during OLAP process analyst is testing hypothesis by moving dimensions into relationships or analyzing specific trends while OLAP analysis provide final reports.

Looking at available groups of data samples there is always large number of combinations which can be used to process OLAP analysis while analyst based on his experience and project nature, execute predefined group of analysis following project scenario. Usage of traditional data mining methods includes predefined steps while looking for hidden knowledge in data. Being used for better data sample understanding or to create final report, basic statistical methods and visualization methods have significant impact on knowledge discovery process.

Churn within the business needs to be quantified. Before doing this, a key step is to define what is really meant by churn. This essentially defines the type of customers that you need to manage. Often, both voluntary and involuntary churn exist. An example of involuntary churn is a bank closing a customer's credit card as a result of non-payment. Usually, for churn management, the focus is on voluntary customer churn. The next consideration is whether to focus on both hard and soft churn. Hard churn is when there is a defined event that signifies churn, for example, the closure of an account. However, this approach may be too simplistic, thereby requiring soft churn to be considered. A customer may be defined as having soft churned if they have not transacted with the organization for a period. The length of time varies depending on the nature of the industry and often on the customer's initial behavior

Table 2. Prepared data sample

User	Age	Age category
A	25	18-25
B	33	25-35
C	46	45-55
D	32	25-35

Table 3. Data processing results, age groups and frequencies

Average user age 41.5 years	Age Category	Frequency
	18-25	10%
	25-35	20%
	35-45	40%
	45-55	10%
	55+	10%

(namely, transactional frequency). For example, a shorter period would be used if focusing on supermarket shopping (as we shop and eat every week) compared to booking a holiday. Consideration should be given as to whether to focus on a specific customer group. The measurement may be limited to customers with the most valuable product, for example home loans for banks, or to another area such as the busiest time of year for seasonal businesses. Restrictions regarding the interface of existing systems may require a product led approach rather than taking a holistic customer view. This definition phase considers the practical issues within your business and should not be left to an analyst to decide in isolation from the business. Once the degree of churn is known, it needs to be expressed as a financial consequence to the business. This assists with getting the right degree of focus from the business, a 5% churn rate could be costing billions of dollars. To assess the financial impact depends on the value or profitability by product, service, and channel and/or customer segment. A number of assumptions based on customer knowledge can be made. For example if the average tenure of a customer is 5 years, the expected future revenue can be built into the assessment. The purpose is to gauge the magnitude of churn on the business, not to provide a highly accurate measure. To understand more about the type of customers that are churning involves profiling by comparing customers who have churned compared to customers that have not churned. This will use all available information, including service history, behavioral, demographics, channel, value, usage etc. Integrating any specific information collected at the point of disconnecting, for example, reason codes, is useful. The behavioral profile identifies the typical customer patterns of behavior and interactions with the business prior to churning. Integrate any qualitative market research that is available to help build understanding of the complete customer landscape for the churn events.

Key findings and recommendations based on the analysis provide the foundation for implementing customer retention and customer loyalty marketing initiatives to minimize the future impact of customer churn. Examples of the type of insight you can expect include the best time to contact a customer based on a moment of truth and a defined demographic profile to help with creative and offer. The combination of likelihood to churn or risk of churn and value provide a powerful basis for marketing action.

Churn analysis is the first essential step towards implementing effective customer retention and customer loyalty programs. More specifically, it will:

- Establish the cost of customer churn to your business and provide justification for appropriate
- investment in customer retention and customer loyalty initiatives
- Target retention efforts on high-value customers with a high risk of churn
- Focus retention efforts on the areas over which your business has most control

Combat churn by providing the data backbone for developing predictive modelling for more proactive customer management

2.5 CHURN MONITORING AS A LONG TERM STRATEGY

There are two basic approaches to modeling churn. The first treats churn as a binary outcome and predicts which customers will leave and which will stay. The second tries to estimate the customers' remaining lifetime.

To predict „who will leave" we need to model churn as a binary outcome, it is necessary to pick some time horizon. If the question is "Who will leave tomorrow?" the answer is hardly anyone. If the question is "Who will have left in 100 years?" the answer, in most businesses, is nearly everyone. Binary outcome churn models usually have a fairly short time horizon such as 60 or 90 days. Of course, the hori-

Figure 4. Finding focus for churn analysis initiatives

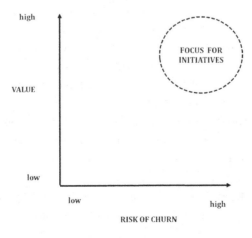

zon cannot be too short or there will be no time to act on the model's predictions. Binary outcome churn models can be built with any of the usual tools for classification including logistic regression, decision trees, and neural networks. Historical data describing a customer population at one time is combined with flag showing whether the customers were still active at some later time. The modeling task is to discriminate between those who left and those who stayed. The outcome of a binary churn model is typically a score that can be used to rank customers in order of their likelihood of churning. The most natural score is simply the probability that the customer will leave within the time horizon used for the model. Those with voluntary churn scores above a certain threshold can be included in a retention program. Those with involuntary churn scores above a certain threshold can be placed on a watch list. Typically, the predictors of churn turn out to be a mixture of things that were known about the customer at acquisition time, such as the acquisition channel and initial credit class, and things that occurred during the customer relationship such as problems with service, late payments, and unexpectedly high or low bills. The first class of churn drivers provides information on how to lower future churn by acquiring fewer churn-prone customers. The second class of churn drivers provides insight into how to reduce the churn risk for customers who are already present.

To predict "who will leave" we will use less common method, although it has some attractive features. In this approach, the goal is to figure out how much longer a customer is likely to stay. This approach provides more information than simply whether the customer is expected to leave within 90 days. Having an estimate of remaining customer tenure is a necessary ingredient for a customer lifetime value model. It can also be the basis for a customer loyalty score that defines a loyal customer as one who will remain for a long time in the future rather than one who has remained a long time up until now. "First 90 days" concept can be found in many areas as crucial period to take control of company, customer, relationship etc. There are several guidelines, depending of industry, on what to pay attention in first 90 days like customers need confirmation that they made good choice or they need to proof price/performance ratio be as they expected.

One approach to mod eling customer longevity would be to take a snapshotof the current customer population, along with data on what these customers looked like when they were first acquired, and try to estimate customer tenure directly by trying to determine what long-lived customers have in common besides an early acquisition date. The problem with this approach, is that the longer customers have been around, the more different market conditions were back when they were acquired. Certainly it is not safe to assume that the characteristics of someone who got a cellular subscription in 1990 are good predictors of which of today's new customers will keep their service for many years. A better approach is to use survival analysis techniques that have been borrowed and adapted from statistics. These

Setting (Realistic) Business Aims

Table 4. CRM processes over customer lifecycle (Filip, 2012)

Marketing	Sales	Service
Market development / lead management • Define target market • Generate leads from campaigns/list/surveys/events/ network marketing/referral marketing/field sales support • Manage and analyze terms • Qualify leads • Closed-loop analysis, reports on leads	*Manage opprtunities* • Manage sales through workflow rules for sales processes (standard sales methods) • Administer and document sales projects • Analyze competition related information • Manage multiple channels	*Manage service requests* • Note and administer service requests via service channels • Manage knowledge
Manage campaigns • Plan campaigns • Prepare and execute campaigns over multiple channels • Analyze and repost on campaigns	*Manage bids and contracts* • Administer enquiries, bids and contracts • Pricing and product configuration • Check availability	*Service bids, manage contracts* • Process service orders and bids • Record/check orders • Pricing
Segment customers, customer value • Segment customers into different tergat groups • Analyze customer potential and behavior • Sampling and grouping, clustering, data mining, decision trees	*Manage agreeements* • Pricing agreements • Cross-selling and up-selling • Monitor status • Administer agreements • Manage key accounts	*Process service agreeements* • Service agreeements • Process/administer agreements • Monitor SLA (to identify new sales opportunities)
Loyalty programs • Register and administer members • Targeted loyalty promotion • Complex reward points earning and redemption processes • Transaction by customer value • Customer and loyalty analysis, recovery campaingns	*Manage pipeline performance* • Analyze sales performance • Plan guidelines, identify pipeline changes and decisive opprtunities • Forecasting • Encourage employees with incentives	*Manage complaints* • Note, process and resolve complaints (direct process) • Evaluate and report complaints, derive activities (indirect process) • Handle returns, recall campaigns • Manage warranties and damages
Manage marketing resources • Strategic planning and budgeting • Manage marketing approvals • Operational planning	*Plan sales, manage territory* • Strategic plans for sales • Segment and assign territory, related schedules, manage for organizations • Cisit customers • Travel expense reports, time tracking	*Plan staff resources and assignments* • Strategic customer service plans • Distribute employees and equipment based on staff assignment plan, availability, site and expense
Manage business patrners and contracts • Complete customer information (companies and contracts) • Manage activities and appointments for contracts • Complete customer history		

Figure 5. First 90 days concept from SundaySky, infographics (Fullen, 2013)

techniques are associated with the medical world where they are used to study patient survival rates after medical interventions and the manufacturing world where they are used to study the expected time to failure of manufactured components (Berry, Linhoff, 2004).

Table 5. Typical churn reduction project timeline (Price Waterhouse Coopers, 2011)

	Phase 1 Hypothesis generation	Phase 2 Analysis	Phase 3 Cost-benefit analysis
Sequence	• Analysis/assessment • Solution brainstorming/ hypotheses generation	• Process analysis • Call monitoring • Primary research • Data analytics	• Prioritization and implementation planning
Duration	1 week	4 to 12 weeks	1 to 2 weeks
Objectives and actions	• Gain understanding of current processes, policies and databases • Determine relative magnitude of churn problem • Interview with key policies owners • Develop hypotheses on root clauses to be tested in second phase	• Identify root clauses and interactions between systems, policies, employee actions and customer expectations • Understand quantitative impact of each churn driver • Establish ability to efficiently test and measure impact of solutions	• Conduct business cases for individual root cause of treatments • Develop roll out schedule and resource requirements • Estimate impact of rollout on key performance indicators

2.6 SETTING EARLY WARNING CHURN SYSTEMS

By looking at the highly competitive markets and changing market demand, we can now conclude that important factor of success for every enterprise is to reduce customer churn to the maximum extent. As a very important part of customer relationship management theory, the core of customer churn management lies in how to conduct effective customer churn early warning system. Technology of data mining is widely used today in the study of customer churn early warning systems. We also show that customer relationship management is in the background of churn management. To establish efficient eary warning churn system we need to eliminate the subjectivity of attribute selection, improve accuracy rate, coverage rate, hit rate and lift coefficient of model to avoid serious overlap of different types of customer attributes in attribute space. Customer churn early warning systems often deals with issues like large volume of data, high dimension of data, unbalanced data set, often subjective and speculative attribute selection which needs to me managed in order to improve prediction performance of model and enhance the accuracy rate of prediction. Efficient models have a good prediction performance especially for dealing with a large quantity of non-equilibrium data set. Models succesfully improves the basic theories and ideas of customer relationship management and enterprise and help enterprises avoid the risk of customer churn, based on a good prediction performance of the model, and effectively guide them to implement customer relationship management to enhance their competitiveness (Wang, 2014).

Despite industry, companies should look for knowledge about churn management especially if their business is related to direct or indirect relationship with large scale customer base. Following advices from this book simple but also more advanced system can be built as starting point for small/medium but also big enterprises.

REFERENCES

Berry, M., & Linoff, G. (2004). *Data Mining Technique for marketing Sales and CRM*. Wiley.

Filip, A. (2012). *Best Practice: Requirements of CRM Processes*. Retrieved from http://www.ec4u.de/en/2012-09-24/best-practice-requirements-of-crm-processes

Fullen, A. (2013). *Live from Mobile World Congress: How to Enhance the Customer Experience in the "First 90 Days"*. Retrieved from http://info.sundaysky.com/blog/bid/271910/Live-from-Mobile-World-Congress-How-to-Enhance-the-Customer-Experience-in-the-First-90-Days

Klepac, G., & Panian, Ž. (2005). *Poslovna inteligencija*. Masmedia Zagreb.

Price Waterhouse Coopers. (2011). *Curing customer churn*. Author.

Wang, Z. J. (2014). *Research On Customer Churn Early-warning Based On Neural Network*. Retrieved from http://www.economics-papers.com/research-on-customer-churn-early-warning-based-on-ig_nn-double-attribute-selection.html

KEY TERMS AND DEFINITIONS

Customer Retention: Activity that a selling organization undertakes in order to reduce customer defections

CRM: System for managing a company's interactions with current and future customers

Hypothesis: Proposed explanation for a phenomenon, scientists generally base scientific hypotheses on previous observations that cannot satisfactorily be explained with the available scientific theories so proposed explanation of a phenomenon still has to be rigorously tested

Chapter 3
Data Mining Techniques for Churn Mitigation/ Detection:
Intrinsic Attributes Approach

ABSTRACT

This chapter overviews data mining starting with an explanation of the data mining methods used the most. Data mining methods are explained together with recommendations of when and how to use them and how to iteratively combine different methods. The methods are explained briefly to understand their role in projects. One of the most important topics that the analysts (readers) have to learn is how to combine different methods in the same analysis and how to use that approach to unlock the synergy effect.

3.1 INTRODUCTION

As shown, customer churn prediction is one of the most important problems in customer relationship management. Its major aim is to retain valuable customers helping to maximize the profit of a company. To predict whether a customer will be a churner or non-churner, there are a number of data mining techniques applied for churn prediction and variety of researches that can be found and are conducting

DOI: 10.4018/978-1-4666-6288-9.ch003

as we are writing this book. Since enterprises in the competitive market mainly rely on the profits which come from customers, companies are trying to focus on confirmed customers that are the most fertile source of data for decision making. We can say that highly competitive organizations realize that retaining existing and valuable customers is their essential resource for surviving to survive in their industries. As shown, to create and retain customers is difficult and costly in terms of marketing. Consequently, this leads to the importance of churn management. As customer churning will likely result in the loss of businesses, churn prediction has received increasing attention in the marketing and management literature over the past time. It shows that a small change in the retention rate can result in significant impact on businesses. Customer churn can be regarded as customers who are intending to move their custom to a competing service provider. Therefore, many companies need to assess their customer's value in order to retain or even cultivate the profit potential of the customers. In order to effectively manage customer churn for companies, it is important to build a more effective and accurate customer churn prediction model. In the literature, data mining techniques have been used to create the prediction models.

Data mining has emerged over recent years as an extremely powerful approach to extracting meaningful information from large databases and data warehouses. Since the increased computerization of business transactions, improvements in storage and processing capacities of computers, as well as significant advances in knowledge discovery algorithms, those all have contributed to the evolution of the data mining. The methodology of data mining views the discovery of information from a database as a four-step process (Tsai, Lu, 2010):

- Business problem must be identified,
- After the problem is defined and related data are collected, the next step is to process the collected data by data transformation, data cleaning, etc. for the later mining process,
- Apply some specific mining algorithm(s) over the processed data (like prediction/classification algorithms),
- Mining result is evaluated to examine whether the finding is useful for the business problem.

The data in the real world is always incomplete, noisy, and inconsistent because of not applicable, human or computer error at data entry, errors in data transmission, or from different data sources, etc. Therefore, the major tasks in data pre-processing includes data cleaning, data integration, data transformation, data reduction, and data discretization. Data cleaning is one of the three biggest problems in data warehousing (Kimball, 1996). In data cleaning process, some tasks may be to fill in missing values, identify outliers, smooth out noisy data, correct inconsistent data, and resolve redundancy caused by data integration. Missing and noisy data are resolved by using attribute mean to fill in, or employing a regression function to find a fitted value generally. Data integration is to combine data from multiple sources into a coherent store. In integration processing, the redundant data problem always occur, since the same real world entity, attribute values from different sources have different names, or one attribute may be a derived attribute in another table. Therefore, researchers should carefully identify real world entities from multiple data sources by using correlation analysis. Otherwise, careful integration of the data from multiple sources may help to reduce/avoid redundancies and inconsistencies and improve mining speed and quality. Data transformation is usually used to smooth the noisy data, summarize, generalize, or normalize the data scale falls within a small, specified range. In addition, data reduction aims to obtain a reduced representation of the data set that is much smaller in volume but yet produce the same (or almost the same) analytical results. Since complex data mining may take a very long time to run on the complete data set, dana reduction is usually employed in the data pre-processing stage. Data reduction tasks include data cube aggregation, dimensions reduction (e.g., removing unimportant attributes), data compression, and to reduce data volume by choosing alternative, smaller forms of data representation. Finally, data discretization divides the range of a continuous attribute into intervals since some classification algorithms only accept categorical attributes. After data preprocessing, data analysis and mining can be proceed efficiently and effectively.

After data are pre-processed, knowledge discovery algorithms can be applied to the processed data. The type of algorithms used, depends on the nature of the problem. If the problem can be viewed as a problem of classification or prediction, and a complete set of training data is available, then the problem is well structured. Supervised learning algorithms like multilayer neural networks, regression, or decision trees can be used to learn the relationship between variables and correct decisions. Neural networks are the popular and widely used algorithm in data mining. It attempts to simulate biological neural systems which learn by changing the strength of the synaptic connection between neurons upon repeated stimulation by the same impulse. Neural networks can be distinguished into single-layer perceptron and multilayer perceptron (MLP). The multilayer perceptron consists of multiple layers of simple, two taste, sigmoid processing nodes or neurons that interact by using weighted connections. The MLP network may contain several intermediary layers between input and output layers. Such intermediary layers are called as hidden layers and composed of a number of nodes embedded in these layers, which are called as hidden nodes. Based on prior research results, multilayer perception is a relatively accurate neural network model. A decision tree is constructed by many nodes and branches on different stages and various conditions. It is a very popular and powerful tool for many prediction and classification problems, since it can produce a number of decision rules. Several algorithms of decision trees have been developed, such as C4.5 and C5.0. Among them, classification and regression trees (CART) are a non-parametric statistical method to construct a decision tree to solve classification and regression problems. Logistic regression is a widely used statistical modeling technique to compare with other data mining algorithms, in which the probability of a dichotomous outcome is related to a set of potential independent variables and it is used to forecast the value of two class labels or sequence variables. Although it is one of the traditional statistical techniques, the logistic regression model does not necessarily require the assumptions of discriminant analysis, but it is as efficient and accurate as discriminant analysis (Tsai, Lu, 2010).

3.2 WHICH IS THE BEST DATA MINING TECHNIQUE FOR CHURN DETECTION?

To answer this question we need to fist ask "is there best" data mining technique for churn detection at all". By looking at researches so far it is obvious that industry and specific environment affect which data mining method we should use to achieve best results. Furthermore, with increasing availability of high performance processing power researchers are combining different methods into hybrid models with best characteristic of every method merged into single iterative methodology. Nevertheless, in literature we can find updated lists of achievements by industry and method as interesting starting point which can create perspective for everyone who is evaluating methods for the first time but also someone who will like to proof its idea or check best practice for its industry (Table 1).

Following idea of „best" data mining method, by looking at researches conducted so far we can easily conclude several important facts for every method helping us to choose among most used ones. Most important conclusion is that there is no „one-size-fits-all" approach. Furthermore, once model is established it needs to be calibrated on annual basis in order to keep its competitiveness among changing influences of modern market (Table 2).

In next chapters, we will briefly explain methods we see most important for understanding further models and discussions presented in this book.

3.2.1 Fuzzy Expert System

Specific characteristics of fuzzy expert systems make them different from other methods mostly because its focus pointed to expert knowledge during model development project and analysis. Unlike traditional expert systems, fuzzy expert

Data Mining Techniques for Churn Mitigation/Detection

Table 1. Application of data mining in customer churns the research literature (Reza, Keyvan, 2012)

Action	Data Mining Techniques	Business	References
C4.5 decision tree to model customer churn	Decision tree C4.5	Telecommunication	(Wei et al, 2002)
Toward use of data mining techniques to predict customer churn	Decision tree C4.5, Neural network and evaluate results	Telecommunication	(Au et al, 2003)
Analysis of customer churn	Association Rule A priori	Banking	(Chiang et al, 2003)
Identify and predict customer churn	Clustering RFM, Decision tree, SVM	Insurance	(Monk and Kopck, 2004)
Models to predict customer churn as part of the customer lifetime value	Logistic regression, Decision trees, Neural network	Telecommunication	(Hwang et al, 2004)
Comparison of techniques for prediction and focus on profitable customers in a non-contractual environment	Logistic regression, Neural network, Random forest	Retail	(Buckinx et al, 2005)
Analysis model with the focus on predicting customer churn	Logistic regression, Decision trees, Neural networks, Bayesian networks	Telecommunication	(Neslin et al, 2006)
Assessment of classification methods for predicting customer churn	Decision trees (C5.0, CART, Tree Net)	Telecommunication	(Chander et al, 2006)
Applying data mining in managing customer churn	Neural network, Decision tree	Telecommunication	(Hung et al, 2006)
Provide a model compound for retaining current customers	Clustering, Decision tree C5.0	Pay TV company	(Chu et al, 2007)
Evaluation of data mining methods to maintain current customers	Markov chain, Random forest, Logistic regression	Pay TV company	(Burez et al, 2007)
Assessment of classification methods for predicting customer churn	SVM, Logistic regression, Random forest	Newspapaer	(Coussement et al, 2008)
Comparison of neural network techniques to predict customer churn	Neural network, SOM clustering	Telecommunication	(Tsai et al, 2009)
Identify customer churn	Fuzzy C-means clustering	Banking	(Popovic et al, 2009)
Improve the marketing structure prediction customer churn	Neural network, Decision trees, Logistic regression	Newspaper	(Coussement et al, 2010)
Identify and predict customer churn	Neural networks, Decision trees, Association Rule A priori	Telecommunication	(Tsai et al, 2010)

Table 2. Strengths and weaknesses of various data mining techniques in modeling customer churn (Reza & Keyvan, 2012)

Data Mining Method	Strengths	Weaknesses
Decision trees	• Very simple technique • Provide reliable results • Provide concrete rules	• Difficulty of extracting classification rules • The stability of their steady the optimal solution
Neural networks	• The ability to predict precisely	• The difficulty of performing construction • Lack of transparency interpret the output results
Regression	• Ease of application performing model • Very rich literature on the use of model	• Inability to express behavior patterns hidden in dana • The inability of the bahavioral patterns of behavioral phenomena
Association rules	• Ability to discover hidden relationships among dana behavioral • The ability to sequence the events, phenoomena customer bahavior	• Total amount of items that do not frequent
Support vector machines	• Accuracy of dana with much better results • The error rate can be controlled	• Does the Time Being
Clustering	• The most widely used method • Initial assesment of customer data	• Metohd's performance alone is not sufficient to predict customer behavior
Random forest	• Stable and steady • The dana subject has good performance	• The difficulty of performing construction
New Bayes	• The number of nominal variables than id the case New Bayes for better performance	• New Bayes method for the case of binary characters fare much less accuracy

systems are much more flexible in analytic model development, and are able to solve problems caused by strict rules during variable grouping process.

Fuzzy expert systems can be used with problems like:

- Scoring,
- Segmentation,
- Classification.

Besides traditional usage, fuzzy expert systems had great potential if we consider them as part of CRM systems or decision support systems. By introducing time component into fuzzy expert system powerful market monitoring tool can be founded. Fuzzy expert systems use preprocessed data as model entry data sample. Preprocessed data can be collected from different databases or external sources like data warehouses or data marts. Data needs to be preprocessed in order to be combined into variables creating rules for model.

To prepare environment for handling simple business rule like

IF

turnover_in_past_six_motnhs = *low*

AND

marketing_costs_in_past_six_months = *high*

THEN

client_perspective = *not nprofitable*

we need to preprocess turnover and marketing costs data for six month period. Based on variable values and promotion costs fuzzy expert system execute category selection and use expert rule set to decide about customer perspective. Like it has been shown in this simple rule set, it is needed to calculate six month data for every unique customer, calculate their promotion investment and store data processed through ETL process into data table, base storage for further fuzzy expert analysis. Data table created by explained process can be further processed using expert system designed with professional software tool or we can develop standalone application based on ActiveX control or we can use customized API function as data interchange layer.

Simplified fuzzy expert system schema can be found in Figure 1.

Final model can be part of more complex system, furthermore is able to communicate with other OLAP tools.

Preprocessing phase for fuzzy expert systems is very complex process. Overall success of that phase is in correlation with efficient targets which directly influence on variable modeling phase which is prior to processing. At this point we also need to consider time frame for every variable which will be processed especially from business perspective of market segment. Following time frame analysis, for volatile retail we can use three months segment while other market segment need to be analyzed in much wider time horizon. In similar way aggregation functions should be selected by type and nature of business and afterwards analyzed to find most appropriate for predefined time horizons (for example summary function, average function etc.)

Like mentioned before, fuzzy expert systems are used in knowledge discovery processes for classification, segmentation and scoring purposes with main focus on

Figure 1. Fuzzy expert system schema

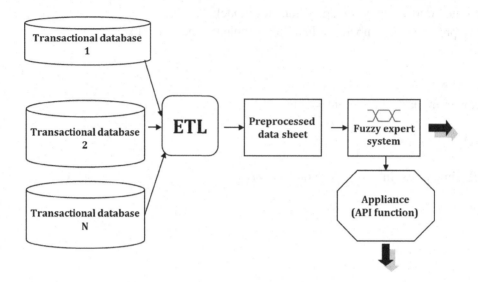

expert knowledge which is implemented into models. Results which are provided from those models are mostly first step for more complex analysis and for usage in combination with other knowledge discovery techniques. If we, for example, execute client scoring using fuzzy expert system, as result we receive information about client classification into specific segment which can help us in better understanding of clients in general but it is not enough for efficient understanding of group of clients or unique client which are part of analyzed category. During analysis process we can move our focus from typical profile of a client who belongs to specific scoring group, can we found smaller segments inside analyzed scoring group, are there any specific behavior characteristics of users who belongs to specific category etc. Only way to get answers to those questions is using further and deeper analysis using other knowledge discovery methods. Those processes are in most cases determined by analysis goals and delivery plan. If our goal is, for example, increase share of most valuable customers, then we firstly need to use expert system to determine who those clients are. This is also ending point for fuzzy expert system and from that point we are using other knowledge discovery methods in order to typical behavior pattern of those customers, to find out main triggers which activate those kind of customers, what are drivers of customers from less valuable groups to be more active, to be loyal and how to influence on other factors which are bringing value to company in order to move as many possible customers into higher (more valuable) scoring group.

Fuzzy expert systems can be also used for market segment layering analysis. Basic procedure include market segment volume analysis. Market segments were created using expert knowledge and fuzzy expert system over similar time segments. By following market segments volume over similar time periods we are able to monitor market activities and trends looking for opportunities and threats. To be able to efficiently monitor market segments we need to combine other knowledge discovery methods. That combination allows us to look for answers on questions like:

- What are the reasons for decreasing trend of most profitable customer segment volume in past 6 months
- What are the reasons for decreasing trend of sales volume in specific customer segment in past 6 months
- Which are basic characteristics of clients who are part of valuable customer segment while they at the same time have decreasing trend of specific product group purchase

Those kinds of events are sometimes correlated with macroeconomic trends while sometimes events can be related to heavy activity made by competitors. Therefore, for efficient analysis, we need to consider all potential causes and test them as hypothesis. It is hard or impossible to influence on macroeconomic trends, from the other side company's microeconomic situation can sometimes be manageable. However, if we are talking about trend caused by competitor activities, we have to be able to recognize those effects on time and be able to proactive react in order to minimize or totally stop negative trends. Since competitor activities are mostly focused on specific market segments, in situations where target market segment is small group of our clients which is hard to determine and manage in same way like our competitors do, fuzzy expert system can be very sufficient in determination of those trends. Segmentation executed using company's expert knowledge in combination with awareness of value of specific market segments together with market layering indicators evaluating in time segments can provide very valuable information about profiles of clients who are moving to less valuable segments or are stopping their relationships with company. Using that information, company management can work on strategy focused on customer retention while using other knowledge discovery methods to gather all kind of data about specific segment group. Using other methods we can expand basic profile onto behavior, buying preferences, purchase drivers etc.

It is very easy to interpret results delivered from fuzzy expert system analysis. Since results are based on values of linguistic variables which are closer to human perception, and are created using expert knowledge, it is very easy to present those data very convenient for people to understand it. Term "easy" include results delivered with fuzzy expert system. In plain language, system is able to explain its conclusions while conclusion is direct consequence of expert knowledge usage represented using business rules in fuzzy syntax.

3.2.2 Neural Networks

Neural networks concept finds its base in neuropsychology. Knowledge about behavior of nerve cell was used for model by simulating activation and synapses potential flow principle. Basic principles of biological model were used to create mathematical model used in practice. Elementary part of mathematical model is unit designed using biological neuron as role model.

Basic learning method for neural network is usage of experimental samples network combined with existing paradigms: auto-associative and hetero-associative learning. For auto-associative one, samples are clustering (combining with themselves) while for hetero-associative two different samples are combining mutually.

Network learning methodology can be divided in three groups (depending of how they use external, back propagation, signals):

- Supervised learning
- Unsupervised learning
- Associative reinforcement learning

Supervised learning (learning with tutor) removes differences between expected outcome and real outcome by invoking back propagation link. Unsupervised learning focused on self-organization or clustering therefore this group does not have back propagation link. Associative reinforcement learning (learning with critics) is based on back propagation link which indicates when actual and estimated samples are overlapping which implicate evolutionary orientation of this group. For better understanding, error back propagation model of supervised learning will be explained in details together with its practical appliance. Preprocessing data for neural network analysis is related to problem type that we are looking to solve. Neural network error back propagation model is mostly used for predictions and classification. Mentioned prediction problems can be related to temporal or non-temporal prediction. While using neural network error propagation model for non-temporal predictions, number of numerical prediction variables determine number of neuron sin entry layer while exit layer neuron represents prediction variable.

For example, if we are looking for prediction of price per m2 in residential area and we are in possession of facts like how real estate is old, where is exact location, garden space in m2, how close building is to public transportation etc. first we need to numerically express all variables, to quantify our data. While doing that, we can plan as many neurons in entry layer as number of variables we have while exit layer neuron represents predicted price per m2 in residential area. All variables which need to be quantified, before learning process has to be normalized (mostly included as default functionality in every neural network analysis software package from major vendors). Explained process can be conceptually expressed in Figure 2.

Same model can be also used for temporal prediction when we are predicting time series Tt value using other time series (At, Bt..). In case of temproal prediction, time series usage for predicting value in moment t+1, has to be adjusted concidering time series value for prodiction using neural networks error backpropagation model as shown in Table 3 and Figure 3.

Explained data adjustments include variable values normalization before analysis.

Neural network creation methodology is similar for classification problems. Only difference is related to exit layer neuron, its value is represented as category. In process of learning, neural network Error back propagation model is processing

Figure 2. Error back propagation model and non-temporal prediction

Case No.	Customer Age	Customer Address	Customer budget	Family budget	...	Purchase in past year
1	25	12	10	1	...	1300
2	15	23	0	0	...	1400
3	38	32	20	1	...	923
4	20	34	10	0	...	1100
n	...	...	...	...	...	...

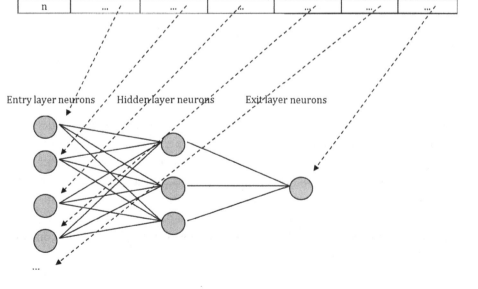

Table 3. Prepared data based on time series T for 3x2x1 neural network architecture

T1	T2	T3	T4	T5	T6	T7	T8	...	Tn
a	b	c	d	e	f	g	h	...	n

Figure 3. Error back propagation model and temporal prediction

Random value	1st entry layer neurons value	2nd entry layer neurons value	3rd entry layer neurons value	Exit layer neurons value
1	a	b	c	d
2	b	c	d	e
3	c	d	e	f
4	d	e	f	g
n	...	...	...	...

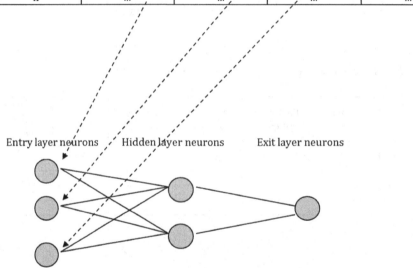

every case with intention to minimize total model error by changing model weight factors. Chosen neural network structure can also be changed during training process in way of increase of neurons in all layers or in way of increase of number of hidden layers. To redesign structure of neural network, we are applying heuristically process which can be executed during learning triggered by iterative inefficient outcomes. Model validation is provided using test data sample before final model confidence decision made by analyst (depending of error level while comparing test and real data sample).

Analysis results which were delivered using neural network error back propagation are generally hard to interpret. Although, things get more complicated if we would like to explain reasons that brought us to results even with very clear targets, to interpret results from business perspective is much easier. Additionally, results generated using non temporal prediction model are easy to interpret. If we follow earlier example, real estate price estimation, it is clear how trained neural network with managed confidence level is able to predict target price using known data used as information for neurons in entry network layer. In similar way we can interpret results delivered from neural network trained for classification purpose. This type of neural network model execute sample classification while it uses analysis result by defining segment category and can be used for further clustering analysis.

3.2.3 Logistic Regression

Regression analysis is a popular technique used by the researchers dealing with predicting customer satisfaction (Whitten & Frank, 2005). It provides a first step in model development. To explain it we need to fist explain concept of linear regression. Linear regression can easily be used for classification in domains with numeric attributes. We can use any regression technique, whether linear or nonlinear, for classification. The idea is to perform a regression for each class, setting the output equal to one for training instances that belong to the class and zero for those that do not. The result is a linear expression for the class. Given a test example of unknown class, we need to calculate the value of each linear expression and choose the one that is largest. This method is sometimes called multi response linear regression. One way of looking at multi response linear regression is to imagine that it approximates a numeric membership function for each class. The membership function is 1 for instances that belong to that class and 0 for other instances. Given a new instance we calculate its membership for each class and select the biggest. Multi response linear regression often yields good results in practice. However, it has two drawbacks. First, the membership values it produces are not proper probabilities because they can fall outside the range 0 to 1. Second, least squares regression assumes that the errors are not only statistically independent, but are also normally distributed with the same standard deviation, an assumption that is blatantly violated when the method is applied to classification problems because the observations only ever take on the values 0 and 1. A related statistical technique called logistic regression does not suffer from these problems. Instead of approximating the 0 and 1 values directly, thereby risking illegitimate probability values when the target is overshot, logistic regression builds a linear model based on a transformed target variable.

Regression is considered to be a good technique for identifying and predicting customer satisfaction. For each of the variables in a regression model the standard error rate is calculated. Then the variables with the most significance in respect to linear regressions for churn prediction are obtained and a regression model is constructed. Since the prediction task in churn prognosis is to identify a customer as a churner or non-churner and therefore the prediction attribute is associated with only two values logistic regression techniques are suitable. While linear regression models are useful for prediction of continuous valued attributes, logistic regression models are suitable for binary attributes. The logistic regression model is simply a non-linear transformation of a liner regression model. The standard representation of logistic regression is referred as logit function. The estimated probability of churn is estimated with the function:

$$\Pr\left[churn\right] = \frac{1}{1 + e^{-T}} \tag{1}$$

where $T = a + BX$. Variable a is a constant term, X represents the predictor attributes vector and B is the coefficient vector for the predictor attributes. If T equals 0 the probability is 0.5. This means that it is equi-probable that a customer is a churner and non-churner. With T growing large the probability comes closer to 1, so the customer becomes a more probable churner, when T is becoming small the probability of churn is tending to be 0 (Lazarov, Capota, 2010).

3.2.4 Survival Analysis

Early similarity diagnostics of churned clients, analysis churn trend, customer lifetime estimation. For that analysis specific data mining models are used, called survival models combined into survival analysis. Those models were first introduced in medicine used to evaluate success of different patient therapies during treatment over time.

Business practice finds powerful analysis tool in those models and it is using same methodology for churn analysis. By using this approach it is possible to very efficiently and very early determine churn trends in products and/or services usage and it is possible to efficiently determine link (if any) between contract terminations. Main focus of survival models is how to estimate probability that someone who "survived" contracted relationship will stop or continue to be active in next time period. Survival models like Cox regression (covered later in book) can provide answers like "what is probability of churn regarding different customer characteristics".

Survival models include so called „*terminal markers*" for any activity like for example churn. Therefore, for example, status marked „1" represents customer who terminated its relationship while status marked „0" represents customer who is still active. Next important model variable is time, number of months of product/service usage. Time variable is calculated as number of months from date of churn looking back until customer signature on starting contract. Regarding nature of survival models (like Cox regression) we can include other attributes into model (like predictive variables) using which it is possible to estimate probability for customer churn.

Survival models are used in situations when we want to estimate churn trends. Specific variants of survival models, like Cox regression, allows us to execute deep analysis using predictive variables, being able to look for interesting segment samples together churned client characteristics (for example most frequent churn clients had 3+ calls to call center while their products were in warranty period, or highest churn trend is linked with youngest customer segment while our competitor focused their sales campaigns to those market segment).

Survival models can be also used from so called inverse logic perspective. That means that terminal mark does not have to point out relationship end but also start of relationship. Using that approach we can analyze characteristics of customers who prefer out product/services and we can provide detailed analysis following every promotion activity. This methodology allows us to monitor campaign efficiency while estimating campaign trend curve as well as monitoring newly acquired customers all related to time segments during campaign. This methodology allows communication channels efficiency analysis together with budget allocation focusing most effective channels.

Analysis results indicate churn trends depending of used algorithm and most important characteristics. That information are affecting decision makers in decisions like stopping negative churn trends of specific customer segment or budget re-allocation onto activities related to increase awareness of most profitable clients. Anyway, no matter of strategy, it is highly recommended (crucial) to have as many structured information regarding customers who churned in order to analyze and manage activities and to create strategy for avoiding those effects.

Reasons for churn can vary but most common ones can be structured as follows:

- Bad service/products
- Competition has better <_____> (...price, customer service etc.)
- Not following contract terms
- Bad or incomplete information about service/product
- Competition has better relationship with customers (cross channel, cross product etc.)

Variety of reasons for churn which are determinable using analytical methods has different consequences to company's costs while company is seeking for managing those reasons. When estimated costs for stopping negative trends are higher comparing to future benefit for total specific product/service customer population, we have to apply selective approach focusing only on specific customer groups, mostly most profitable ones.

Relevant and permanent usage of survival methods for monitoring can be used as efficient early warning system providing valuable information to company which is then able to interact and avoid negative effects. Specific situations shows that is possible that, despite early warning systems, negative trends can increase mostly caused by aggressive and unexpected activities from competition (like „price wars"). In those situations survival models provide us efficient help in understanding of churned customers and churn prediction based on most important customer characteristics.

3.2.5 Self-Organizing Maps

Self-organizing maps (SOM) are one of data mining methods, by type SOMs are neural network subcategory. Because of its type, SOMs are often explained as part of neural networks. However, because of its specific algorithm and field of use, SOMs are also covered independently. Usual usage of SOMs covers clustering problems although it has wide application in analysis. One of very efficient fields of usage is for combinatory explosion management (reduction). Process itself includes activation of neuron using two dimensional frames. By increase of sensitivity coefficient of neuron in frame, activation frequency for neurons inside frame is changed. Activation is furthermore caused by shortest distance between analyzed value and value of neuron in frame. To calculate distance we use distance function. Values inside frames are adapting during iterative learning process based on topological principle. Many learning algorithms are available today which uses topological approach to adapt elements in network following nearest neighbor around activated neuron.

Self-organizing maps use numerical attributes as entry values for analysis. Preprocessing phase for SOM include transformation non numerical values into numerical similar to preprocessing for clustering analysis. Main difference while comparing to clustering process is coming from method principle considering that data are „hitting" network frames and in those „hits" values surrounding „hits" are modified. For specific purpose, it is also possible to transform categorical values in numerical ones. Considering transformation rules, attention should be pointed on range of values inside network frame which will be adapted during SOM learning process.

Self-organizing maps are used in business environment for visualization and data clustering, both depending on method characteristics. Visualized clusters in network frame can provide basic overview of analyzed sample, mostly shown in two dimensional spaces. Generally, even by expanding overview to three dimensions it uses topological data concentration principles, results provided by this method are very easy to interpret. Self-organizing maps are also used to reduce combinatory explosion especially in cases which include temporal sample search. As mentioned before, topological principle in combination with data held in network frame provides recognition concentration areas and indicates dominant clusters. In that way we are able to recognize top frequent areas based on pre-defined indicators (like age or salary). Data groups selected in that way can be deeper analyzed using other methods in order to find additional knowledge. Basically, SOMs are mostly used to explore clusters in data because of possibility to easily interpret data delivered from analysis using this method.

3.2.6 Decision Trees

Decision trees are data mining method used to classify attributes based on outcome target variable. Other method usages include appliance in prediction models. Decision trees represent analysis results in form of tree, simple to understand and interpret. Also, delivery crated by this approach can be easily transformed into rule based results. There is wide range of algorithms used to create decision tree. Most known are ID3, c4.5, CHAID, CR&T and QUEST.

Basic methodology to create decision tree include following steps:

- Tree starts with unique root (target variable) which represents overall sample
- If all samples are part of same class, then know become leaf and is market with that class
- If not, algorithm uses measure based on entropy (information gain) to select attribute which will most suitably/efficiently divide sample into sub classes, that attribute is known as test knot attribute, algorithms in this phase are mostly divided by capability to work with different variable types
- Tree is expanding for every value of test attribute

Explained steps are repeating recursively until any recursion stopping indicator is reached. Basic method usage includes problems of classification and prediction. Decision trees, based on wide range of available algorithms can use categorical, discrete but also continuous variables in analysis. Considering that, focus during preprocessing phase is moved to selection of target variable and selection of predictive variables. Every database variable, depending of analysis goal and characteristics of analysis, can became target variable as well as any database variable can become predictive variable.

Preprocessing phase for decision tree analysis can be point towards creation of additional variables which will be used on further analysis. Decision trees are also used in problems of prediction and classification. In plain language, we use those when we are looking for answer on questions like:

- Which are basic characteristics of customer who bought textile products?
- Which are basic characteristics of market segment A?
- Which customers preferable buy life insurance policy?

Decision trees are often used in combination with other knowledge discovery methods, like clustering because delivered clusters can sometimes be used and interpreted as simple results. Decision trees are become very efficient in researches so far in discovery of basic cluster characteristics.

Based in its character, decision trees is part of data mining methods which results are easy to interpret also because it can be transformed into rule set as follows:

IF (GENDER = "W") AND (AGE = "30-40")

AND (LIFE_INSURANCE != "YES")

THEN

PROPERTY_INSURANCE = "YES"

P(probability) = 0.816667   (2)

Rule interpretation shoes that it is preferable to offer real estate insurance policy to clients who do not have life insurance policy, are women and have between 30 and 40 years of age. Probability that that segment will accept our offer is high, 82%.

Rules expressed int his way are very familiar with human perception which also express knowledge in form of rule set. Analysis results can be used as guidelines in campaign planning but also can be used for building rule set sin expert systems. Modern software packages based on decision tree include pre generated sample partitioning tools which separate sample into training set, testing set and model validation set. Using that approach it is possible to evaluate relevancy of decision tree models that we are creating.

3.3 PUTTING IT ALL TOGETHER

Commercially known software packages and tools for data mining with special user interface for analytic modeling by combining different methods provide easy to understand and use approach for method linking. On contrary, by using unique methods manually we need to pay attention to every step, to every preprocessing phase and delivered results. No matter of development environment that we are using, everything is always based on data. It is all about quality of preparation and quality of data.

Data can be processes in iterative cycles and can be treated with all kind of methods with intention to reach goals targeted by analyst. An outcome from one usage does not guarantee applicability to next phase. Sometimes we need to adapt data between phases. If, for example, we apply neural network to classify client risk level for insurance company, and we made that classification for several 6 month periods, and afterwards we will look for trend in market segmentation for every time period and segment – we clearly need to prepare data in order to process it through decision tree analysis. Those preparations and adjustments can be simple operations like additional categorization, normalization or grouping but can also include more complex processes like data partitioning, values interpolation, creating new values etc.

Looking from its characteristics, preparation can be executed in three ways as follows:

- Locally
- On database server
- Combination of first two

Local adjustment includes data preparation on local data storage medium while data can be stored in different formats, preferable ones that can be read with most available applications. We can often found that software package understand and is able to import data from competitors application but if that option is not provided, so called standard data structures are used (like CSV or TAB). Before we prepare data for import into another software package, it is more important to organize data in way that it will be suitable for usage in next method that we are planning to use. Sometimes it is not possible to assure direct connection between two software packages which are based on different mind sets and different data mining methods using plain text files without using specific program language to transform data. Conceptually that process can be expressed as follows:

Preparation using database server includes database, server and outcome data stored in data sheets and in structured way/data format. This approach makes export process easier while data organization problem (preparing data for next method) still remains. Software packages for data mining based on unique methods are able to connect to most available databases. In this case, usage of programming language is even more important to prepare data for further analysis. Conceptually that process can be expressed as follows:

Figure 4. Method connection technique, local

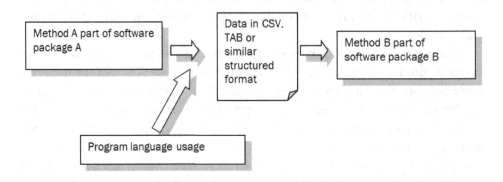

Figure 5. Method connection technique, using database

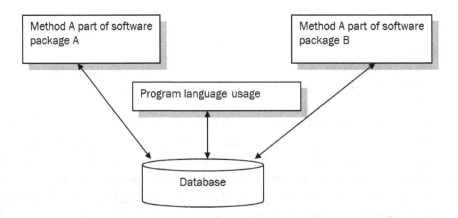

Technique which combines two explained approaches is most commonly used. It overlaps local and methods which use database server. Weight of every part of preparation (local: database) depends of analysis and methods that we are preparing to use. This classification represents illustration into methods connection methodologies while it has to be pointed out that physical and logical data compatibility is priority for efficient method connection.

Complex commercial packages for data mining analysis like IBM SPSS Clemetine or SAS Enterprise Miner, resolve methods connection inside application. Available are also integrated software solutions based on academic initiatives like Orange Modul for Python however they often misses wide number of methods leaving us

Figure 6. Method connection technique, using software package and ActiveX/API service

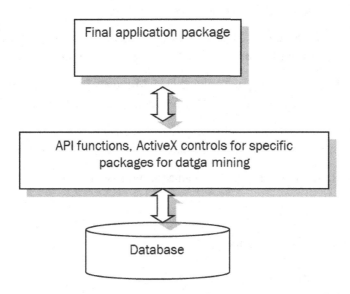

to combine data interchange manually like explained earlier. It is also familiar that software packages include functionality like ActiveX or API functions implementation for further integration into custom packages for data mining. Conceptually that process can be expressed as follows:

This approach is specific and is related only for cases in which we are creating software package for data mining analysis. Of course, it is possible to integrate these functions in specific analysis while results will be stored back in database for further analysis. By using this approach, we are widening applicability of advanced analytics implementation however under more complex environment.

Considering everything explained in this chapter, we can recognize complexity in putting methods together. Although we were mostly explaining problems in physical data interchange, logical one is also crucial but is related to specific analysis and methodology so we will cover that part inside every method and in case studies later in book.

REFERENCES

Kimball, R. (1996). *Data Warehouse Toolkit*. Wiley.

Lazarov, V., & Capota, M. (2010). *Churn Prediction*. Retrieved from http://home. in.tum.de/~lazarov/files/research/papers/churn-prediction.pdf

Reza, A., & Keyvan, R. (2012). Applying Data Mining to Insurance Customer Churn Management. In *Proceedings of 2012 IACSIT Hong Kong Conferences*. IACSIT Press.

Tsai, C., & Lu, Y. (2010). Data Mining Techniques in Customer Churn Prediction. Taiwan: Department of Information Management, National Central University.

Whitten, I. H., & Frank, T. (2005). Data Mining. Elsevier.

KEY TERMS AND DEFINITIONS

CART: Classification and Regression Trees.

CHAID: Type of decision tree technique, based upon adjusted significance testing.

CR&T: Recursive partitioning method, builds classification and regression trees for predicting continuous dependent variables (regression) and categorical predictor variables (classification).

QUEST: Tree-structured classification algorithm that yields a binary decision tree.

SOM: Type of neural network that is trained using unsupervised learning to produce a low-dimensional/two-dimensional discretized representation called a map.

Chapter 4
Social Network Analysis (SNA) for Churn Mitigation/Detection:
Introduction and Metrics

ABSTRACT

Social network analysis[1] is intentionally covered in a separate chapter for two reasons. First, the importance of this method has rapidly increased in past few years, and second, there are very few useable studies that cover social network analysis concepts in churn management. By understanding the methods explained in Chapter 3 and combining them with knowledge of SNA concepts, the analysts (readers) can unlock the full potential of advanced analytics in one of the most important fields of research today, customer relationship and especially churn analysis. With the ability to understand how those metrics can be used, integration of those methods into more complex environments is explained regarding the key topic, churn management.

4.1 INTRODUCTION TO SOCIAL NETWORK ANALYSIS

"All the world's a *network*," William Shakespeare would surely conclude if he were a modern scientist, and John Donne would readily continue: "No man is an island entire of itself...any man's death diminishes me, because I am involved in a *network*...", and they would both start following the direction of the rapidly growing number of contemporary scientist and analysts from fields as different as biology and

DOI: 10.4018/978-1-4666-6288-9.ch004

mathematics, sociology and physics, or geography and psychology. This direction is characterized by the network way of thinking and perceiving the world around us in terms of numberless interconnected entities forming networks of different densities, shapes, and sizes. All types of relations, those among people or animals, their movements and interactions, virtual relations and links, and even relations among genes and neurons, or protein reactions in human body can be perceived as different types of networks functioning in a similar way, and therefore analyzed using same tools and models.

However, to be able to understand full complexity of the social network analysis (SNA), we shall start by defining general concept and component parts. *Social network* is formally defined as a group of interconnected individuals. These individuals are connected by one or more types of relations whose patterns occupy the attention of scientists and researchers. They relate to each other by either some kind of cooperation, or competition/conflict, and are referred to as *entities* or *actors*. Their relations can be depicted by a graph in which each entity (actor or individual) is depicted as what is in graph theory called a *node*, and their relations are depicted as *links* (ties). In terms of social network analysis, actors can be any sets of related entities, whereby entities need not be only persons - the scope of analyzing social networks also includes animals, genomes, and even inanimate systems, such as traffic lines and electric power grids.

4.1.1 Evolution of Social Network Analysis

With a history of almost one hundred years, SNA developed under many influences from various fields, primarily sociology, and mathematics, but its implementation as an interdisciplinary technique ranges from physics and computer science, to communication science, economics, and even psychology.

Social network analysis as an academic discipline was generated in 1920s–1930s, in the research field of anthropology in Britain. Term *social network* was first coined by anthropologist Roger Brown who suggested that social structure is similar to a network and that interpersonal communication among individuals resembles the relationship between a node and another nesting in the network (Zhang, 2010; Scott, 1987).

At the turn of the twentieth century Georg Simmel was the first scholar to think directly in social network terms. He advanced the idea that society consists of a network of patterned interactions, and argued that society is merely the name for a number of individuals, connected by interaction. All human behavior is behavior of individuals, but Simmel suggested that much of it can be explained in terms of the individual's group affiliation, and constraints imposed upon him by particular forms of interaction (Coser, 1977; Simmel, 1908/1971).

The visualization of networks and the early sociograms began with social psychologist of Romanian origins Jacob Levy Moreno with his *Sociometry Method* created in 1930s. This method introduced systematic analysis of social interaction in small groups, and as such paved the way for quantitative analysis in social network approach.

In his 1934 book, Moreno used the term "network" in the sense that it is used today. According to Freeman, the work of Moreno – with the help of Jennings and Lazarsfeld - had displayed "all four of the features that define contemporary social network analysis" (Freeman, 2004). In Moreno's images, each actor was represented by a point, and each link was shown by a line connecting a pair of points (Figure 1).

Sociometry measures the "socius" – the interpersonal connection between two people (Moreno 1951). Moreno conceived three levels of sociometry:

- Theoretical system or *sociatry*, including role, social atom, spontaneity/encounter, psychodrama/enactment, and sociometry theories;
- Sub theory of theoretical system, and
- Assessment method and intervention (Hale, 1981; Remer, 2006).

Sociometry had a crucial influence on sociology and related fields, but overtime its influence has significantly diminished. However, "a complete understanding of

Figure 1. Moreno's early network (Carrington et al., 2005)

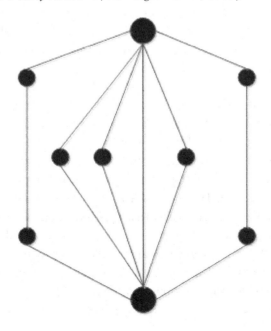

sociometry provides tremendously powerful structures and tools for use not only in small group interactions but also wherever and whenever interpersonal dynamics come into play" (Remer, 2008).

The period between 1940s and 1960s is considered by some as "the Dark Ages" in the history of the development of SNA. In this period, there was no generally recognized approach to social research that included the "structural paradigm". Freeman argues that social network analysis was still "not identifiable either as a theoretical perspective or as an approach to data collection and analysis". After that, there was a period of a rapid growth in number of scholars who focused their work on combining different tracks and traditions in studying social networks. One large group gathered around Harrison White and his students at Harvard University: Ivan Chase, Bonnie Erickson, Harriet Friedmann, Mark Granovetter, Nancy Howell, Joel Levine, Nicholas Mullins, John Padgett, Michael Schwartz and Barry Wellman. The so-called Renaissance of SNA spread among Harvard scholars resulting in a number of important articles that influenced social scientists everywhere, regardless of their field (Freeman, 2004).

4.1.2 "The Small World" of Stanley Milgram

Network patterns have been researched and studied even more intensively in the past decade, and the idea that underlies all the research is the idea of the small world attributed to Stanley Milgram.

In mid 20th century, Stanley Milgram conducted a number of experiments connected with human behavior, and the most important one for the development of SNA is known as *small world problem* (Milgram, 1967). Foundation of the experiment, later named *six degrees of separation*, is the question "What is the probability that any two persons know each other?"

The motif for the research is the situation which happens surprisingly often: two people meeting for the first time discovering that they have common acquaintances, the co-called small world phenomenon. Milgram formulated a general question applicable for each of these cases: Starting with any two people in the world, what is the probability that they will know each other? And another question one may ask is: Given any two people in the world, person X and person Z, how many intermediate acquaintance links are needed before these two people are connected? (Blass, 2004)

However, Milgram was not the first to ask these questions. Conclusions of physicist Guglielmo Marconi, stemming from his work on wireless telegraphy from the beginning of the 20th century, and articulated in his speech for the Nobel Prize reception ceremony (Marconi, 1909), inspired Hungarian writer, dramatist and journalist Frigyes Karinthy (1929), who mentions this small world concept in his novel titled "Chains". One of his characters suggests a game experiment to prove the theory of the existence of a link between any two persons in the form of the chain of at most 5 people. At that time, Budapest was already acquainted with the belief that people are separated by the six degrees of social contact. This belief was mostly based on at that time very important demographic work of statists, who had considerable influence in urban planning of Eastern European cities of the time. Mathematician Benoit Mandelbrot, born in Poland, travelled around Eastern Europe, where he got acquainted with the practical statist rule of degrees of separation. Simultaneously, Mandelbrot was linked with De Sola Pool, Kochen, and Milgram – his colleagues at the Paris University from the beginning of the 1950s. They were all in a way fascinated by interconnectedness and the social capital of social networks.

It is obvious that Milgram's experiment was devised in times when scientific circles were already aware of growing connectedness of the world. Michael Gurevich conducted a research on the structure of social networks in his doctoral thesis mentored by De Sola Pool at the Massachusetts Institute of Technology (MIT). Political scientist De Sola Pool and Austrian mathematician Manfred Kochen, who was at that time dealing with urban planning, investigated empirical results of Gurevich's work and introduced their findings in mathematical manuscript titled "*Contacts and Influence*" (De Sola Pool and Kochen, 1978). This manuscript circulated among scientists for 20 years before it was published in Elsevier magazine "Social Networks" in 1978. De Sola Pool and Kochen based their results on a theoretical model that suggested that any two randomly chosen strangers could be linked with a small chain of acquaintances. In the population of the size of American that has no social structure, they concluded, it is almost certain that any two individuals can contact one another through at least two intermediaries. But social structure posed a big problem in their experiment and influenced their results. If person A has 500 acquaintances, and his friend has about the same number of acquaintances, then many of those 500 of each of them may actually be friends or acquaintances among themselves. The acquaintances of person A will "simply feed back into his own circle and fail to bring any new contacts into it." In other words, "though poor people always have acquaintances, it would probably turn put that they tend to be among other poor people, and that the rich speak mostly to the rich. It is exceedingly difficult to assess the impact of social structure on a model of this sort" (Milgram, 1967). In a socially structured population these results are less probable, but still possible, while for the entire world population it would take only one intermediary more (De Sola Pool and Kochen, 1978). Based on Gurevich's data the two scientists designed Monte Carlo simulations, which proved that both weak and strong ties of acquaintances are needed to model social structure. Simulations were limited in scope due to slowness of computers at the time they were made (it was in 1973!), but they were a good predictive model for somewhat more realistic 3 degrees of separation within the American population, which was also the value that foreboded later Milgram's discoveries.

This work formally articulated the mechanics of social networks and investigated their mathematical consequences, including connectedness, but many important questions regarding networks remained open, including the number of degrees of separation in real social networks.

At that time Milgram visited Paris University and collaborated with De Sola Pool and Kochen on their project, where he got attracted by this counterintuitive nature of the small world, and he decided to empirically test it himself. In his experiments started at the Harvard University in 1967, Milgram used the results of earlier Gurevich's experiments with acquaintances' networks. Milgram developed his experiment out of the desire to find out more about the likelihood that two randomly selected people would know each other. Another way of studying small world problem is to imagine the population as a social network and try to find the average path length between any two nodes. Milgram's experiment is designed to calculate the length of these paths by finding a model that would help calculate the number of links between any two persons.

In the first study, Milgram picked a certain number of persons from the Wichita (Kansas) as the starting points and the target person who lived in Cambridge (Massachusetts). For the second study starting points were from Omaha (Nebraska), and Sharon/Boston (Massachusetts) as the finishing point of the correspondence chain. The reason why these particular cities were chosen was their distance, geographic as well as social.

The next step was to disseminate packages with information among randomly selected individuals in Omaha or Wichita. When receiving invitations for participating in the experiment, the receiver would be asked whether he personally knew the contact person mentioned in the letter. If the answer was positive, the candidate had to send the package directly to that person. For the purpose of the experiment notion "know personally" was defined as the person whom the sender knew on a first name basis.

Packages contained documents with details about the aim of the research and some basic information about the target person in Boston. To help trace its path the envelope also included the roster which had to be signed by each participant, along with "tracer" cards addressed to Harvard that had to be sent to Milgram and the team of scientists leading the experiment.

In most cases the sender did not personally know the target person, and had to send the package to a friend, cousin, or acquaintance for whom he thought might have known the target person. He had to add his name to the list enclosed then, and send the tracer card to Harvard so that the scientists had continuous feedback on the progress of each chain.

In cases when the package reached the target, the roster helped count the number of times the package was forwarded from one person to another. For packages that did not reach the target, tracer cards were used to identify the point in which the chain was broken.

Shortly after the experiment had started, packages started to reach the target addresses, and Harvard scientists to receive the postcards. In some cases, packages reached their target in only a few steps, while other chains had as much as nine or ten links. It was discovered also that only one part of chains was finished. Significant problem that the experiment encountered posed situations in which people did not want to forward the package, which resulted in breaking the chain. Of 160 chains that started in Nebraska, 126 dropped out. However, the remaining 44 packages reached the target contact person. In this study, the chain length varied from two to ten intermediate acquaintances, with the median at five. Over many trials, the results of Milgram's experiment indicate that the average number of intermediate connections in a successful chain was between five and six. Based on that, the conclusion of the experiment was that people in the US were separated by 6 people on average.

Scientists also used tracer cards for a qualitative research about the relevant sociological characteristics of the senders of the cards and types of chains created during the experiment. They discovered that packages reached geographically closer destinations relatively soon, but they circulated around the target almost randomly until they found a narrower circle of friends or acquaintances of the target person. The results point to the fact that participants mostly preferred geographical characteristics when choosing the appropriate next person in the chain, but also that social communication is sometimes restricted less by physical distance than by social distance. Also, the experiment discovered that the participants were three times as likely to send the package to someone of the same sex, which suggests that some kinds of communication are strongly conditioned by sex roles. Kansas study revealed another interesting aspect of social structure: of the 145 participants 123 sent the folder to friends or acquaintances and only 22 sent it to their relatives. Milgram suggests that in societies which do not possess extended kinship systems, such as US, "acquaintance and friendship links provide preponderant basis for reaching the target persons" (Milgram, 1967; Travers and Milgram, 1969).

What is even more important, Milgram discovered that in our social world, some people are "more important" in terms of establishing contacts possessing a wide circle of friends and acquaintances, and contact with them puts us in a far-ranging network of additional persons. This idea was later developed into a concept of "hubs". Foundation for Milgram's conclusions were findings from Nebraska study which revealed that the target person - a stock-broker living in Sharon and working in Boston - got 16 out of 24 packages from the same person – a clothing merchant in town. At his place of work in Boston, 48% of the chains reached him by three persons. This tells us that there appear to be highly popular channels for the transmission of the chain, and Milgram called them "sociometric stars with specialized contact possibilities". This also suggests that "six degrees of separation" does not mean that every person is only six steps apart form every other person, but rather that there is a small minority connecting vast majority, and we call them *connectors*. In Tipping Point, Gladwell argues that connectors are not important only because of the number of people they know, but also because of the type of people they are acquainted with. "These people who link us up with the world, who bridge Omaha and Sharon, who introduce us to our social circles — these people on whom we rely more heavily than we realize — are Connectors, people with a special gift for bringing the world together" (Gladwell, 2002).

This only confirms the fact that complex networks, and social networks in general, are dominated by the hubs - socially successful people whose connections make shortcuts which shrink the world we live in into various "small worlds".

Milgram's basic small-world experiment remains the foundation of the research in social networks and the framework for the majority of recent network models. Although there was a number of scientists who harshly criticized his methodology, the findings were important for two reasons. Firstly, he was the first who actually counted the number of acquaintances needed to link two randomly selected strangers, and to do so he used inventive methodology. Secondly, the fact is that lots of people have at least one or two personal experiences connected with the small world idea, but Milgram was the one who proved that this type of close connectedness is a general and calculable feature of our social world. And this discovery is counterintuitive: Milgram asked an intelligent friend how many links would take to send a letter from his starters in Nebraska to the target person in Boston, and the reply was about one hundred.

In the 1980s, a number of sociologists began to use SNA as analytical technique to examine social and economic phenomena. The most prominent among them, the one with the crucial role in reviving SNA approach within the mainstream social research field was American sociologist and Stanford University professor Mark Granovetter. In 1970s and 1980s, Granovetter developed several theories that earned him the title of the leader in the field of economic sociology, and the father of "new economic sociology". In mid 1980s, he proposed the concept of "embeddedness"[2], arguing that economic relations between individuals or firms are embedded in actual social networks and do not exist in an abstract idealized market. Unlike traditional economic interpretations of interactions between people, which assume rational, self-interested behavior affected only marginally by social relations, Granovetter believes that it is more accurate to view economic rationality as "embedded" within social structure, and that the core social structure is, in fact, individuals' social networks.

However, more important work for the study of social networks is his "The Strength of Weak Ties" (Granovetter, 1973), a seminal paper in contemporary social network analysis, and also a groundbreaking work in sociology in general. In this paper he uses SNA as a tool in elaborating the macro implications of the strength of dyadic ties. He argues that "the degree of overlap of two individuals' networks varies directly with the strength of their tie to one another", and further explores the impact of this principle on "diffusion of influence and information, mobility opportunity, and community organization" (Granovetter, 1973)[3]. In this context, Granovetter emphasizes the strength and cohesive power of weak ties in relations between groups. There are two important hypotheses emanating from Granovetter's discussion. Firstly, if we consider any two arbitrarily selected individuals, say *A* and *B*, in the set *S=C, D, E,...*, of all persons with ties to either *A* or *B*, or to both of them, a certain number of persons from the set will also be connected - the stronger the tie between *A* and *B*, the larger the proportion of individuals in *S* to whom they both will be tied, by either a strong or weak tie. In other words, in our close circle of friends, our friends are also friends among themselves. Granovetter suggests that this overlap in friendship circles will be least when the tie between *A* and *B* is absent, most when it is strong and intermediate when the tie is weak. Secondly, Granovetter suggests that some ties can act as a bridge that bypasses parts of social networks and connects otherwise disconnected social groups. Defining the bridge as "a line in a network which provides the only path between two points," he argues that "no strong tie is a bridge," except under unlikely conditions, and that weak ties are most valuable for the diffusion across network. "A strong tie can be a bridge only if neither party to it has any other strong ties, unlikely in a social network of any size (though possible in small groups). Weak ties suffer no such restriction, though they are certainly not automatically bridges. What is important, rather, is that all bridges are weak ties." Based on these hypotheses, Granovetter concludes that "whatever is to be diffused can reach a larger number of people, and traverse greater social distance, when passed through weak ties rather than strong." Granovetter managed to prove the significance of weak ties at both the individual and community level. In his world, weak ties have a better cohesive power because they connect groups of people with other groups of people. Thanks to weak ties that serve as bridges between different groups, information or rumour will spread easier and faster to different groups. Besides, weak ties are crucial because they help opening a wide set of options. They are a cohesive factor in terms of individual's integration in various social groups (Figure 2).

Another problem that he studied was the structure of ego networks (Granovetter, 1973). The point he discussed was whether ego's network should be treated as composed only of ego and those with whom he is directly connected, or should it include contacts of their contacts as well. At the time Granovetter developed his

Figure 2. Granovetter's scheme of strong and weak ties (Granovetter, 1973)

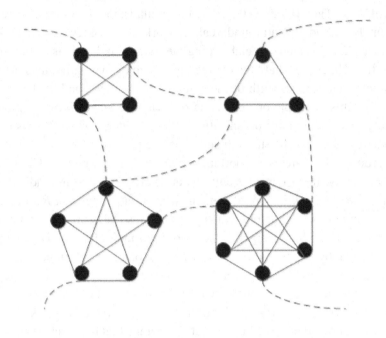

theory, there were two different approaches to the analysis of social networks. One emphasized encapsulation of ego by his network, and the other manipulation of entire networks, since the information and services accessible through direct contacts might depend on who these contacts are. According to Granovetter, the structure of a social network formed around a person (ego) is quite general. Ego will have a group of close friends, most of which are also connected with each other, which makes a densely woven society structure network. Furthermore, ego will also have a set of acquaintances among which only few might know each other. However, each of those contacts will also have his own close friends, which means he will also be a part of a densely woven network of society, but different from ego's. Granovetter concludes his discussion by dividing ego's network into "that part made up of strong and nonbridging weak ties on the one hand, and on that of bridging weak ties on the other (...)" (Granovetter, 1973). Ties in the former part would consist of people who know one another, but also some of their contacts not tied to ego. In the latter part, ego's contacts will not be tied to one another, but will be tied to individuals not tied to ego.

In this way, indirect contacts would be reachable through ties, and consequently, these ties would be important not only to ego's manipulation of networks, but would also be channels through which ideas, information and influence would reach ego although socially distant from him. "The fewer indirect contacts one has the more encapsulated he will be in terms of knowledge of the world beyond his own friendship circle; thus, bridging weak ties (and the consequent indirect contacts) are important in both ways," Granovetter concludes (Figure 3).

Granovetter proves this argument with the results of his study on labor market and the use of personal social networks for this purpose, specifically the nature of the tie between a job seeker and his contact person, the one who told him about the job vacancy. The research was based on two assumptions: first, the person we knew personally will be more motivated to help us and give us the necessary information about the job; second, people whom we meet rarely or occasionally (weak ties) move in circles different from ours, and, accordingly, have access to different information from those we receive. He used empirical data from a survey of job seekers, asking those who had found a job through personal contacts how often they saw the person who passed on job information to them. Only 16.7% of those finding a job trough contacts said that they saw their contacts often, while more than 83% said occasionally or rarely. In many cases the contact was only marginally included in the current network of contacts, with whom only sporadic contact was kept.

Granovetter's findings are an upgrade of Milgram's small-world experiment (Milgram, 1967) and Rapoport-Horvath study (Rapoport and Horvath, 1961). In an empirical study related to the small world problem Rapoport and Horvath examined sociometric networks in the sample of 861 Michigan junior high school students. They asked each student to name their eight best friends within the school in order of preference. Then they traced the acquaintance chains created by the students' choices. They proved that the smallest total number of people were reached through

Figure 3. Ego network (Granovetter, 1973)

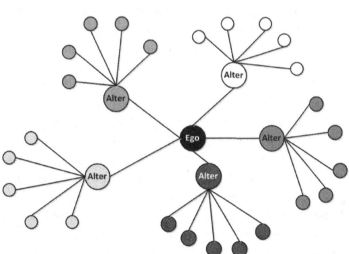

the networks generated by first and second choices (strong ties), while the largest number were reached through seventh and eight choices (weak ties), which confirms Granovetter's assertion that more people can be reached through weak ties.

4.1.3 Graphs and Networks

The study of social networks develops parallelly on two tracks – sociological (networks), and mathematical (graphs), and consequently, social network analysis is based on two different approaches. Apart from the mentioned sociological aspect with small-world phenomenon, equally important aspect for the development of SNA is the mathematical one, namely combinatorics, or more precisely, graph theory.

Graph theory is a mathematical tool for depicting and explaining social networks. Mathematical foundation for the SNA came from Hungarian mathematicians Pál Erdős and Alfréd Rényi with their model of generating random graphs, or in terms of SNA – random networks. A few years prior to Milgram's small-world experiment, in 1959, Erdős and Rényi suggested the first algorithm for random graph generation, which uses same probability to chose node pairs from a given set of nodes, and links them based on the previously defined probability. According to this model, the set that has n nodes forms every connection with a given probability of p, and the formation is independent across links (Erdős and Rényi, 1959, 1960, and 1961).

Erdős-Rényi model is one of the oldest and most intensely studied random network models, whose basic feature is the possibility to mathematically calculate most of its average properties. This model has intuitive structure and was a starting point to most of later models. Since it presumes that connections in a network are the result of a completely random process, properties of random networks may help to get insights in properties of some other networks, social or economic for example. Some of these properties, intensively studied today, are the ways of distribution of connections over nodes, ways in which networks are connected in terms of their capability to find ways from one node to another, average and maximum path lengths, number of isolated nodes, etc. Random networks therefore can be a useful benchmark for comparing observed networks because these comparisons help identify those elements of social structure that are not the result of mere randomness, but must rather be assigned to some other factors. Two key points which differentiate this model from real-world networks are low network clustering and unrealistic degree distribution.

Origins of graph theory as a branch of combinatorics are attributed to Leonhard Euler, who proposed the solution for the problem of the seven bridges of Köningsberg (today known as Kaliningrad) in 1735 (Figure City map of Köningsberg (Kaliningrad))[4]. This problem was discussed in Albert-László Barabási's book Linked (Barabasi, 2002) (Figure 4).

Figure 4. City map of Köningsberg (Kaliningrad) (Barabási A. L. 2002)

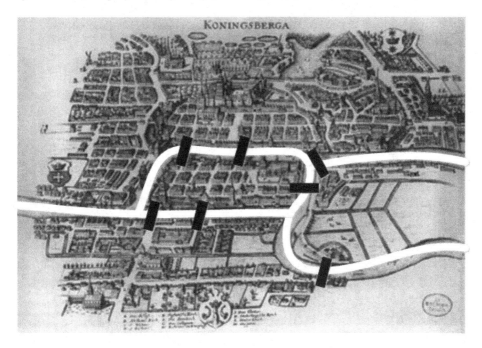

As most European cities, Köningsberg is situated on the banks of a river. River Pregel passes through the center of the city which includes two big islands connected with the rest of the mainland with seven bridges. The problem that Euler set was to find a way through the city by crossing each of the bridges only once. Islands could not be reached by any other route, except cross the bridges. The only important feature for Euler was the sequence at which bridges should be crossed. Therefore, it was possible to discard all other features but the bridges which connected two pieces of land. This problem is considered as a foundation of the graph theory.

In the bridge problem Euler noticed that any time the pedestrian would make the connection and reach the node by bridge, he would also leave the node by bridge. In practice it meant that during any walk around the city pedestrian would enter the bridge as many times as he would leave it. Mathematically speaking, Euler discovered that the existence of a path in a graph depended on node degrees. What counts is the number of connections touching a certain node. Euler also noticed that a necessary condition for a particular walk-through is that the graph be connected and have zero or two nodes with odd degrees. This solution is called Euler path: a continuous path that passes through every link once and only once. Alternative formulation of the bridge problem is to discover the path which would include crossing all the bridges,

Figure 5. Problem of the seven bridges of Köningsberg (Barabási, 2002)

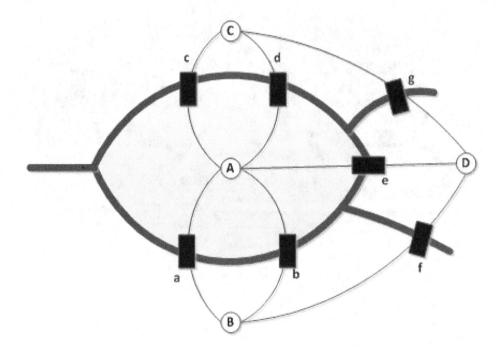

whereby the same point would be starting as well as finishing. Such a path is called Euler circuit: a Euler path which begins and ends in the same node (Figure 5).

So, Euler's first theorem says that if a graph has any nodes with odd degrees, than it cannot have any Euler circuit. Also, if a graph is connected and every node has an even degree, then it has at least one Euler circuit. Accordingly, Euler's second theorem says that if a graph has more than two nodes with odd degree, it cannot have an Euler path. Furthermore, if a graph is connected and has exactly two nodes with odd degree, then it has at least one Euler path. Any such path must start at one of the odd degree nodes and must end at the other odd degree node.

Euler's theorems as applied to directed graphs suggest that if at each node the *number in* equals *number out*, then there is an Euler circuit. Also, if at one node *number in* equals *number out+1*, and at one other node *number in* equals *number out-1*, and all other nodes have *number in* equal to *number out*, then there is an Euler path (Figure 6).

Extrapolating this concept to SNA, every piece of land would be marked as a vertex, and bridges as edges. Mathematical structure of the problem is known as a graph, while in the context of social sciences, its components form a network. In this type of problem the only relevant information is that of connecting. Graph can

Figure 6. Euler path (a path that traverses each link exactly once)[5]

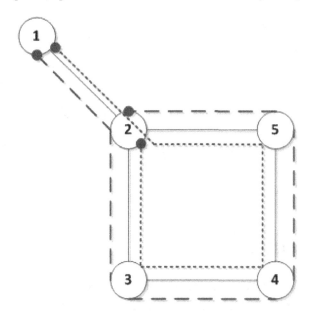

be depicted in various forms, but with no changes in the graph itself, i.e. links between nodes must remain unchanged. Therefore, the only thing we are interested in in SNA is the existence or lack of edges between a pair of vertices. Even when we want to calculate network metrics of certain vertices, to be able to do that we need to consider edges. Connected vertices are determined by the edges between a pair of vertices, the original one and the one with which it is connected, regardless of whether the connection comes to the vertex or leaves from it. The degree of a vertex in a network is the number of edges the vertex has to other vertices, or, in other words, the total number of vertices adjacent to the vertex. If a network is directed, meaning that edges point in one direction from one vertex to another vertex, then vertices have two different degrees: the in-degree (indicating the number of incoming edges), and the out-degree (the number of outgoing edges). In undirected network the edges go in both directions (Figure 7)..

Social network analysis is the study of relations between vertices, and this relation in this context is defined by edges. Accordingly, the degree distribution $P(k)$ of a network is defined as the fraction of vertices in the network with degree k. We can then say that if there are n vertices in a network and n_k of them have degree k, then $P(k) = n_k/n$

This example of network analysis have spread recently in various directions, primarily thanks to computer sciences, statistical physics, and the capacity of implementation in economic sciences.

Figure 7. Directed and undirected network

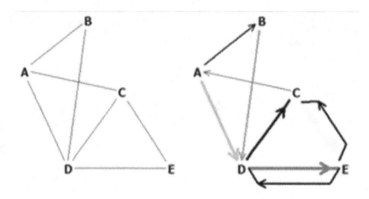

4.1.4 Complex Networks

Granovetter's society in the form of fragmented network of closely connected groups communicating among themselves through bridging weak ties is much closer to actual social structure than a completely random picture designed by Erdős and Rényi with their random graphs. Almost three decades after Granovetter's research was published, these two completely different theories on social structure have come to shape a new network model.

In the past fifteen years, from the late 1990s onwards, the research of networks has diffused over a number of scientific fields through the study of complex networks. As mentioned earlier, graph theory in its original form designed by Erdős and Rényi, their model of random graphs and some other mathematical models of networks that have been studied in the past lacked certain properties that occur in real networks, such as heavy tail in the degree distribution[6], high clustering coefficient, assortativity or disassortativity among vertices, community structure, and hierarchical structure. The study of these non-trivial topological features, however, have brought together researchers from many areas in an attempt to try and discover patterns of connection and other specific structural features of real networks, that are neither purely random nor purely regular in their nature.

Two much studied classes of complex networks are scale-free and small-world networks, the former characterized by power-law degree distributions, and the latter by short path lengths and high clustering. Short path lengths refer to the fact that any two random persons can be connected through a relatively small number of acquaintances, as confirmed by Milgram's six degrees of separation, while high clustering can be illustrated with a group of friends where our friends are also friends among themselves.

Many naturally occurring networks are small-world networks because we can reach a given node from another one in a very small number of steps, or, in terms of SNA, following a path with a small number of edges between the vertices (Figures 8 and 9).

Results of Watts-Strogatz model suggest that a few random links in an otherwise clustered graph give an average shortest path close to that of a random graph.

The Watts-Strogatz random model includes two parameters: the probability of re-arrangement (p), and the number of "ring" neighbors (k). We start with a ring adding nodes or vertices, with each node being connected to k successive neighbors. To get a random network, for each edge in turn we flip a p-biased coin. If heads, we replace an edge with a random edge from one of its nodes to a random other node.

Properties of such networks are as follows:

- For p = 0, we get a regular structure (ring-like), also called ordered lattice.
- As p increases, there is more randomness.
- For p = 1, it becomes the standard Erdős-Rényi random graph.
- The regular structure (ring) has high clustering coefficient and long path lengths.
- Erdős-Rényi has small characteristic path length and low clustering coefficient.
- For a range of p, we get small path length and high clustering coefficient, i.e. small-world graph.

Application of Watts-Strogatz model is wide. It ranges from biology (modeling of disease epidemics); epidemiology (efficacy of needle-exchange programs in AIDS prevention), and economics (modeling of fads, momentum investing), to business

Figure 8. Schematic of the Watts-Strogatz model (Watts & Strogatz, 2004)

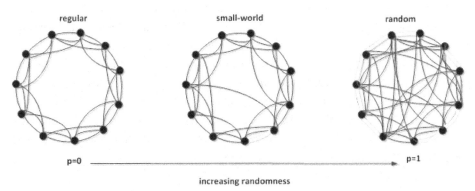

Figure 9. Normalized average shortest path length L and clustering coefficient C as a function of the random rewiring parameter p for the Watts-Strogatz model with N = 1000, and k =10 (Watts and Strogatz, 2004)

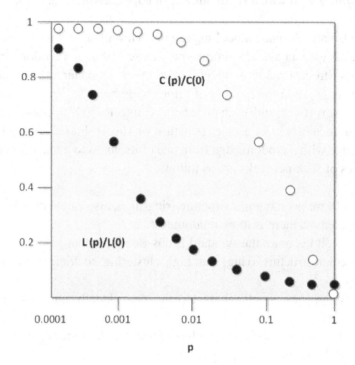

(organizational hierarchy), and commercial application (meetup.com, friendster. com, tribe.com, linkedin.com, etc.).[7]

Another important property in the study of complex networks is the power-law function, which implies that the degree distribution of these networks has no characteristic scale. In contrast, random graphs or lattices have single well-defined scale, which means that every vertex has roughly the same degree. In a network with a scale-free distribution some vertices have a degree that is orders of magnitude larger than the average. These vertices are often called hubs. Scale-free networks are specially attractive to researchers because some of them show two very interesting properties: high resistance to the random deletion of vertices, which means that the vast majority of vertices remain connected in a giant component, but on the other hand, they can be highly sensitive to targeted attacks aimed at destroying the network quickly through high-degree vertices known as hubs. Scale-free networks are widely spread in real-life and human-made systems, such as the Internet and World Wide Web, citation networks and social networks.

Difference between small-world and scale-free networks is the type of degree distribution, and can be illustrated by Figure 10.

Small-world networks have the bell curve shape (normal or Gaussian distribution), while real-world (scale-free) networks the so-called heavy tailed shape. In such distributions there are lots of vertices with tiny values and a few of them with enormous values. The heavy tail of the distribution refers to the fact that a small, but not insignificant number of vertices in the distribution take on extremely large values relative to the mean.

Graph theory is today regularly used for finding communities in networks. The number of algorithms for detecting communities grows rapidly on a daily basis, which provides for resolving everyday real and business problems using this methodology. By detecting small networks, communities and subgraphs, but also their structures – hierarchical, circular or other – it is possible to apply SNA in various types of problems, e.g. cross-sell in marketing, or fraud and money laundering in revenue insurance. Understanding of small communities and their structures enables understanding of network behavior, and consequently helps in some sorts of forecasting (Pinheiro, 2011: 19-22).

The term "small world" suggests the idea that big networks have small diameter and short average path length (Watts, 1999). The example that supports this idea is the work of Cornell scientists Duncan J. Watts and Steven Strogatz (Duncan & Strogatz,1998), who calculated the average path length of 3.7 degrees in the network of Hollywood actors, whereby the connection meant that they played in the same movie. It has been discovered that small communities, such as those of mathematicians and actors, are densely connected with chains of personal and professional

Figure 10. Small-world and scale free networks (Barabási, 2002)

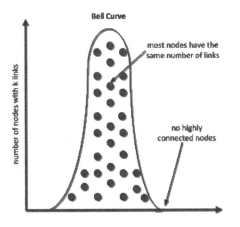
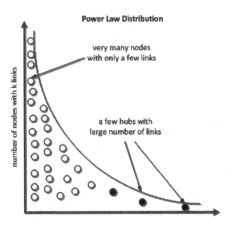

ties. Mathematicians came up with the so-called Erdős number which describes their connection with Pál Erdős based on common publications. For example, author who collaborated with Erdős on an article or published his work in the same publication as Erdős will have Erdős number 1. Correspondingly, an author who never collaborated with Erdős, but collaborated with an author who did will have Erdős number 2, etc.

Similar game was created for American actor Kevin Bacon. In mid 1990s three Albright College students Craig Fass, Brian Turtle, and Mike Ginelli devised a trivia game based around the idea of linking every actor to just one star – Kevin Bacon, and called it Six Degrees of Kevin Bacon. After that a computer student at the University of Virginia Brett Tjaden turned the Kevin Bacon game into a web site. He wrote a program that would extract the path from every actor or actress to Kevin Bacon. Soon the site became a huge hit with a tremendous number of visitors. Thanks to Tjaden, Kevin Bacon became a cult figure, and inspired a big scientific breakthrough later on made by Duncan J. Watts and Steven Strogatz.

Networks such as those of mathematicians or Hollywood actors show some interesting patterns regarding the ways they grow. They are interesting to scientists because they can help discover the ways a research is conducted, or how innovations or information may be transferred.

Structure of these networks can be illustrated and explained by some statistical research of co-authorship networks shown in Table 1.

Table 1 shows that in spite of significant differences in some dimensions (e.g. average degree, clustering, and fraction of nodes in the largest components), there is also big resemblance between the average path length and the diameter of the largest component of each of the networks. Besides, these are of an order substantially smaller than the number of nodes in the network, which confirms the hypothesis of the small world in social networks.

Inspired by the desire to discover the mechanism of synchronization of cricket chirps, which show high degree of coordination over long ranges, Watts and Strogatz

Table 1. Co-authorship networks (Jackson, 2010)

	Biology	**Economics**	**Math**	**Physics**
Number of nodes	1520521	81217	253339	52909
Average degree	15.5	1.7	3.9	9.3
Average path length	4.9	9.5	7.6	6.2
Diametar of the largest component	24	29	27	20
Overall clustering	0.09	0.16	0.15	0.45
Fraction of nodes in the largest component	0.92	0.41	0.82	0.85

published the first network model based on small-world phenomenon in 1998. To be able to understand the way in which crickets synchronize their chirps, Watts realized that the question he had to ask himself was in fact how crickets paid attention to one another. Do they listen to every other cricket, or they just pick one cricket from the crowd and synchronize with it? Another question was what was the structure of the network through which crickets (or humans) influence one another. Watts started to think more of networks and less of crickets and turned to Strogatz for help. Two scientists adopted the Granovetter's concept of clustered society in which everybody knows everybody else. For Watts, who is a mathematician, and Strogatz, a physician, the only acceptable solution was to find a way in which this clustering could be measured. Most important assumption to be explained was that the world, although small in its nature (six degrees of separation), was highly clustered. Studying the small-world phenomenon, they discovered that there was a certain paradox at the heart of it: the world is very small, with everyone only a few steps from everyone else, and at the same time very clustered. It means that although people as individuals are connected with only a small number of connections with any other individual in the world, these individuals form closed groups (clusters) of interconnected individuals. Each of them may be connected with only a hundred people, but there is a high probability that out of these hundred a significant number of them appears among connections of other friends or acquaintances from the same group. Trying to explain this paradox and empirically prove their hypotheses, the two scientists went a step further from Erdős-Renyi graph theory and introduced the idea of clustering coefficient.

Barabásí explains clustering coefficient in the following way: "Let's assume that you have four good friends. If they are all friends with each other as well, you can connect each of them with a link, obtaining six friendship links. Chances are, however, that some of your friends are not friends with each other. Then the real count will give fewer than six links – let's say, four. In this case the clustering coefficient for your circle of friends is 0.66, obtained by dividing the number of actual links between your friends (four) by the number of links that they could have if they were all friends with each other (six). The clustering coefficient tells you how closely knit your circle of friends is. A number close to 1.0 means that all your friends are friends with each other. On the other hand, if the clustering coefficient is zero, then you are the only person who holds your friends together (...)" (Barabási, 2002).

To prove that social networks have some generic properties common to all networks we can find in the nature, Watts and Strogatz have chosen to study one network from animal world (*C. elegans* neural network), one from human (Hollywood actors' network), and a power grid network, and proved the existence of the small-world phenomenon. Power grid graph was relevant for the efficiency and robustness of electricity networks, while *C. elegans* was picked as an example of a completely mapped neural network.

In all three examples of networks, Watts and Strogatz have managed to prove that they do not differ much from other networks around us, or the society in general, and that the small-world phenomenon is not specific for social networks only, nor does it present an ideal model, but it is rather a generic presentation of many big, scattered networks that can be found in the nature. Their examples also show extremely high clustering degree. In *C. elegans*, for example, they noticed that the probability of connecting neighboring neurons is five times higher than in random networks. They got similar results in other two examples – power grid and Hollywood actors' network.

Based on the data shown in Table 2, we can conclude that all three graphs show characteristics of small-world networks.

The table includes empirical data for the characteristic path length L and clustering coefficient C for the three real networks, compared to random graphs with the same number of vertices (n) and average number of edges per vertex (k) (Actors: $n = 225.226$, $k = 61$; power grid: $n = 4.941$, $k = 2,67$; *C. elegans*: $n = 282$, $k = 14$). Watts and Strogatz define their graphs in the following way:

- "Two actors are joined by an edge if they have acted in a film together. We restricted attention to the giant connected component8 of this graph, which includes approximately 90% of all actors listed in the Internet Movie Database, as of April 1997.
- For the power grid, vertices represent generators, transformers and substations, and edges represent high-voltage transmission lines between them.
- For C. elegans an edge joins two neurons if they are connected by either a synapse or a gap junction."

In all three examples of networks, Watts and strogatz treat all edges as undirected and unweighted, and all vertices as identical.

All three networks show the small-world phenomenon: L is almost greater than L_{random}, but C is greater than C_{random} (Watts & Strogatz, 1998)

Table 2. Empirical examples of small-world networks (Watts and Strogatz, 1998)

	L_{actual}	L_{random}	C_{actual}	C_{random}
Film actors	3.65	2.99	0.79	0.00027
Power grid	18.7	12.4	0.080	0.005
C. elegans	2.65	2.25	0.28	0.05

To show the network with high clustering coefficient, Watts and Strogatz have designed a simple model showing a circle of vertices in which each vertex is connected with its first and second neighbours. To prove the idea of the small world, they added a few random edges connecting distant vertices thereby shortening drastically the average distance between all vertices.

This way they have proved that each of the small-world networks contains some characteristics of a regular graph, such as clustering density, as well as some properties of random networks, such as typically small path length. Watts and Strogatz have shown that adding a small number of random links would reduce the network diameter, that is, it would shorten the longest direct path between any two vertices in the network. In Barabási's example with the circle of friends, it would mean that every one of us has a friend or acquaintance in some remote part of the world, and instead of going from door to door knocking to our immediate neighbors to reach the other part of the world, we can use such "random" connections which make the world we live in really small.

Strogatz once said that this type of architecture, this "beautiful application of the small-world property" can be easily seen in the national electric power network, Internet, human brain or genome. This architecture, present in all types of interaction enables rapid data dissemination, coordination of all types of activities globally, but also some undesirable effects, such as computer viruses. Generally speaking, this model demonstrates Granovetter's conclusions that the strength of weak ties keeps social networks together, and is considered to be a pioneering work in the area of complex networks.

In network theory, the model of small-world networks continues being intensively researched. Some results in this domain suggest that even those network with no real topological structure exhibit the small-world phenomenon. This phenomenon can be mathematically expressed as the network diameter growing with the logarithm of the number of nodes, rather than proportionally to the number of vertices, this being the case in Watts-Strogatz lattice. Apart from being the focus of the interest of scientists, and the inspiration and reason for numerous experiments in various fields, primarily mathematics, physics, and biology, the idea of small-world networks has also been introduced in the vocabulary of popular culture as "six degrees of separation". Although Milgram never mentioned this term, his findings contributed to its wide acceptance many years later (Guare, 1990).

Similar results can be observed in networks with power-law degree distribution, such as scale-free networks. One of several proposed models that generate scale-free networks is the Barabási-Albert model - an algorithm for generating random scale-free networks that incorporates two important general concepts: growth and preferential attachment. Growth means that the number of nodes in the network increases over time, and preferential attachment means that the more connected a node is, the more likely it is to receive new links, i.e. nodes with higher degree have stronger ability to grab links added to the network. An excellent example is the web, where new pages link preferentially to hubs, well known sites as Google or Wikipedia, rather than to "smaller", unknown sites.

Furthermore, Ravasz and Barabási (Ravasz and Barabási 2003) showed that "the scale-free nature and high clustering of real networks are the consequence of a hierarchical organization, implying that small groups of nodes organize in a hierarchical manner into increasingly large groups, while maintaining a scale-free topology. In hierarchical networks, the degree of clustering characterizing the different groups follows a strict scaling law, which can be used to identify the presence of a hierarchical organization in real networks" (Figure 11).

"Starting from a fully connected cluster of five nodes shown in (a) (note that the diagonal nodes are also connected—links not visible), we create four identical replicas, connecting the peripheral nodes of each cluster to the central node of the original cluster, obtaining a network of N=25 nodes. (b) In the next step, we create four replicas of the obtained cluster, and connect the peripheral nodes again, as shown in (c), to the central node of the original module, obtaining a N=125-node network. This process can be continued indefinitely."

They also find that several real networks, such as the World Wide Web, actor network, the Internet at the domain level, and the semantic web "obey this scaling law, indicating that hierarchy is a fundamental characteristic of many complex systems".

Figure 11. The iterative construction leading to a hierarchical network (Ravasz & Barabási, 2003)

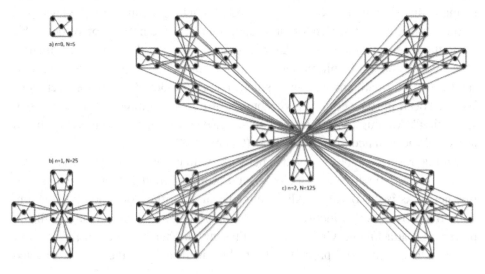

The way networks have captured the imagination and attention of business analysts can be illustrated with the research of the American corporate elite network (Davis et al., 2003). Since the information flow across organizations is heavily dependent on connections between managers, networks created by overlapping board memberships have become an important medium for the spread of corporate practices and structures, from acquisitions (Haunschild, 1993) and takeovers (Davis and Greve, 1997), to investments (Rao and Sivakumar, 1999) and market positions (Rao et al., 2000). In this case, the architecture of social networks is important because it shapes the dynamics of contagion and information flow (Coleman, 1964). The authors also suggest that changes in the structure of the network should have important consequences for the strategies adopted by organizations.

The study on the degree of stability in the structure of the corporate elite network in the US during the 1980s and 1990s, conducted among several hundred largest US corporations and their several thousand directors, also revealed a dense network of interconnected individuals. The study shows that the population of the largest firms and their directors were rather different at the end of the 1990s from the beginning of the 1980s: less than one-third of the largest firms in 1999 were among the largest in 1982, and less than 5% of the directorships were constant across this time. Moreover, less than 2% of the ties among firms that were created by particular shared directors in 1999 could be traced back to the beginning of the 1980s (Davis et al., 2003). However, in spite of these considerable changes in the structure of boards and among directors, and nearly complete turnover in ties, distances among the corporate elite remained virtually constant. The authors of the article argue that their findings should be attributed to the small-world property of networks. The results show that "the aggregate connectivity of the network is remarkably stable and appears to be an intrinsic property of the interlock network, resilient to major changes in corporate governance". Namely, their results show that on average, any two of the 4538 directors of the 516 largest US firms in the largest component in 1999 could be connected by 4.3 links, and any two of the boards are 3.5 degrees distant. They conclude that corporate America is "overseen by a network of individuals who to a great extent know each other or have acquaintances in common. (...) It appears that nearly any collection of firms that share directors with a few random ties will end up appearing like a well-connected elite, without intentional design." Such design, tough, is possible, but they suggest that it is not necessary.

Also interesting network analysis of business environment is the study of Tomohiko Konno from Princeton University on Japanese firms' transaction network (Konno, 2008). The study encompasses 800,000 firms, their financial data and network relationships: buy, sell and shareholder relationship. He discovered following important properties:

- The network is not a random graph but a scale-free network;
- The network has hierarchical structure;
- Degree-degree correlation (Table 3 and Figure 12).

There is a great number of articles and books that would be worth mentioning here in the context of SNA evolution. However, for fear of undeservedly omitting some of them due to the lack of space, we just mentioned those names and works whose pioneering contribution to the development of the SNA had to be explained for easier understanding of the general idea of the SNA and guiding principles in studying social networks.

4.2 SOCIAL NETWORK ANALYSIS (SNA) METHODS AND METRICS

You can't find a new land with an old map! (English proverb)

As the world has rapidly become a "global village" due to technological advances, connections between people, businesses, or information have become more complex and complicated than ever. This in part justifies growing fascination with this complex "connectedness" among different entities, and the degrees and ways in which associations between individuals or groups, human, animal or even inanimate entities can be strengthened or weakened. Network analysis is the tool that helps visualize, identify, understand, define, and measure connections between entities, and can be broken down into three stages (Heuer and Pherson, 2010: 68-75):

- Network or Link Charting is the process and technique of drawing links between individuals, groups, things, places, and events of interest (nodes) based on various types of association. It is used to literally "connect the dots" between people, groups or other entities;
- Network Analysis is the process and technique that analyzes data from the chart by sorting them and identifying patterns among entities. It puts the dots in context;

Table 3. Estimation results: Degree correlation (Konno, 2008)

Variable	Coefficient	(Std.Err.)
Log degree	-0.546	(0.014)
Intercept	7.162	(0.080)

Figure 12. Degree correlation (Konno, 2008)

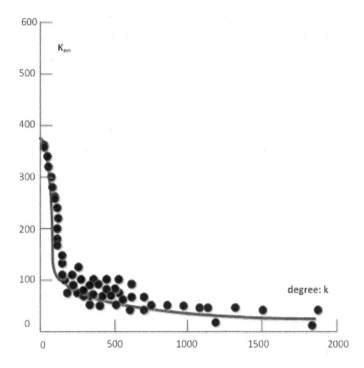

- Social Network Analysis (SNA) is the structured analysis of social networks, using mathematical tools and computer software it helps measure different types of variables related to the distance between the nodes (vertices) and the types of their associations, or links (edges), in order to determine the degree and type of influence one vertex has on another, SNA helps identify hidden associations and degrees of influence between the dots.

Although there is this general division to different stages, in most cases these three intertwine and the term "network analysis" is often used as a generic name for all three stages, and as such generally deals with the patterns of connection in a wide range of physical and social phenomena. Network analysis observes individual entities (nodes or vertices) as nested within larger networks of interrelations. Network perspective provides the tools and methods for answering "standard social and behavioral science research questions by giving precise formal definition to aspects of the political, economic, or social structural environment. From the view of social network analysis, the social environment can be expressed as patterns or regularities in relationships among interacting units" (Wasserman and Faust, 1994: 4-5). Social networks are created from any collection of connections among a group of people and things, and therefore the unit of analysis in network analysis becomes an entity of a collection of individuals and their connections, rather than the individual. This fact has a crucial role in the development of methods for social network analysis.

4.2.1 Modality and Levels of Analysis

Generally speaking, a social network is a social structure made up of actors (individuals or organizations) called "nodes", which are tied (connected) by one or more specific types of interdependency, such as friendship, kinship, common interest, financial exchange, dislike, or relationships of beliefs, knowledge or prestige. In other words, social network analysis views social relationships in terms of network theory consisting of nodes and ties (also called edges, links, or connections). Nodes are the individual actors within the networks, and ties are the relationships between the actors.

In SNA, graphs and matrices are typically used to represent social network data. In the network structure modeled as a graph, vertices represent actors, and edges represent ties, which show the existence of a relation between two actors. Apart from indicating the links between vertices, the data also provide us with additional information on directionality and link weights (de Nooy et al., 2008: 7). The network can also be used to measure social capital – the value that an individual gets from the social network (Figure 13).

Social network analysis has now become a scientific field, with its own theoretical statements, methods, software, and researchers. Analysts reason from whole to part; from structure to relation to individual; from behavior to attitude. They typically either study whole or complete networks, meaning all of the ties containing specified relations in a defined population, or personal or egocentric networks, meaning the ties that specified people have, such as their "personal communities" (Wellman and Berkowitz, 1998). A group of individuals with connections to other

Figure 13. Illustration of a network with matrix

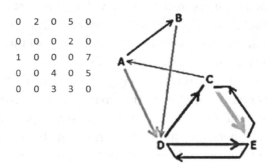

social worlds is likely to have access to a wider range of information. It is better for individual success to have connections to a variety of networks rather than many connections within a single network. Similarly, individuals can exercise thier influence or act as brokers within their social networks by bridging two networks that are not directly linked. The latter concept is called "filling structural holes" (Scott, 1991).

Network thinking and methodology help the analyst deal with multiple levels of analysis simultaneously. Differences among actors arise from their attributes and the nature of their relations, and these relations depend on how they are embedded in the network. On the other hand, the structure and behavior of the network depends on local interactions among actors. This dichotomy of the individual and structure is the first major emphasis of social network analysis. Another emphasis is to see how individual choices lead to patterns which in turn give rise to more holistic patterns (Hanneman and Riddle, 2005).

SNA combines organizational theories with mathematical models to help understand the dynamics of groups and organizations in which we are interested. The structure of a network can determine:

- The performance of the network as a whole and its ability to achieve its key goals.
- Characteristics of the network which are not immediately obvious, such as the existence of a smaller sub-network operating within the network.
- The relationships between prominent actors of interest whose position may provide the greatest influence over the rest of the network.
- How directly and quickly information flows between actors in different parts of the network (IBM, 2012).

SNA is equally used in mathematical sociology and quantitative analysis. Major difference in approach is the fact that statistical analysis methods need probabilistic approach to calculate probability distributions of relationship strengths. Mathematical approaches to the analysis of networks use structural descriptive (deterministic) methods, assuming that the measured relationships and their strengths represent the real or final status of the network. Crucial advantage of statistic models according to Wasserman and Faust is that they "can cope easily with some lack-of-fit of a model to data", while descriptive or deterministic models "cannot be relaxed in this way". "Deterministic models usually force the aspect of social structure of interest (such as reciprocity, or complete transitivity or structural equivalence) to be present in the model, while statistical models assume these aspects to be absent" (Wasserman and Faust, 1994: 505-506)

Analysis of social network data can be focused on five separate levels, depending on the aim and purpose of the analysis (Wasserman and Faust, 1994):

- Individual actor level: centrality, prestige and roles (isolates, liaisons, bridges, etc.);
- Dyadic level (two actors and their ties): distance and reachability, structural and other notions of equivalence, and tendencies toward reciprocity;
- Triadic level (three actors and their ties): balance and transitivity;
- Subgroup or subset level: cliques, cohesive subgroups, components, and
- Global or network level: connectedness, diameter, centralization, density, prestige.

Each of these levels requires different analytical approach, and the use of different tools correspondingly. Social network analysts have developed a number of tools and metrics that help conceptualize and calculate variations in relations within the structures they analyze. Most of the time people interact with a small number of others, and in most cases they know one another. In other cases, people are connected through some shared attributes or memberships in "categorical social units" or "sub-populations" (Hanneman and Riddle, 2005). There are different patterns specific for different populations, and many different approaches to defining the form and extent of embedddedness of actors in their populations.

Two decades ago scientists from different fields (mathematicians, sociologists, physicists, etc.) started collaborating on designing new algorithms for calculating SNA metrics that help analysts systematically examine the world of complex networks. These metrics has become a solid foundation for comparing different types of networks, examining changes in networks in time, or analyze positions and behaviors of actors in a network, and their impact on other actors, clusters, and the network in general. Advantages of SNA and reasons why it receives such enormous attention of scientists, among other, are easy handling the rapidly growing data sets, quickly identifying key individuals/groups and their positions and role within a group/network, understanding their relationships and how they affect the group/network, deeper understanding of target networks and their characteristics, etc.

In line with that, some measures are used for defining and describing the network in general, while other are applied for determining relative and absolute position of a node within a network. In following passages we shall discuss properties and metrics relevant for each of the five levels of SNA along with basic ideas and features of corresponding levels of analysis. Some of them include basic cohesion (e.g. density, degree, components), brokerage (e.g. degree, closeness, betweenness), or ranking (e.g. prestige, acyclic decomposition) metrics.

4.2.2 Actor Level

If we want to identify key player in a group of individuals for example, the one who exerts the largest influence, we are going to analyze our network at the individual actor level (Katzmair, 2004). In business application, outcome and utility of the analysis at this level will, according to Katzmair, give answers to following questions (Katzmair, 2004):

- Who has the best overview about what is going on in the markets?
- Who is the first to know about news and innovations?
- Whom should I first address when starting a campaign?
- Whom should I invite to an event?
- Who is a good target for below-the-line and pre-launch activities?
- Who is already congested and overburdened by information overflow and by
- The quantity of relationships?
- Who are the insiders who can bring me into contact with key player?
- Who are the key players of today, who are the key players of tomorrow?
- Get more knowledge about your markets and the network of your customers!

Structural properties at which we aim at this level are centrality (through which we can get the information about the activity of individuals, access, control, influence, etc.), prestige (in-degree, proximity prestige, authority weight, etc.), roles, and structural holes (Burt, 1992).

Centrality. Centrality is a key concept in social network analysis. This measure gives a rough indication of the social power of a node based on how well they "connect" the network. "Betweenness", "closeness", and "degree" are all measures of centrality (Figure 14).

A highly centralized network is dominated by one person who controls information flow and may become a single point of communication failure. A less centralized network has no single point of failure, so people can still pass on information even if some communication channels are blocked. SNA software allows us to calculate betweenness, closeness and degree centrality measures to provide different perspectives on the social relationships within the network. You can also influence the centrality measures by taking into account the direction of links and the weightings applied to them.

Betweenness centrality is based on the importance of intermediaries in the communication network. By asking ourselves "How crucial is a person to the transmission of information through a network? How many flows of information are disrupted or must make longer detours if a person stops passing on information or disappears from the network? To what extent may a person control the flow of information due

Figure 14. Centrality measures in a simple network

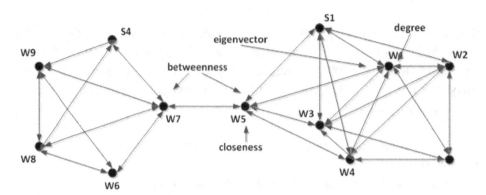

to his or her position in the communication network?" (de Nooy et al., 2005: 131) we can determine the extent of the importance of an actor in the network. Betweenness centrality stands for the extent to which a node lies between other nodes in the network. It measures the number of paths that pass through each entity. It takes into account the connectivity of the node's neighbors, giving a higher value for nodes which bridge clusters. The measure reflects the number of people who a person is connecting indirectly through their direct links. In this sense, betweenness centrality measures the control that an individual has over the interaction of others, who are not directly connected. This may identify entities with the ability to control information flow between different parts of the network. These are called gatekeeper entities.

Gatekeepers may have many paths running through them, allowing them to channel information to most of the others in the network. Alternatively, they may have few paths running through them but still play a powerful communication role if they exist between different network clusters (IBM, 2012).

In the Figure 15, the circled entity has the highest measure of betweenness.

His position in the network means he may play a strong role in controlling the flow of information between its different parts.

Link betweenness centrality measures the number of paths that pass through each link. This can help to identify key connections of influence within the network. A link through which many paths pass may be a significant route for information exchange between entities. In Figure 16, the circled link has the highest measure of betweenness because it provides a key path through which information may flow between different parts of the network.

Closeness centrality is based on the reachability of a person within a network: "How easily can information reach a person?" It measures the proximity of an entity to the other entities in the social network (directly or indirectly). Thus, closeness

Figure 15. Betweenness centrality (IBM, 2012)

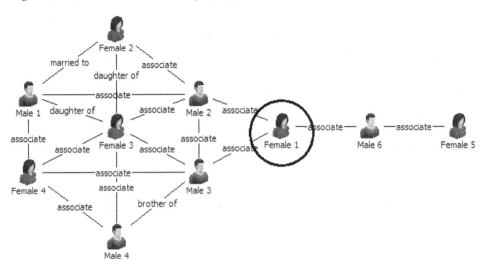

Figure 16. Link betweenness centrality (IBM, 2012)

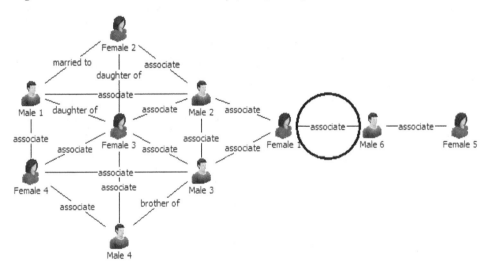

is the inverse of the sum of the shortest distances between each individual and every other person in the network. The closeness centrality of a vertex is higher if the total distance to all other vertices is shorter. An entity with a high measure of closeness centrality has the shortest paths to the other entities, allowing them to pass on and receive communications more quickly than anybody else in the organization. Information has to travel much further to and from an entity on the edge of a network that is attached only to few other entities, so they will have a lower measure of closeness centrality.

One of the most common and important approaches to indexing the distances between actors is the geodesic. The *geodesic distance* or *diameter* between pairs of actors is the measure of closeness used to describe the minimum distance between actors. In simplest terms, geodesic is the shortest path between two vertices. However, the geodesic distance describes only a single connection between a pair of actors (or, in some cases several actors), and sometimes we are not interested in the shortest connection, but rather in the sum of all connections between actors. In directed networks, when measuring the diameter, the direction of the edge needs to be considered.

In the following figure the diameter between two nodes (Ivan and Marija or Bozo) is shown with a red directed line. It is also the shortest path between the two entities in which we can still follow the direction of connections. If we remove arrows from the graph and consider it as undirected, the diameter would significantly change. In the latter case the diameter has the value of 5 steps and is shown in green. Since direction is no longer important, we can observe the diameter from entities named Borislav, Božo or Marija to entities Tonka, Biserka or Ksenija (Kopal & Korkut, 2011) (Figure 17).

Average geodesic distance is the measure that explains the closeness in the network, i.e. the average distance value between the entities. If the value is high, it means that a small number of entities has close contacts and there is a large number of steps/entities between them. On the other had, if the value is low, entities in the network are close. This measure reminds us of Stanley Milgram and his "six degrees of separation".

Figure 17. Maximum geodesic distance in directed and undirected network

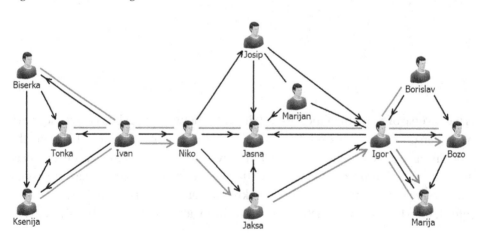

Closeness centrality measures both direct and indirect closeness:

- Direct closeness is when two entities are connected by a link.
- Indirect closeness exists when information can only pass from one entity to another via a path that runs through one or more entities.

In Figure 18, the two circled entities have equal highest measures of closeness. Their position in the network means they have the shortest paths to all other entities which may provide them with the best visibility of network activity.

Degree centrality is a basic measure that measures how well connected an entity is by counting the number of direct links each entity has to others in the network. In undirected networks, entities have only one degree value, while in directed networks, each vertex can have three values for each entity:

- Out-Degree, whose number depends on the number of links going from the entity,
- In-Degree, whose number depends on the number of links coming to the entity,
- Degree or Total Degree, standing for the total of the sum of Out-Degree and In-Degree number of links.

This can reveal how much activity is going on and who are its most active members. In the example below, the circled entity has the highest measure of degree. This

Figure 18. Closeness (IBM, 2012)

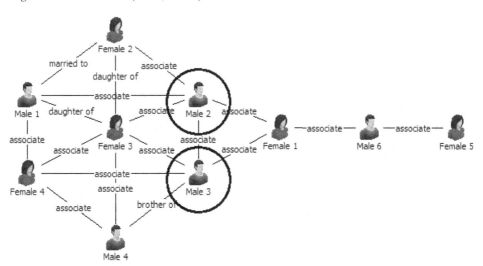

measure can be defined as a certain social capital of the entity, and the entity with the highest number of direct links can be considered as a central entity (Figure 19).

The position in the network of the entity in red circle means he has more direct links than any other entity and may play the most active role.

Link degree: Directed links can be taken into consideration when calculating centrality measures. A link with arrows added to it represents the directed flow of information between entities; either in a single direction or in both directions. This may have an important bearing on how quickly information is passed from one part of the network to another. For example, a person may receive information from many others in the network but only send information to a select few. The centrality measures for an entity through which information is channeled in both directions will be higher than the measures for an entity through which information is channeled one way (IBM, 2012).

In Figure 20, the circled entity has the lowest measure of betweenness and closeness. The inbound direction of the links attached to her mean that she is only capable of receiving information, not passing it on to others in the network.

If link direction was both inbound and outbound as it is between the other network entities, she would have the highest measure of betweenness and the second highest measure of closeness.

Link weightings. Not all relationships in a network are equal. For example, the link between two people connected through a family relationship may be stronger than a link between two business associates. These links can be weighted so that they represent real-world strengths when carrying out social network analysis. Weight-

Figure 19. Degree centrality (IBM, 2012)

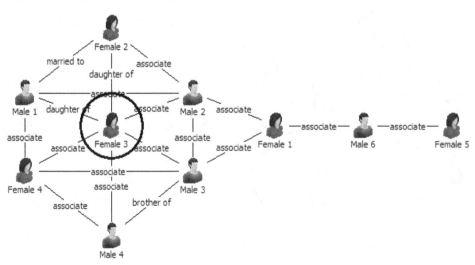

Figure 20. Link degree (IBM, 2012)

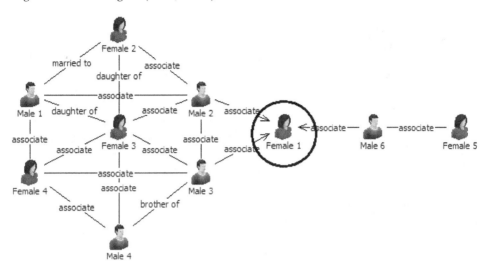

ing key paths in the network may also infer that the entities using them to channel information have key roles to play. For this reason, centrality measure results are affected by link weightings.

In Figure 21, the selected links represent family relationships.

It may be inferred that these links are stronger than those between associates, so they can be weighted to ensure that the paths that run through them are treated as more reliable than others.

A somewhat more sophisticated measure of centrality is the measure of the importance of a node in a network called *Eigenvector*. By singling out the entity with the highest score, eigenvector makes it possible to identify who in the network mobilizes other entities and indirectly controls the network. It assigns relative scores to all nodes in the network based on the principle that connections to nodes having a high score contribute more to the score of the node in question. Google's PageRank is a variant of the Eigenvector centrality measure (Figure 22).

Ranking deals with the notions *prestige* and *ranking through acyclic decomposition*. In a directed graph prestige is the term used to describe a node's centrality. *Degree prestige*, *proximity prestige*, and *status prestige* are all measures of prestige. In social networks there are many techniques to calculate the so-called structural prestige of a person. It is important to distinguish structural prestige and social prestige: the first depends on the data from which we are able to infer a structure so that the structural prestige of a person only reflects his or her actual social prestige.

Figure 21. Family relations (IBM, 2012)

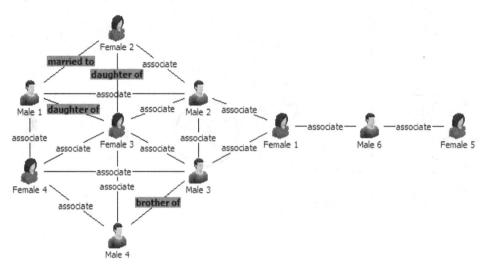

Figure 22. Centrality measures in a simple directed network[9]

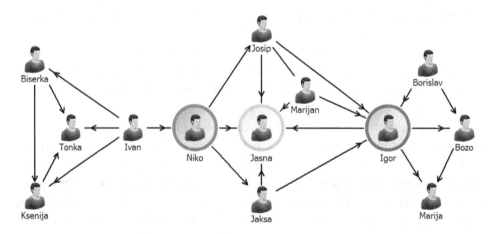

The *in-degree* of a vertex represents the popularity of the person represented by the vertex. To measure popularity, we need to have a directed network.

Domains represent extended prestige to indirect in-links so that the overall structure of the network is taken into account. The input domain of a vertex is defined as the number or percentage of all other vertices that are connected by a path to this vertex. A restricted input domain restricts the maximum path length. In well-connected networks it is recommended to limit the input domain to direct neighbors (i.e., to use popularity instead) or to those at a predefined maximum distance (e.g., 2).

Proximity prestige of a vertex is defined as the proportion of all vertices (except itself) in its input domain divided by the mean distance from all vertices in its input domain. It ranges from 0 (no proximity prestige) to 1 (highest proximity prestige) (Abraham et al., 2010: 143).

Once we have determined the nature of our network, we can start discovering the clusters and the hierarchy. Technique used for extracting discrete ranks from social relations and for determining the hierarchy, is called *acyclic decomposition*. While cyclic sub-networks (i.e., strong components) represent clusters of equals, acyclic sub-networks perfectly reflect the hierarchy. Following steps are used in determining the hierarchy:

1.   Partition the network into strong components (i.e., clusters of equals).
2.   Create a new network in which each vertex represents one cluster.
3.   Compute the maximum depth of each vertex to determine the hierarchy.

With this procedure we have decomposed each strong component into smaller clusters of people that are interconnected (Abraham et al., 2010: 144).

In directed networks we can usually identify two types of important vertices: hubs and authorities. A vertex is a good *hub*, if it points to many good authorities, and it is a good *authority*, if it is pointed to by many good hubs (Figure 23).

Authority centrality and *hub centrality* measures are first introduced by Kleinberg (1998) for information retrieval purposes in directed (and acyclic[10]) networks. These metrics are suitable for simultaneously measuring mutually reinforcing centrality arising from nodes pointing to other nodes (hubs), and from nodes being pointed to by other nodes (authorities).

To understand networks and their participants, the location of actors in the network needs to be measured. Measuring the network location is finding the centrality of a node. These measures determine the various *roles* and groups in a network: the *connectors, specialists, leaders, bridges* (connections in the graph which, if removed, would result in a disconnected structure, i.e. their removal increases the number of components in a network (de Nooy et al., 2011: 162)), *liaisons* (relation is called a "liaison" when brokering a relation between two groups, and is not part of either), *isolates* (actors in a network that are not connected to any other actors), etc. Other important questions that can be analyzed using this metrics are, for example, where the clusters are and who is in them, who is in the core of the network, and who is on the periphery, etc. (Abraham et al., 2010: 151)

Wasserman and Faust suggest that "the notion of social role is conceptually, theoretically, and formally dependent on the notion of social position". Whereas network position refers to a collection of actors who are similar in social activity, ties, or interactions, with respect to actors in other positions, network role refers to

Figure 23. Hub vs. authority

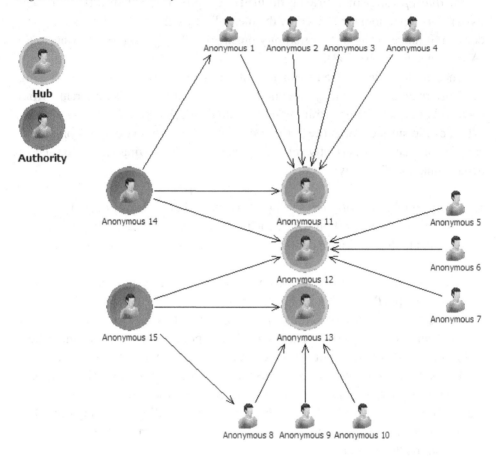

the patterns of relations which exist between actors or between positions. "Thus, role is defined in terms of collections of relations and the associations among relations" (Wasserman and Faust, 1994: 349).

These metrics are very useful in studying the possibilities of the diffusion of information inside the network. When analyzing the diffusion process, it is critical to determine the number of nodes that can be connected, and, what is even more important, to identify the nodes that have better chances to diffuse information through the social structure using their connections. To be able to identify such nodes, we first need to recognize which nodes within the network have a high first degree of centrality with a good sequence of nodes in their connection paths. To determine how far could the information spread inside the network through the connections of the original connections, we need to use second-order centrality. First-order centrality can be expressed by the question "How many friends do I have?", and second-order centrality as "How many friends do my friends have?" (Pinheiro, 2011: 74).

Structural holes are areas of no connection between nodes that could be used for advantage or opportunity. Ronald Burt describes the social structural theory of competition that has developed through the 70s and 80s of the 20th century. The contrast between perfect competition and monopoly is replaced with a network model of competition. The basic element in this account is the "structural hole", the "empty space" in the network between two sets of nodes that do not otherwise interact closely. In other words, a structural hole is a gap between two individuals with complementary resources or information. When the two are connected through a third individual as entrepreneur, the gap is filled, creating important advantages for the entrepreneur (Burt, 1992) (Figure 24).

Burt invented this term to explain how the position of actors in their neighbor-hood[11] can influence their constraints or opportunities, and their behavior. Burt formalizes very important property called redundancy when he explains structural holes: "I use the term structural hole" for the "separation between non-redundant contacts. Non-redundant contacts are connected by a structural hole." In other words, "a structural hole is a relationship of non-redundancy between two contacts" (Burt, 1992: 65). Criteria that govern the creation of a structural hole are cohesion and equivalence. "Cohesion says redundancy arises when the two of the ego's relations share a direct link. The greater the cohesion (or density), the fewer structural holes" (Degenne and Forsé, 1999: 118). Cliques have no structural holes, which means that there is no obstacle for information flow. "The equivalence criterion takes into account indirect relations between the ego and the people in his networks. (...) They may not be in mutual contact but their relations are still identical because they can access the same information sources" (Degenne and Forsé, 1999: 118). In other words, they are redundant from the ego's standpoint.

4.2.3 Dyads and Triads

Most of the time most social actors are engaged in interactions in very local contexts. Analysis on the local level studies smaller units than the entire graph or network. In such cases, when the purpose of the analysis is the local aspect of the network, we analyze dyads and triads and their properties. There have been many studies over the past two decades about structural properties which are manifested at the structural level of dyads and triads. For analyzing key connections, for example, in order to find out who influences whom and how strongly in a certain network-structured group, we need to analyze the network at the dyadic or triadic level.

Apart from the individuals' behavior, local connections of actors are important for understanding the social behavior of the whole population as well. In studying the connections of actors, important indicators of the stability and institutionaliza-

Figure 24. Structural hole

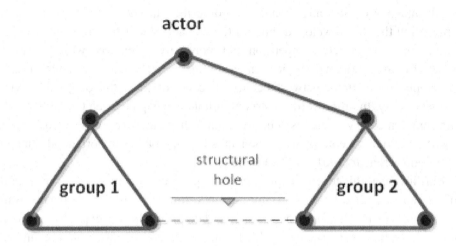

tion of actor's positions in social networks, such as the degree of "reciprocity" and "balance" and "transitivity" in relations need to be considered.

The smallest social structure in which an individual can be embedded and a basic unit of social network theory and analysis is a pair of actors called *dyad*, or pair of parties who may or may not share a social relation with one another. In other words, there are two possibilities for each pair in the population - either they have a tie, or they don't.

German sociologist and philosopher Georg Simmel argued that "the size of a social group was key to understanding the interactions among the group's constituents". He also said that "dyads are the most basic form of interaction and exchange, involving immediate reciprocity between the two social actors involved" (Simmel, 1950). We can characterize the whole population in terms of the prevalence of these dyadic "structures." This is what the density measure does.

In directed relations, there are three kinds of dyads - no tie, one likes the other but not vice versa, or both like the other. The extent to which a population is characterized by "reciprocated" ties (each actor directs a tie to the other) helps us determine the degree of cohesion, trust, and social capital that is present (Hanneman and Riddle, 2005) (Figure 25).

A triad is a set of three parties, which also consists of three dyads. Simmel (1908/1971) argues that the *triad* is the fundamental unit of social analysis, and that patterns of relations that appear in these small parts of the network can result in larger structural patterns that influence the whole network. In other words, triads, i.e. any "triple" {A, B, C} of actors, are considered to be the smallest social struc-

Figure 25. Dyads (IBM, 2012)

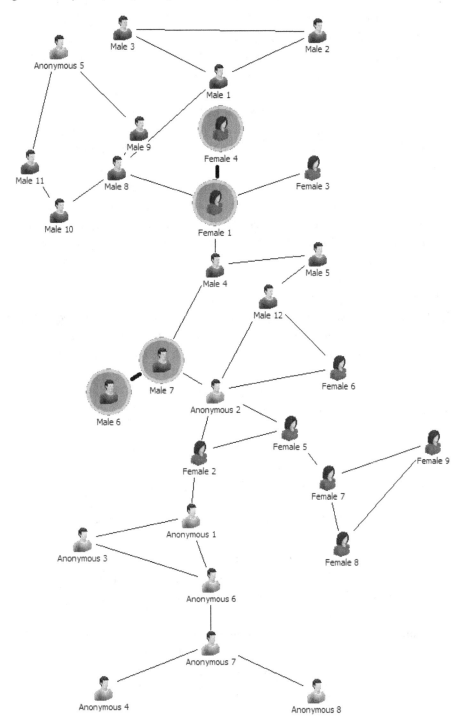

ture that has the true character of a "society". Such a structure "embeds" dyadic relations in a structure where "other" is present along with "ego" and "alter" (Hanneman & Riddle, 2005) (Figure 26).

Simmel further argues that three actors in a triad may allow qualitatively different social dynamics that cannot be reduced to individuals or dyads. For example, among three parties A, B, and C, party A may have a dyadic relation to C but also may have an indirect relation to C through B. Party B may then serve to alter the strength or the nature of the relation between A and C, such as solidifying an alliance or mediating a conflict. If A and C do not interact directly, party B may broker a transaction between them and may derive power from this intermediary position (Wolf, 1950). Simmel also argues that triads may serve as an analytical foundation for understanding larger social groups. The analysis of different types of triads in populations has been the principal element of social network analysis.

A number of works have analyzed the structure of networks by measuring the distribution of relations at the triadic level. Qualitatively distinct sets of relations for triads in a given network have been employed to assess an overall tendency toward sociability, hierarchy, or transitivity in large social networks.

In directed triads, we can see the emergence of tendencies toward equilibrium and consistency, i.e. institutionalization of social structures (balance and transitivity). Triads are also the simplest structures in which we can see the emergence of hierarchy.

Katzmair suggests that in business application outcome and utility of the analysis at this level will answer the following questions:

- Which already existing relationship is the best for reaching new customers?
- Whom should I influence in the 1- and 2-step surroundings of my key players?
- Which connections most likely indicate a strong relationship based on trust?
- Who most likely shares common attitudes, norms and beliefs?
- Who is most likely forced to be on good terms with somebody else?
- Which connections are most likely only formal relationships?
- Who most likely has the strongest influence on whom?
- What are most likely to be "frozen" and strong relationships?
- Which relationships could most likely be easily destabilized?

Structural properties that we need to consider at this level of network data analysis are distance and reachability, structural and other notions of equivalence, tendencies toward reciprocity, balance, robustness and transitivity.

Figure 26. Triads (IBM, 2012)

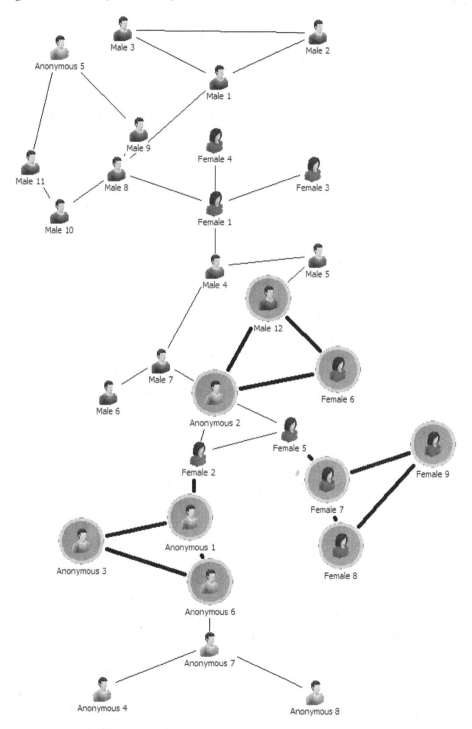

4.2.4 Distance and Reachability

The *distance* that one actor is from others shows how individuals are embedded in networks. If two actors are adjacent, the distance between them is 1 (it takes one step for the information to go from A to B). If A tells B, and B tells C, then actors A and C are at a distance of 2. Distances among actors can be important for understanding the differences among actors in the constraints and opportunities they have as a result of their position. Sometimes we are also interested in how many ways two actors can be connected, at a given distance. That is, can actor A reach actor B in more than one way?

The distances among actors in a network may indicate some important macro characteristics of the network. For example, if distances are great, it may take a long time for information to diffuse across a population. The differences between actors based on distances that they have from other actors may be a basis for differentiation and stratification - actors who are closer to more others may be able to exert more power than those who are more distant. Forms of connection which represent the distance among actors are walks, paths, semi-paths, etc.

An actor is *"reachable"* by another if there exists any set of connections by which we can trace from the source to the target actor, regardless of how many others fall between them. If the data are asymmetric or directed, it is possible that actor A can reach actor B, but that actor B cannot reach actor A. With symmetric or undirected data each pair of actors either are, or are not reachable to one another. If some actors in a network cannot reach others, there is the potential of a division of the network. Or, it may indicate that the population we are studying is really composed of more than one sub-populations (Hanneman and Riddle, 2005).

4.2.5 Structural and Other Notions of Equivalence

The notions of equivalence provide ways of defining and examining core analytical tools in sociology: social roles, individual's positions in groups, and types of structures.

Structural equivalence determines which nodes play similar roles in the network. Two nodes are said to be exactly structurally equivalent if they have the same relationships to all other nodes, the same ties to exactly the same other individual actors. In other words, two actors must be exactly substitutable in order to be structurally equivalent. Actors that are structurally equivalent are in identical "positions" in the structure of the diagram with regard to all other actors, and are facing the same sets of opportunities and constraints. Exact structural equivalence can rarely be found in practice (particularly in large networks). Therefore, the degree of structural equivalence is examined instead of the simple presence or absence of equivalence. It means that two actors who are approximately structurally equivalent are in approximately the same position in a structure.

Apart form structural equivalence, analysts often examine other, a bit more "relaxed" patterns of equivalence, such as *automorphic* and *regular equivalence* (Hanneman and Riddle, 2005).

Automorphic equivalence means that sets of actors can be equivalent by being embedded in local structures that have the same patterns of ties - "parallel" structures. It simply means that structures are identical, but the actors are different. With automorphic equivalence, we are searching for classes of actors who are at the same distance from other sets of actors, that is, we are trying to find substitutable substructures, rather than substitutable individuals. Large scale populations display a great deal of this sort of structural replication.

Two nodes are said to be *regularly equivalent* if they have the same profile of ties with members of other sets of actors that are also regularly equivalent. This is a complicated way of saying something that we recognize intuitively. Hanneman (2005) provides the example with two mothers – they are "equivalent" because "each has a certain pattern of ties with a husband, children, and in-laws, for example. The two mothers do not have ties to the same husband or the same children or in-laws" - they are not structurally equivalent. They are neither automorphically equivalent because different mothers may have different numbers of husbands, children, and in-laws. But they are similar because they have the same relationships with some members of another set of actors. Regular equivalence describes the "social roles" that are fundamental to all social institutions. Actors that are regularly equivalent do not necessarily occupy the same network positions or locations in relation to other individual actor, but they have the same kinds of relationships with some members of other sets of actors. Approximate regular equivalence is particularly interesting pattern because it helps determine the role that an actor plays and the ways in which social roles relate to one another.

One of the important aspects in human relations is the *reciprocity*, or mutuality. Reciprocity can be defined as a social norm of in-kind responses to the behavior of others. It is the tendency towards forming mutual connections with one another by returning similar acts. In a highly reciprocal relationship both parties share equal interest in keeping up their relationship, while in a relationship with low reciprocity one person is much more active than the other (Akoglu et al., 2012). Nguyen et al. (2010) show that reciprocity related behaviors provide good features for ranking and classification-based methods for trust prediction.

The idea of *balance* was first introduced by Fritz Heider (1946). In the study of an individual's cognition of social relations, Heider focused on how individual's attitudes and opinions coincided with attitudes and opinions of other actors or "entities" in the network. In this regard Heider considered ties in the social structures of dyads and triads, and argued: "In the case of two entities, a balanced state exists if the ties between them are positive (or negative) in all aspects... In the case of three entities, a balanced state exists if all three possible ties are positive in all respects, or if two are negative, and one positive" (Heider, 1946).

This *cognitive balance* soon came to be known as *structural balance*, which focuses on a set of people or a group, rather than on the single individual. The group is, then, structurally balanced if, when two people like each other, then they are consistent in their evaluation of all other people (Figure 27).

Cartwright and Harary (1956) used graph theory to quantify Heider's balance theory, and proposed theorem that implied that in a structurally balanced group, set of actors can be divided into two subsets in such a way that within subsets all ties are positive and between them all are negative (Wasserman and Faust, 1994: 221-233) (Figure 28).

The eight graphs shown in the previous figure fall naturally into two subsets: one with four graphs with positive cycles (first row), and one set containing the four graphs with negative cycles (second row).

One of the ideas that have emerged in the literature is that node centrality can be evaluated based on how much the removal of the node "disrupts" the graph structure. This idea provides also a notion of *robustness* of the network: if removing few nodes has no noticeable impact, then the network structure is clearly robust in a very strong sense (Boldi et al., 2011). Although the idea of robustness has no unique definition, the term unambiguously refers to resilience of networks to random errors, i.e. the fragility to attacks.

Figure 27. Structural balance (Degenne and Forsé, 1999: 174)

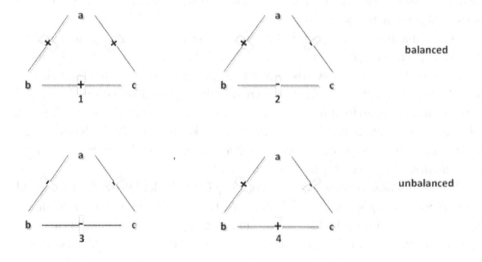

Figure 28. The eight possible P-O-X triples (Wasserman and Faust, 1994: 224)

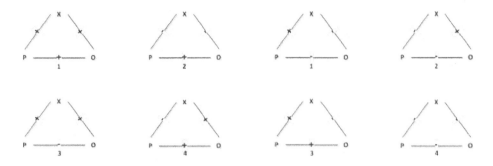

A principal interest in the study of triads is the phenomenon of *transitivity*. In a triple of actors, a triad involving actors A, B, and C is transitive if whenever A→B and B→C, then there is also a tie from A→C. If the A-B and B-C ties both exist, but A is not tied to C, then the triad is intransitive. Transitivity is typically studied for directed relations, where a tie from A to B (A→B) is directional and does not imply the same relation from B to A. For directed networks, if the A→B and B→C ties both exist, but A→C does not, then the triad is intransitive. Some directed relations have a pervasive tendency toward transitivity: If A dominates B and B dominates C, then A is also likely to dominate C. Some undirected relations also tend to be transitive, as represented by the adage, "a friend of a friend is a friend" (Kitts and Huang, 2010) (Figure 29).

With undirected data, there are 4 possible types of triadic relations (no ties, one tie, two ties, or all three ties), which are manifested within a population in the form of isolation, couples only, structural holes, or clusters. With directed data, there are 16 possible types of relations among 3 actors, including relationships that exhibit hierarchy, equality, and the formation of exclusive groups. Of the 16 possible types of directed triads, six involve zero, one, or two relations - and can't display transitivity because there are not enough ties to do so. One type with 3 relations (AB, BC, CB) does not have any ordered triples (AB, BC) and therefore cannot display transitivity. In three more types of triads, there are ordered triples (AB, BC) but the relation between A and C is not transitive. The remaining types of triads display varying degrees of transitivity.

The triads that are "transitive" are those displaying a type of balance where, if A → B, and B →C, then also A→C. Such transitive or balanced triads are argued to be the "equilibrium" or natural state toward which triadic relationships tend (Hanneman and Riddle, 2005).

These methods, referred to as "local" methods, are designed for analyses of subgraphs embedded within the graph for the entire network. It means that that

Figure 29. The sixteen possible triads for transitivity in a digraph (Wasserman & Faust, 1994: 244)

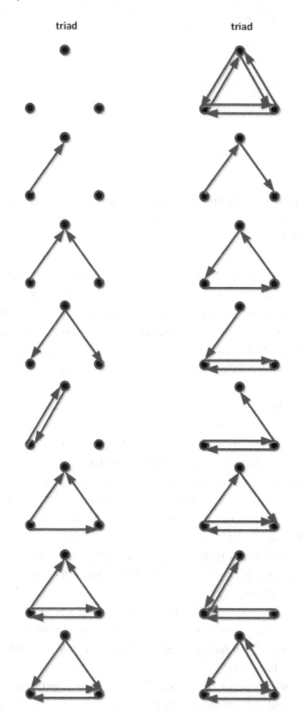

they deal with subsets of actors, rather than the properties of the entire collection of actors simultaneously (Wasserman and Faust, 1994: 506).

4.2.6 Subset Level

One of the aspects of studying social networks is the analysis of groups and substructures present in a network. Divisions of actors in groups and substructures may be important for understanding the behavior of the entire network: individual actors can be embedded in networks in different ways and this variation has important impact on his behavior within that group, which will then influence the behavior of that group, but also the behavior of the network he is embedded in as a whole.

If the aim of our analysis is the opposition analysis, for example, if we want to discover "who opposes whom", we need to conduct a subset-level network analysis, with cliques, cohesive subgroups, components, and islands as the properties that will be analyzed.

Katzmair again suggests outcome and utility of the analysis at this level (Katzmair, 2004):

- Who is most likely a friend / an enemy of whom?
- In what regions of my network should I launch a simultaneous campaign?
- Whom should I invite to an event at the same time?
- Which of my customers should I bring together?
- How robust is your competitor's network?
- Who are good partners for joint projects?

A *clique* is a subset of a network in which the actors are more closely and intensely tied to one another than they are to other members of the network. "A clique in a graph is a maximal complete subgraph of three or more nodes. It consists of a subset of nodes, all of which are adjacent to each other, and there are no other nodes that are also adjacent to all of the members of the clique(Luce and Perry, 1949; Harary et al., 1965)." Some scientists suggest that mutual dyads could not be considered as cliques and that the clique should contain at least three nodes. In the context of human networks, people may form cliques on the basis of gender, age, ethnicity, race, religion, or some other criteria (Figure 30).

Simply put, a clique is a collection of actors all of whom "choose" each other, and there is no other actor in the group who also "chooses" and is "chosen" by all of the members of the clique (Wasserman and Faust, 1994: 254). Cliques in a graph may overlap, i.e. the same node or set of nodes might belong to more than one clique, or there may also be nodes which do not belong to any of the cliques, but no clique can be antirely contained within another clique.

Figure 30. A graph and its cliques (Wasserman and Faust, 1994: 255)

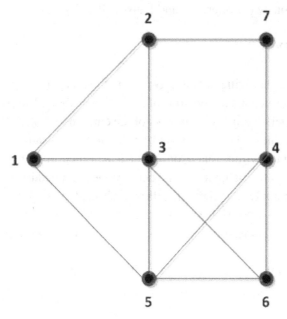

cliques: {1,2,3}, {1,3,5}, and {3,4,5,6}

"*Cohesive subgroups* are subsets of actors among whom there are relatively strong, direct, intense, frequent, or positive ties",(Wasserman and Faust, 1994: 249) and they represent an important part of social network analysis.

Wasserman and Faust (1994) mention the four general properties of cohesive subgroups:

- The mutuality of ties – all pairs of subgroup members must "choose" each other or must be adjacent;
- The closeness or reachability of subgroup members – all subgroup members should be reachable to each other, and not necessarily adjacent;
- The frequency of ties among members – subgroup member should have ties to many other within the subgroup, and
- The relative frequency of ties among subgroup members compared to non-members – the subgroups should be relatively cohesive compared to the rest of the network.

The number of *components* constituting a network is a measure that tells us of how many separate components our network is designed. Components of a graph are subgraphs that are connected within, but disconnected between subgraphs. If a graph contains one or more "isolates," these actors are components. If all entities in the network are connected in such a way that any entity can reach any other entity in the network (regardless of the number of steps), this network is made of one component. If there is a group of interconnected entities, which cannot be connected to any other group of entities, the network is said to be made of two components, etc. This metrics help us see the consistency of the network we analyze.

More interesting components are those which divide the network into separate parts, and where each part has several actors who are connected to one another. In case of directed graphs, there are two different kinds of components: weak and strong components. A *weak component* is a set of nodes that are connected, regardless of the direction of ties, i.e. it is a maximal (weakly) connected network. In this context, term *maximal* stands for the situation in which no other vertex can be added to the subnetwork without destroying its defining characteristic (de Nooy et al., 2005: 68). A *strong component* requires that there be a directed path from A to B in order for the two to be in the same component. If, for example, ego was connected to A and B, who are connected among themselves, and ego is connected to C and D, who are also connected to one another, but A and B are not connected in any way to C and D, then there would be two "weak components" in ego's neighborhood (Hanneman & Riddle, 2005).

De Nooy et al. (2011) argue that multiple lines are more important because they are less personal and more institutional, and larger the number of interlocks between two actors, the stronger or more cohesive their tie, the more similar or interdependent they are. The concept of an *island* is a subnetwork defined by the multiplicity of lines. "An island is a maximal subnetwork of vertices connected directly or indirectly by lines with a value greater that the lines to vertices outside the subnetwork" (de Nooy et al., 2011).

4.2.7 Network Level

Global or network analyses focus on properties of complete sets of graphs. Structural properties that we need to look into at this level of analysis are connectedness and diameter, density, prestige, and network centralization. We have already spoken about some of them in the context of the "lower" levels of analysis, and will here provide definitions and explanations for those not mentioned previously.

A network is *connected*, or weakly connected, if all vertices are connected by a semipath. In a (weakly) connected network, we can "walk" from each vertex to all other vertices if we neglect the direction of the arcs. In directed networks, there is a second type of connectedness: a strongly connected network - each pair of vertices is connected by a path.

In a strongly connected network, you can travel from each vertex to any other vertex obeying the direction of the arcs. Strong connectedness is more restricted than weak connectedness: each strongly connected network is also weakly connected but a weakly connected network is not necessarily strongly connected. Our example is not weakly connected, so it cannot be strongly connected (de Nooy et al., 2005).

Measuring the *density* of a network provides us with the index of the degree of dyadic connection in a population. Density measure can have a value between 0 and 1, and is usually defined as the sum of the values of all ties divided by the number of possible ties. That is, with valued data, density is usually defined as the average strength of ties across all possible (not all actual) ties. This metrics can enable comparison between two or more networks. However, we need to consider the fact that the growth of the number of entities, diminishes the density of the network, and it is not advisable therefore to compare networks with big differences in the number of entities. This happens because in persons' networks, when the number of entities/actors in the network grows, falls the number of connections a person can absorb. This can be explained by the fact that in real life a person is limited by the number of possible friendships/acquaintances (Hanneman & Riddle, 2005).

Individual network centralities provide insight into the individual's location in the network. The relationship between the centralities of all nodes provides us with the insight into the overall network structure. A very *centralized network* is dominated by one or a few hubs. If hubs are removed or damaged, the network quickly fragments into unconnected sub-networks. A network centralized around a well connected hub can fail abruptly if that hub is disabled or removed.

A less centralized network has no single points of failure. It is resilient in the face of intentional attacks or random failures - many nodes or links can fail while allowing the remaining nodes to still reach each other over other network paths (IBM, 2012).

Other network metrics include:

Network reach. Not all network paths are created equal. More and more research shows that the shorter paths in the network are more important. Friedkin (Friedkin and Johnsen, 1999 and 2011; Friedkin, 1998), Burt (Burt, 1992; Burt & Minor, 1983) and other researchers have shown that networks have horizons over which we cannot see, nor influence. They propose that the key paths in networks are 1 and 2 steps and on rare occasions, three steps: the "small world" in which we live is not one of "six degrees of separation" but of direct and indirect connections < 3 steps away.

Therefore, it is important to know: Who is in your network neighborhood? and Who are you aware of, and whom can you reach?

Boundary spanners. Nodes that connect their group to others usually end up with high network metrics. Boundary spanners such as Fernando, Garth, and Heather are more central than their immediate neighbors whose connections are only local, within their immediate cluster (Figure 31).

Figure 31. Boundary spanners (IBM, 2012)

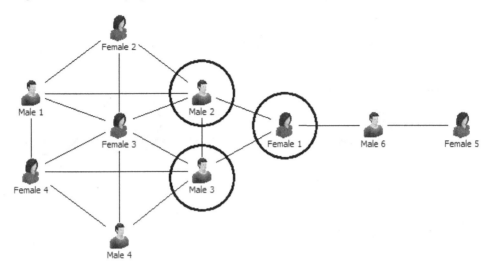

Boundary spanners are well-positioned to be innovators, since they have access to ideas and information flowing in other clusters. They are in a position to combine different ideas and knowledge into new products and services.

Peripheral Players. Most people would view the nodes on the periphery of a network as not being very important. In fact, Ike and Jane receive very low centrality scores for this network. Yet, peripheral nodes are often connected to networks that are not currently mapped (Figure 32).

One measure in networks is the global *clustering coefficient*. The clustering coefficient measure, introduced by Watts and Strogatz, varies from centrality measures, and is close to density. It measures how connected a vertex's neighbors are to one another. It is the number of edges connecting a vertex's neighbors divided by the total number of possible edges between the vertex's neighbors. It is used in ego-centric networks: ego has a high clustering coefficient if most or all of his neighbors (alters) are connected with one another.

The "overall" graph clustering coefficient is simply the average of the densities of the neighborhoods of all of the actors. While the *local* clustering coefficient of a vertex in a graph is based on ego's network density or local density, *global* clustering coefficient is concerned with the density of triplets of nodes in a network, and it is defined as the number of closed triplets over the total number of triplets (Figure 33).

Figure 32. Peripheral players (IBM; 2012)

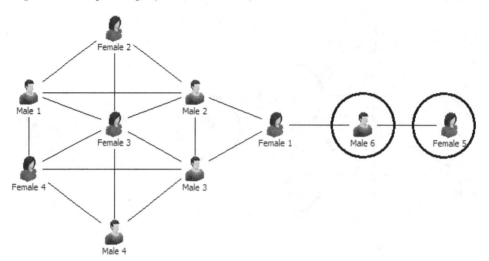

4.3 POWER OVER INFLUENCE

Fundamental objective of the analysis of social networks is to understand relationships within a social structure composed of different types of actors, and examining how these actors influence one another. SNA tools and metrics help us visually analyze networks, thus enabling us to detect and single out the actors that are capable of influencing other actors in the network, their behavior, and the behavior of the entire network correspondingly. Social network analysis offers an alternative approach to examining the relationship between actors in a telecommunication business and providing a means to identify key players in a network of users.

There are several aspects of analysis that we should consider in an attempt to analyze churn by using SNA methodology: firstly, we need to recognize the nodes in the network with highest degree centrality (hubs); secondly, these hubs have to be put in some context in order to determine their power, and detect ways and directions of their influence on other actors in the network; and thirdly, we need to establish the scope of their influence.

Not all members of a network are equally capable of exerting influence over other actors in the network, their decisions, behavior or opinions (Degenne and Forsé, 1999). Some are leaders, others are followers. Difference between them is the matter of power and influence, or homophily. *Homophily* stands for the idea that people show the tendency to stay together with people similar to them. If we define *influence* as a force that person A (i.e., the influencer) exerts on person B to

Figure 33. Local clustering coefficient in an undirected network[12]

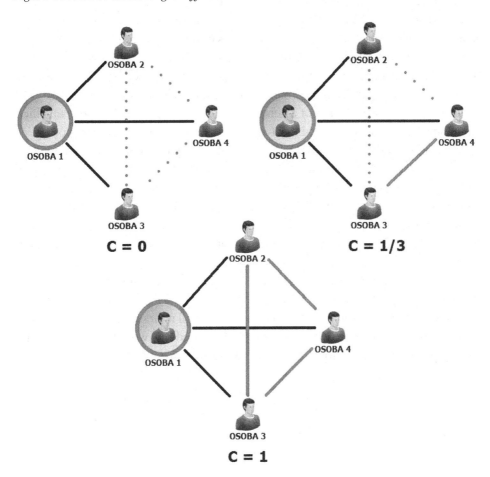

introduce a change of the behavior and/or opinion of B, we can say that homophily is one form of social influence, which is just the opposite side of the same medal.

Power and influence are measured by analyzing the social structures. One of the most important means of analyzing social networks is measures of centrality. Centrality is a key concept in social network analysis, and a critical metrics for determining power and influence, because it provides us with the information about the social power of a node based on how well he connects the network. *Power* is, thus, calculated by a "particular node's connections, the strength of its links, and the length of its path to the other nodes within the network, among other factors. The measure of power is a network metric that indicates which nodes hold high values in relation to their social structure" (Pinheiro, 2011).

We have already spoken about centrality measures in previous chapters of this book, but for the purpose of putting this SNA metrics into the context of churn analysis, we shall here provide short reminders of their definitions and application. However, to understand how centrality is used in examining power and influence, first we shall consider three simple network structures proposed by Wasserman and Faust (1994): star-, circle-, and line networks (Figure 34).

The *star structure* consists of a central node and several satellite nodes in which the central figure occupies strongest position relative to other nodes. Node A is connected to all other nodes (B, C, D, E, F, and G), which means it has six connections whereas all other nodes have just one, and is only one step away from each of the other nodes. This position enables node A to influence six other nodes, and probably in a quick way, due to the short length of his connections. "Any sort of information or message can flow widely and quickly throughout this particular social structure if it is triggered by node A" (Pinheiro, 2011: 68) On the other hand, if we remove node A in this particular structure, all other nodes will no longer be able to reach each other, since node A is the one that keeps the network together. In other words, node A acts as a hub.

In the second type of network, shaped as a *circle*, all nodes have the same number of connections – one with each of their neighbors, and this would indicate they are equally powerful in terms of the number of related nodes. However, to determine

Figure 34. Three illustrative networks for the study of centrality

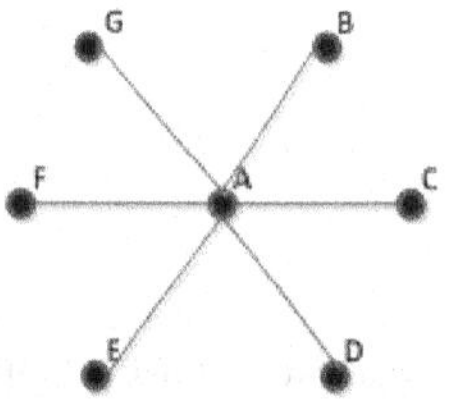

star graph

0	1	1	1	1	1	1
1	0	0	0	0	0	0
1	0	0	0	0	0	0
1	0	0	0	0	0	0
1	0	0	0	0	0	0
1	0	0	0	0	0	0
1	0	0	0	0	0	0

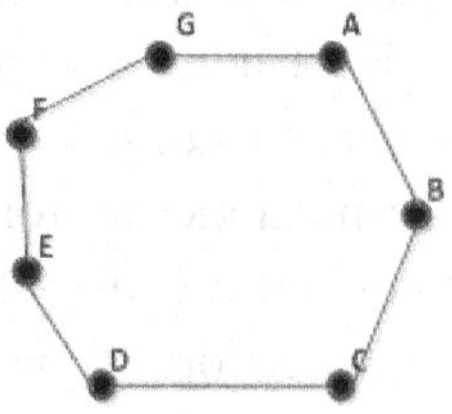

circle graph

0	1	0	0	0	0	1
1	0	1	0	0	0	0
0	1	0	1	0	0	0
0	0	1	0	1	0	0
0	0	0	1	0	1	0
0	0	0	0	1	0	1
1	0	0	0	0	1	0

line graph

0	1	1	0	0	0	0
1	0	0	1	0	0	0
1	1	0	0	1	0	0
0	1	0	0	0	1	0
0	0	1	0	0	0	1
0	0	0	1	0	0	0
0	0	0	0	1	0	0

the power and influence of a certain node, we also need to consider their position in the network. In circle networks, all nodes have the same number of connections and the same average path length (position). Therefore, they all have an equal amount of power.

In a *line-shaped* network, node A is at the end of the network, and thus unable to influence other nodes. Nodes B, C, D, E, and F have two connections, whereas nodes A, and G have just one. Based on the number of nodes, we could conclude that nodes B, C, D, E, and F have the same power within the network. However, node D is in the center of the network, one step away from nodes C and E, two steps from nodes B and F, and three steps from nodes A and G. By calculating his average path length (adding all of the steps needed to reach the other nodes in the network), we conclude that node D is the most powerful node in this social structure, as its average path length is the shortest (12 steps away from every other node).

Centrality measures are used to establish and identify "important or prominent actors" (Knoke & Yang, 2008; Wasserman & Faust, 1997), and also to establish the influence that a particular actor may exercise within a network (Scott, 2000). Based on previous examples of network structures we shall explain the role and purpose of centrality measures in calculating power and influence.

Three centrality measures are used to determine power and influence: *degree* – measures how well connected an entity is by counting the number of direct links each entity has to others in the network; *betweenness* – which measures the number of paths that pass through each entity, and reflects the number of people who a person is connecting indirectly through their direct links, and *closeness* – which measures the proximity of an entity to the other entities in the social network (directly or indirectly).

Degree centrality in a network indicates actor's influence and power potential. Hanneman and Riddle (2005) explain that actors who have more ties than other actors may be in advantageous positions. When referring to degree, Wasserman and Faust (Wasserman & Faust, 1994) explain that the central actors in the network are "the most active in the sense that they have the most ties to the other actors in the network". The star graph is maximally central, since its "one central actor has direct contact with all others, who are not in contact with each other" (Wasserman & Faust, 1994). Namely, in this type of social structure node A has a degree of centrality of 6, and all other nodes, B, C, D, E, F, and G, have a degree of centrality of 1.

In the other two graphs, the degree of centralization can vary just by changing a few ties in the network. In the case of circle network, nodes are interchangeable, having the same a degree of centrality of 2, because each one of them is directly connected to two other nodes. Since all of them have the same measure of power, it makes them equally good starting points for a diffusion process. In line network, however, some nodes make a better choice for diffusion as they can move information through the network more efficiently. Nodes B, C, D, E, and F, for example, have two related nodes, and correspondingly a degree of centrality of 2. Nodes A and G have a degree of centrality of 1. Furthermore, despite the fact that nodes B, C, D, E, and F have the same degree of centrality, node D has, on average, the shortest path to the rest of the social structure, making it the best choice for diffusion (Pinheiro, 2011).

In a real-world example of telecommunications, for example, if we want to target the best set of customers, we would need to consider some additional information about the customers. Pinheiro (Pinheiro, 2011) explains why: "in a telecommunications network, the degree of centrality is equal to the number of customers who make or receive calls to or from a particular customer. For instance, if John is a customer and makes calls to 5 friends, and receives calls from another 5 friends, he has a degree of centrality of 10." He further argues that the number of calls he makes or receives is not important to this network measure, but we should rather investigate how many other customers he is connected to within the network (Pinheiro 2011). So, in the case of global degree centrality it is not important who calls whom, and how many times. What counts is the number of phone numbers you communicated with. For example if John makes 5 phone calls to Mary and Mary makes 14 phone calls to John, they would both still have the global degree of centrality of 1.

However, if we want to introduce directions into the story, and say that John makes calls to Mary, Stephen, Cathy, and Bill, and receives calls from another set of friends, say Barbra, Sam, and Jack, than he would have an in-degree of 3, and out-degree of 4. The global degree centrality would be the sum of the in- and out-degrees, and it would equal 7.

In-degree and out-degree centralities are important metrics for the analysis of telecommunications networks because they tell us about power and influence in analyzed social structure: the person who makes calls to a number of other customers may be a potential leader, and the one who receives calls from leaders may be a potential follower (Pinheiro 2011). Therefore, directed graphs should be used to represent the customers and their relationships within a network.

When the analysis goes beyond a single network, in-degree and out-degree centrality values may lead in a different direction. Pinheiro (Pinheiro, 2011) mentions just a few possibilities: "a customer who receives a call from outside the network can be an anchor to capture new customers or, in terms of revenue, can collect a substantial amount of interconnection rates from other operators. A customer who makes a call outside the network can be a high-risk customer in terms of churn if the majority of his connections are outside. He may eventually decide to move to another operator." In such cases, in the analysis of internetwork connections, additional network metrics should be applied.

By measuring the number of paths that pass through each entity, *betweenness* centrality provides information on the node's role within the network. It measures the possibility that the particular node can operate as a point of dominance in the communication and interaction (Leydesdorff, 2007).

A person with a high *betweenness* score occupies one of the best locations in the network, and the higher the score, the more significant his role in the network. He plays a broker role in the network, which means that he is located on a path between two important constituencies, and occupies a controlling position. It means that a node in the network need not have many ties to be powerful. What is important is that he occupies potential controlling position which ensures power and influence in controlling the interactions and communications between all other actors in the network. These nodes are essential for the communication and interaction within the network. However, a node with high *betweenness* score represents a single point of failure in the network because if an actor with a high *betweenness* score were deleted, there is the possibility that the network might fall apart (Leydesdorff, 2007).

It measures the proximity of an entity to the other entities in the social network (directly or indirectly), "how close an actor is to the other actors in the network" (Wasserman & Faust, 1997). It measures "how quickly an actor can interact with others, for example, by communicating directly or through very few intermediaries" (Knoke & Yang, 2008). One of the most common and important approaches to indexing the distances between actors is the geodesic. The geodesic distance or diameter between pairs of actors is the measure of closeness used to describe the minimum distance between actors. In simplest terms, geodesic is the shortest path between two vertices.

Hanneman and Riddle (Hanneman and Riddle, 2005) explain the importance of centrality measures in calculating power and influence: "Power can be exerted by direct bargaining and exchange. But power also comes from acting as a "reference point" by which other actors judge themselves, and by being a center of attention whose views are heard by larger numbers of actors. Actors who are able to reach other actors at shorter path lengths, or who are more reachable by other actors at shorter path lengths have favored positions. This structural advantage can be translated into power." The measure of power is closely related to graph theory. It is a "property of social structures, and hence it relies on the shape of the structure being analyzed" (Pinheiro, 2011). As mentioned earlier, different types of social networks require variations in approach to computing power. The measure of power depends solely on a node's relationships within the network: their number (*degree*), distance between them (*closseness*), and their location (*betweenness*).

Pinheiro defines influence as "a form of power, suggestion, or domination" (Pinheiro, 2011). In the context of telecommunications, "influence is the capacity of one particular customer to induce others to follow him or her in a specific business event (e.g. churn, purchase, etc.). Influence needs to be observed over time as it describes how the behavior of an individual customer induces others to behave similarly (Pinheiro, 2011: 66). In business structures connections, positions, and relations are crucial to calculate power because they determine how many customers might be influenced, how quickly, and by whom.

4.4 APPLICATION OF SNA IN CHURN ANALYSIS

Why use social network analysis in churn? The answer to that question rests on three premises. First premise refers to the fact that the information flows rapidly within well connected groups, which makes it reliable for the members of the groups. In this context it is interesting to mention research results of Kalakota and Robinson (2000: 170) who argue that it is 5-8 times more expensive to sell a product/service to the new customer than to an existing one; that dissatisfied customers will tell an average of 8-10 people about their negative experience; of the 15 the most-cited complaints, 12 were related to poor customer service; 70% of complaining customers will do business with the company again if the complaint is quickly addressed; the odds of selling a product to a new customer are 15%, whereas odds of selling a product to an existing customer are 50%.

Another premise is the tendency of the members of well-connected networks to make frequent calls among themselves, which is the reason why they hang on to the same carrier. The third premise is that smaller social groups often have a dominant leader with strong influence on the preferences of the entire group, and consequently the group members' decisions on churn. In this chapter, we shall consider social network analysis to illustrate churn prediction on several examples.

Recent work in the area of churn prediction has shown that using SNA tools and analyzing customers' interactions by "assessing the social vicinity of recent churners" can improve the accuracy of churn prediction. Richter et al. (2010) proposed "a novel framework, termed Group-First Churn Prediction, which eliminates the *a priori* requirement of knowing who recently churned". Their approach "exploits the structure of customer interactions to predict which groups of subscribers are most prone to churn, before even a single member in the group has churned". Method they used to identify closely-knit groups of subscribers was second-order social metrics. They kept only the strongest connections, and divided the network into a collection of small disjoint clusters, each representing a dense social group. Then they analyzed the social interactions within each cluster and established the relative social status of each of its members. The most important step was to identify social leaders. Based on Key Performance Indicators derived from these groups, they proposed a novel statistical model to predict the churn of the groups and their members. They provide empirical evidence that their method "captures social phenomena in a highly significant manner". They further suggest: "A good churn prediction system should not only pinpoint potential churners successfully, but further provide a sufficiently long horizon forecast in its predictions. Once a potential churner is identified, the retention department usually makes contact and, if the customer is established to be a churn risk, takes appropriate measures to preserve her business. Thus, a long forecast horizon is an obvious advantage since the further away the customer is from actually making the churn decision, the easier it is to prevent that decision at a significantly lower cost."

There are two important aspects that distinguish this approach from other mainstream analyses: first is group-based analysis vs. global analysis of the social structure, which facilitates deeper analysis of each group, and "allows advanced machine learning techniques to be applied at the group-level," as demonstrated in their results; second aspect is that they aim to predict the beginning of a churn process rather than predicting behavior in the next period based on the last one. Therefore, their approach deals with a more difficult problem - early identification of potential churners (longer forecast horizon), but a larger expected payback as early detected churners are easier to retain.

The goal was to predict the future churners over a predefined forecast horizon, given the data associated with each subscriber in the network. Input they used for the analysis included data on past calls for each mobile subscriber, together with all personal and business information that is maintained by the carrier.

Performance is measured using the ratio called lift. For any given fraction $0 < T < 1$, lift is defined as "the ratio between the number of churners among the fraction of T subscribers that are ranked highest by the proposed system, and the expected number of churners in a random sample from the general subscribers pool of equal size" (Richter et al., 2010).

The analysis was performed on data of a large mobile operator, which has an average of 117 million call data records every day. The sample included 28 days of the data, and approximately 28 million subscribers for that period. The subscribers' base included those of the operator and people who had called them. Approximately 16 million of them were subscribers of the analyzed operator. In the month after the data was collected, 800,000 people churned. Analysts were provided with the last day on which each of the subscribers made a call, and this was the indicator for the day of churn. For each of the subscribers, they analyzed last 100 calls they made in the previous 3 days.

The results are as follows:

- Probability of churn for subscribers who are member of a smaller group (20 or less) is 2.7 times greater than in subscribers who are members of larger groups.
- They define that a group has a leader "when its highest ranked member has a social strength that is larger by at least 0.2 compared with the weakest member in the group". Under such circumstances:
  - 70% of the groups have a leader.
  - In 99% of the groups, the leader is a member of the telecom provider analyzed.
- In the remaining 1% of groups, the probability of churn is 19.4 times greater than in groups where the leaders are from the provider analyzed.
- Members of these groups are 1.6 times more likely to churn compared to their peers in groups where the leader is from the company analyzed.
- Leader strength has an important effect on the probability of group churn, i.e. the leader seems to be an indicator of churn likelihood in the group:
  - There is a high correlation between the strength of a leader and the increase in churn probability, indicating that the stronger the leader, the more likely there is to be churn from her group.
  - The most likely person to churn in a group is the leader, who is 3 times more likely to churn compared to the churn probability of other group members.
  - In groups where two subscribers churned, the probability that one of them is a leader is 12 times that expected by chance.
  - In groups where more than two subscribers churned, the probability that one of them is the leader is 11.8 times that expected by chance (Figure 35).

Analysis of the decision tree reveals that the groups with more than four members are less likely to churn, while groups at a higher risk of churn are those where the "leader made and received few calls, groups with few non-voice interactions (i.e., SMS messages), and groups where the leader is not a subscriber of the analyzed carrier".

Advantages of this analysis in relation to other SNA-based models is that it predicts whole group churn and therefore does not require knowing which customers have churned recently. Furthermore, since only call data records are used, they do not require the use of financial indicators and demographic information (used in most individual-based models), which means that this method is applicable to both pre- and post-paid customers without the need to retrain the model. Also, this prediction being based on the last calls made by each customer in a relatively short

Figure 35. Lift obtained by the churn prediction model for four coverage levels (Richter et al., 2010)

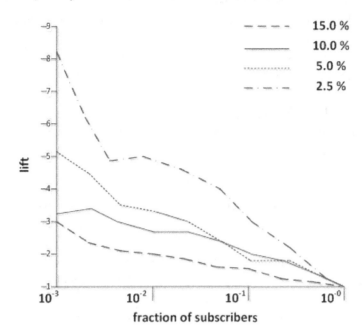

time period means that the method can be applied before the data passes through the operator's data warehouse, saving thus both time and effort.

The results presented in Richter et al. (2010) indicate that their group-based model is very successful in accurate prediction of churn in large populations.

Another research conducted by Richter, Yom-Tov, and Slonim (Richter et. al., 2010) analyzed churn in two segments: prepaid churn, with SIM change instead of renewal, and postpaid churn resulting in subscriber moving to another carrier, but keeping his mobile number. Key assumption they based their research on was that mobile networks are composed of underlying distinct social groups, which made SNA a perfectly adequate tool for the analysis due to its network approach.

As the mobile market Richter et al. analyzed was mostly saturated, and gaining new business much more expensive than retaining the existing one, they set a goal to predict potential churners as early as possible, which is both an easier, and a cheaper option. All traditional approaches used in such cases were inappropriate and defective because they treated customers as individuals, while churn has a "strong social aspect to it", which is not captured by individual models.

In analyzing customer churn, the input IBM analysts used was customer associated data with only two weeks of customer calls, and the aim of the analysis included predicting churn in the following 3-month time.

By using lift metric they measured the effectiveness of their model aimed at improving targeting of customers likely to churn. Lift was calculated by dividing the number of churners in their sample divided by the number of churners in the subset of the population.

Methodology they used in constructing social reference groups consists of several steps:

- Quantify links between people (edges);
- Partition groups according to strongest links (identify clusters);
- Link "stragglers" (using second-order interactions analysis), and
- Analyze each group (leaders, followers, etc.).

The results they got proved that most groups have a leader, and in 87% of groups the leader was from the carrier. In other 13%, in cases where leader was not from carrier, group churn likelihood grew 2.2 times. Leader (from carrier) is proved to be the most risky member of the group for he is 10.6 times more likely to leave than all other members of his group. If the leader (from carrier) leaves, the results show that another churner is 2.4 times more likely to leave also, and the likelihood of more than one group member to leave is almost 7 times higher compared with cases when leader does not leave. Richter et al. (Richter et al., 2010) also proved that early adopters[13] churn earlier, and that there is a 92% certainty that opinion leaders determine the carrier of choice for their group members.

The general conclusion of the analysis was that churn had certain social aspects, which was the key argument for the use of SNA. The methodology used has many advantages in relation to other churn prediction approaches: it allows social analysis of disjoint social groups, a modular approach, and easy integration with statistical analysis, and can be used in synergy with the existing solutions.

Pinheiro presents several case studies primarily on churn and bundle acquisition, but emphasizes that similar models can be equally applied in sales campaigns and cross- and up-selling initiatives. He argues that this type of analysis may help in understanding the evolution of different types of social structures within telecommunication environment, which would in turn help prepare appropriate marketing and sales campaigns "based not just on the behavior of the social networks but also on their possible evolution".

The focus of the model Pinehiro proposes is recognizing the customer behavior and the consequences of such behavior on community correlated to some particular event. This reveals the power and influence of particular customers based on which companies will be able to establish effective processes for determining customer loyalty and bundle adoption. Pinheiro (2011) describes correlation between the customer-influence factor and business events on examples of churn and bundle acquisition. In this respect, following procedures needed to be established to evaluate the strength of those correlations, relating the customer-influence factor to past events of churning and bundle diffusion.

Monitoring and analysis of networks helps companies to see what impact different business events have in terms of revenue. Also, based on likelihood of churn and the influence of analyzed customers, SNA enables telecommunication companies to plan activities aimed at decreasing churn and increasing bundle diffusion. These activities should incorporate marketing and other campaigns targeting influential customers as they can lead other customers, and trigger some other events in a chain process (e.g. churn). "Influential customers inside the telecommunications network," argues Pinheiro (Pinheiro, 2011) "would be in a strong position in relation to the social structure being analyzed, both in terms of their number of connections and the length of their path to other customers."

Pinheiro proposes use of an SNA model (call-detail records - CDR) to be applied to distinguish influential customers from the ordinary ones.

The methodology Pinheiro used to calculate customer-influence factor includes two traditional measures of network topology for depicting social networks – first-order centrality and second-order centrality. The first describes the number of direct connections from a particular node, and the latter refers to the number of connections that the nodes related to the original one have. In Figure 36 first-order centrality is shown in black and the second-order centrality in grey color.

Figure 36. First- and second-order centrality

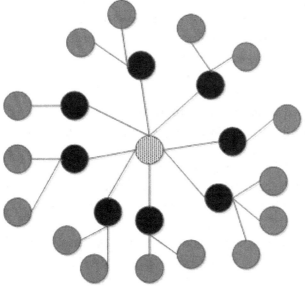

First-order centrality represents the number of nodes a particular customer can reach directly, and this measure is particularly relevant for churn, because churn involves exactly this type of influence.

The second element that needs to be considered is the direction of the relationship. Therefore, the formula used to calculate customer-influence factor must consider first- and second- order centrality data of the incoming and outgoing calls separately, whereas call duration values are added to represent customer behavior when receiving calls within the social network.

Since outgoing calls hold a different value than incoming calls when certain corporate dimensions are considered (e.g. revenue), different weights are assigned to first-order centrality, second-order centrality, and duration factor, depending on their value to the company.

These three attributes - first-order centrality, second-order centrality, and an equation of call duration divided by the amount of calls - are being considered to calculate the customer-influence factor.

The values of the attributes can vary widely, and to normalize the calculations, the coefficient of variation for some specific factors inside the formula is applied to the first-order centrality, second-order centrality, and the relation between the number of calls and total duration. This calculation should help decrease the dispersion of the metrics and facilitate the scores that are applicable for real-world business problems.

The first step of the analysis is to extract the call-detail records from the corporate data warehouse together with some additional data regarding customer attributes such as where they live, how long they have been customers, which products they have purchased and when, etc., which help build knowledge about customer behavior and recognize patterns.

At this point of data preparation, Pinheiro proposes collection of information about customers, accounts, fixed lines, call-detail records, products, and billing history from the data warehouse. Usually this information is dispersed, and it should be organized in a single document. After that, each attribute is analyzed in terms of distribution, and the outliers are removed from the sample in order to guarantee a more normalized sample. Dataset for the model development process is now created, and it is possible to start the modeling activity, which includes following steps:

- Computing the basic social network measures;
- Computing the customer-influence factor, and
- Adjusting the influence factor according to past events.

The following and the most important stage is the assessment of the social network model. This process should evaluate the network analysis's possibilities for corporate applications answering the following questions: "How can the network analysis be applied to improve the business process?" and "How can the network measures be deployed in order to avoid churn and to improve bundle diffusion?"

Pinheiro's model computed and evaluated the network outcomes, particularly the network measures, in terms of the business events of churning and bundle diffusion. As formerly said the customer-influence factor was built based on the network measures, weighted by their call value, and normalized by the coefficient of variation. The customer-influence factor was computed taking into account each node's average behavior over the last four months.

The evaluation process took into consideration the following six months of similar business events of churning and bundle diffusion. The assessment was based on the comparison of the most influential customers, based on their influence factor, with a random subset of customers, like a control group. For each influential customer who left the company (leader), an evaluation of the following six months was performed, identifying the number of correlated customers (followers) who left the company as well. The same evaluation was done for random customers who left the company and their followers, and for the same period. The comparison was performed in absolute terms, considering the number of correlated customers who left the company in the following months, but also on a relative basis, considering the percentage of customers who left the company in the following months.

Next are the figures for customer-influence in churn events. The results of the analysis revealed the following:

- The average customer-influence factor was calculated using 769,104 residential customers. In a specific month, 10,624 left the company.
- Considering the almost 11,000 residential customers who left the company in a specific month:
  - Random 1,000 residential customers from that number have led additional 18 residential customers to churn;
  - The top 1,000 residential customers have led an additional 19 residential customers to churn;
  - The top 1,000 influential residential customers from the same 11,000 residential customers who left the company have led an additional 130 residential customers to churn;

Considering the subset of 1,000 residential customers who have left the company in a particular month, from the random process, every 56 residential customers who left the company have led another 1 to follow them in the churn event.

From revenue ranking, every 53 residential customers who left the company have led another 1 residential customer to follow in the churn event.

Finally, from the influence-factor ranking, every 8 residential customers who left the company have led another 1 to follow in the churn event.

Additionally, Pinheiro's results say that every 56 residential customers, on average, will affect or lead another one residential customer to churn. Also, every eight influential residential customers will affect or lead another residential customer to churn.

Although the performance is greater when influential residential customers are considered - 622 percent higher than the random process - the hit rate of the influence factor is also more effective.

Comparing the subsets of influential and random customers, there are more than 5,000 customers related to the influential ones and just a little bit more than 1,000 customers related to the randomly chosen or average ones.

Considering the random subset of customers, from the 1,000 related customers, just 18 customers churned in the subsequent months, representing just 1.3 percent of the possible affected customers.

As the above examples show social network approach may help companies develop marketing and sales programs for retaining the best and most profitable customers, improve their sales campaigns, and increase revenue by offering new services and products adjusted to the social community of a particular customer. Pinheiro suggests that SNA approach be used to help the loyalty program by supporting the process of cross-selling and up-selling products and services through a diffusion approach. He also claims that the retention and sales campaigns can be significantly enhanced by "accurately targeting the customer base, which means selecting the right clients or prospects for responses, thereby reducing the costs of operations and increasing profit" (Pinheiro, 2011).

To learn about customer behavior, Pinheiro suggests developing and implementing solutions based on artificial neural networks and other techniques that will provide predictive models, such as decision trees and regressions. All models can achieve good results, and the choice of which to use is based on the type and format of the data and the data miners' experience.

4.5 DATA MINING METHODS AND SNA: AN INTEGRATED APPROACH

Different models can be developed and implemented for analyzing customer behavior and predicting various business events. These models can include traditional tools and techniques based on artificial neural networks used for predictive modeling, or they can combine several methodologies aimed at prediction and retention of valuable customers.

Pinheiro (Pinheiro, 2011), for example, proposes a two dimensional model, combining traditional models based on artificial neural networks to predict business events acquisition, and social network analysis to "realize the magnitude of impact and influence of particular customers over others". He suggests that this combination of models can help companies establish effective processes for determining customer loyalty and bundle adoption. Some other techniques can also be used to develop predictive models, such as decision trees and regressions. All of the mentioned models have proved to achieve good results, and their use depends solely on the type and format of the collected data.

Regarding the type of data, SNA also differs from other analytical models in that it requires data about observations, as well as data that describe the relationship among these observations. In other words, analyzing data about connections among the nodes in the network helps us learn not only about customer's behavior but also about customers' relationship behaviors (Pinheiro, 2011). It is these sorts of data that differentiate network data from the other models' data: data about links reveal important attributes about the network and the data about the nodes tell us a lot about the importance of the nodes in the networks and as such provide overall analysis of customers. The major difference between conventional and network data is that "conventional data focus on observations and attributes, whereas network data focus on observations and relations" (Pinheiro, 2011).

However, as mentioned earlier, business events like churn and bundle acquisition are chain processes, and should be approached from a chain perspective to be able to assess the impact and the correlation among those business events inside the database. In such cases a specific model should be used and adjusted to specific needs of the event analysis. Social network analysis is the best approach to the perspective of a chain process, although combining SNA with traditional models should give optimal results in predictive modeling and analyzing customer behavior. "Also, some simple approaches, such as average billing or type of products and plans," Pinheiro (Pinheiro, 2011) suggests "can be used to categorize customers into distinct segments. The prediction score assigned to the client's segment can be a good way to define and perform distinct actions for customer retention, thereby decreasing the costs related to loyalty campaigns."

To sum it up, Pinheiro proposes a different sort of statistical approach based on data mining techniques to be applied for analyzing various patterns of behavior for a particular social network. If we use temporal analysis that observes networks over time, predictive techniques such as regression, decision tree, and artificial neural networks can be implemented for defining possible scenarios of evolution for the social network. According to Pinheiro there are several ways to establish customer value - based on average billing, revenue, usage, or even behavior. He, thus, proposes that this type of customer value be determined by clustering models or even by simple statistical processes. The combination of the customer value and the score assigned to a particular business event, such as churning, allows companies to recognize good customers who are likely to leave and then take action to prevent the churn.

In this context, best results can be achieved by using an integrated hybrid approach, which includes data integration (data vs. intelligence), integration of the subject of interest (individual vs. community), and methodology integration (predictive modeling vs. SNA), as presented in Figure 37.

This integrated hybrid model can result in numerous specific (2D, 3D,...nD) applicative models, and we recommend as many dimensions as possible (Figure 38).

For example, we calculate client influence by using SNA methodology, client probability by predictive data mining models and score (value of client) by fuzzy expert systems. As mentioned in previous chapters, fuzzy expert systems are used in knowledge discovery processes for classification, segmentation and scoring purposes with main focus on expert knowledge which is implemented into models. Results which are provided from those models are mostly first step for more complex analysis and for usage in combination with other knowledge discovery techniques.

Very often the profitability of client (in advanced systems observed as score) and client probability of churn have been taken as key parameters of the imperative of targeting clients in preventing and controlling churn. However, by introducing the third axis shown in the figure (client influence) it becomes quite clear that some clients will have to be kept although they have low score values (i.e. they are not profitable). These are the clients who have a large influence measures. On the other hand, we are well aware of the fact that marketing campaigns have restricted

Figure 37. Integrated hybrid model

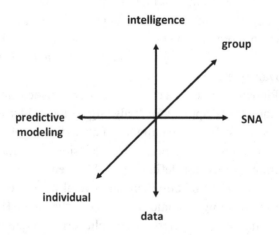

Figure 38. An example of the application of an integrated 3D hybrid model

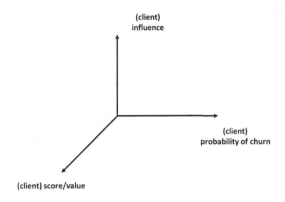

resources, but also aim at maximum efficiency. It means that they need to be as accurate in their campaigns as possible. Now, who are we going to target in a specific subset of clients if all of them have an equal scoring value (e.g. highly profitable), and we do not have enough resources to target all of them equally? We shall target leaders, i.e. clients with the largest influence. Or, what if the leader churns and there is a real danger that he will drag his followers along? We have to target those followers and prevent them from churning, but as we have already said, we do not have enough money to keep them all. Nevertheless, we would like to keep our customers and hopefully halt the diffusion of the "bad vibe" caused, for example, by an unsatisfied customer (leader) who has just churned.

In line with this, the million dollar question is: Whom of his followers shall we primarily try to keep? The answer is: The gatekeeper entity, i.e., the client with the highest *betweenness* score. If we manage to keep this person and make him/her happy, we shall be able to prevent the diffusion of the "bad vibe", and hopefully stimulate the diffusion of the "good vibe".

Additionally, integrated data mining and SNA approach should be observed as a two-way model. It means that, for example, SNA metrics of each node (calculated by SNA methodology) could and should be used as an intensifier of predictive data mining models. On the other hand, results of classification and segmentation of data mining models, for example, can be used as additional attributes on the node or edge levels in SNA methodology.

This sort of approach can lead companies to significant changes in terms of marketing and sales. It can certainly achieve a synergy effect as its overall result will be significantly better than any other individual result.

REFERENCES

Barabási, A. L. (2002). Linked: The New Science of Networks. Cambridge, MA: Perseus. Available at http:\\barabasilab.com\networksciencebook

Barabási, A. L. (2002). *Linked: The New Science of Networks*. Cambridge, MA: Perseus.

Blass, T. (2004). *The Man Who Shocked the World: the life and legacy of Stanley Milgram*. New York, NY: Basic Books.

Bollobás, B. (2001). *Random Graphs* (2nd ed.). Cambridge, UK: Cambridge University Press. doi:10.1017/CBO9780511814068

Carrington, P. J., Scott, J., & Wasserman, S. (Eds.). (2005). *Models and Methods in Social Network Analysis*. Cambridge, UK: Cambridge University Press. doi:10.1017/CBO9780511811395

Coleman, J. S. (1964). *Introduction to Mathematical Sociology*. Glencoe, IL: Free Press.

Coser, L. A. (1977). *Masters of Sociological Thought: Ideas in Historical and Social Context* (2nd ed.). New York, NY: Harcourt.

Davis, G. F., Yoo, M., & Baker, W.E. (2003). The small world of the American corporate elite, 1982–2001. *Strategic Organization, 1*(3).

Davis, G. F., & Greve, H. R. (1997). Corporate Elite Networks and Governance Changes in the 1980s. *American Journal of Sociology, 103*(1), 1–37. doi:10.1086/231170

De Sola Pool, I., & Kochen, M. (1978). *Contacts and Influence. In Social Networks*. Amsterdam: Elsevier.

Erdös, P., & Rényi, A. (1959). *On random graphs*. Debrecen: Math.

Erdös, P., & Rényi, A. (1960). *On the Evolution of Random Graphs*. Mathematical Institute of the Hungarian Academy of Sciences.

Erdös, P., & Rényi, A. (1961). On the strength of connectedness of a random graph. *Acta Math. Acad. Sci. Hungar., 12*.

Freeman, L. C. (2004). The Development of Social Network Analysis: A Study in The Sociology of Science. Vancouver, Canada: Empirical Press.

Freeman, L. C. (2004). *The Development of Social Network Analysis: A Study in The Sociology of Science*. Vancouver, Canada: Empirical Press.

Gladwell, M. (2002). *The Tipping Point: How Little Things Can Make a Big Difference*. New York, NY: Back Bay Books.

Granovetter, M. S. (1973). The strength of weak ties. *American Journal of Sociology*, *78*(6), 1360. doi:10.1086/225469

Guare, J. (1990). *Six Degrees of Separation: A Play*. New York, NY: Vintage Books.

Hale, A. E. (1981). *Conducting Clinical Sociometric Explorations: A Manual for Psychodramatists and Sociometrists*. Roanoke, VA: Royal.

Haunschild, P. R. (1993). Interorganizational Imitation: The Impact of Interlocks on Corporate Acquisition Activity. *Administrative Science Quarterly*, *38*(4), 564. doi:10.2307/2393337

Jackson, M. O. (2010). *Social and Economic Networks*. Princeton, NJ: Princeton University Press.

Karinthy, F. (1929). *Láncszemek: Minden másképpen van (Ötvenkét vasárnap)*. Budapest: Athenaeum, Irodalmi és Nyomdai Rt.

Konno, T. (2008). *Network Structure of Japanese Firms: Analysis from 800,000 Companies*. Academic Press.

Marconi, G. (1967). Wireless telegraphic communication. In *Nobel Lectures, Physics 1901-1921*. Amsterdam: Elsevier Publishing Company. Available at http://www.nobelprize.org/nobel_prizes/physics/laureates/1909/marconi-lecture.html

Milgram, S. (1967). The Small-World Problem. *Psychology Today*, *1*(1), 61–67.

Milgram, S. (1967). The Small-World Problem. *Psychology Today*, *1*(1).

Moreno, J. L. (1951). *Sociometry, Experimental Method, and the Science of Society*. Ambler, PA: Beacon House.

Pinheiro, C. A. R. (2011). *Social Network Analysis in Telecommunications*. Hoboken, NJ: John Wiley and Sons Inc.

Rao, H., Davis, G. F., & Ward, A. (2000). Embeddedness, Social Identity and Mobility: Why Firms Leave the NASDAQ and Join the New York Stock Exchange. *Administrative Science Quarterly*, 45.

Rao, H., & Sivakumar, K. (1999). Institutional Sources of Boundary-spanning Structures: The Establishment of Investor Relations Departments in the Fortune 500 Industrials. *Organization Science*, 10.

Rapoport, A., & Horvath, W. J. (1961). A Study of a large sociogram. *Behavioral Science*, 6(4), 279–291. doi:10.1002/bs.3830060402 PMID:14490358

Ravasz, E., & Barabási, A. L. (2003). Hierarchical organization in complex networks. *Physical Review E: Statistical, Nonlinear, and Soft Matter Physics*, 67(2), 026112. doi:10.1103/PhysRevE.67.026112 PMID:12636753

Remer, R. (2006). Chaos Theory Links to Morenean Theory: A Synergistic Relationship. *Journal of Group Psychotherapy, Psychodrama, and Sociometry*, 59.

Remer, R. (2008). Sociometry. In W. A. Darity (Ed.), *International Encyclopedia of the Social Sciences* (2nd ed.). Detroit, MI: Macmillan Reference.

Scott, J. (1987). *Social Network Analysis: A Handbook*. London: Sage Publications.

Simmel, G. (1971). How is Society Possible? In *On Individuality and Social Forms*. Chicago, IL: University of Chicago Press.

Travers, J., & Milgram, S. (1969). An experimental study of the small world problem. *Sociometry*, 32.

Watts, D. J. (1999). *Small Worlds: The Dynamics of Networks between Order and Randomness*. Princeton, NJ: Princeton University Press.

Watts, D. J. (2004). The "New" Science Of Networks. *Annual Review of Sociology*, 30(1), 243–270. doi:10.1146/annurev.soc.30.020404.104342

Watts, D. J., & Strogatz, S. H. (1998). Collective dynamics of "small-world" networks. *Nature*, 393(6684), 440–442. doi:10.1038/30918 PMID:9623998

Watts, D. J., & Strogatz, S. H. (1998). Collective dynamics of 'small-world' networks. *Nature*, 393(6684), 440–442. doi:10.1038/30918 PMID:9623998

Zhang, M. (2010). Social Network Analysis: History, Concepts, and Research. In *Handbook of Social Network Technologies and Applications*. New York, NY: Springer. doi:10.1007/978-1-4419-7142-5_1

KEY TERMS AND DEFINITIONS

Betweenness: The extent to which a node lies between other nodes in the network, this measure takes into account the connectivity of the node's neighbors, giving a higher value for nodes which bridge clusters, the measure reflects the number of people who a person is connecting indirectly through their direct links.

Bridge: An edge is said to be a bridge if deleting it would cause its endpoints to lie in different components of a graph

Centrality: This measure gives a rough indication of the social power of a node based on how well they "connect" the network. "Betweenness", "Closeness", and "Degree" are all measures of centrality.

Centralization: The difference between the number of links for each node divided by maximum possible sum of differences, a centralized network will have many of its links dispersed around one or a few nodes, while a decentralized network is one in which there is little variation between the number of links each node possesses

Closeness: The degree an individual is near all other individuals in a network (directly or indirectly). It reflects the ability to access information through the "grapevine" of network members. Thus, closeness is the inverse of the sum of the shortest distances between each individual and every other person in the network, the shortest path may also be known as the "geodesic distance."

Clustering Coefficient: A measure of the likelihood that two associates of a node are associates them. A higher clustering coefficient indicates a greater "cliquishness."

Cohesion: The degree to which actors are connected directly to each other by cohesive bonds. Groups are identified as 'cliques' if every individual is directly tied to every other individual, "social circles" if there is less stringency of direct contact, which is imprecise, or as structurally cohesive blocks if precision is wanted.

Degree: The count of the number of ties to other actors in the network

Density: The degree a respondent's ties know one another proportion of ties among an individual's nominees. Network or global-level density is the proportion of ties in a network relative to the total number possible (sparse versus dense networks).

Flow Betweenness Centrality: The degree that a node contributes to sum of maximum flow between all pairs of nodes (not that node).

Eigenvector Centrality: A measure of the importance of a node in a network. It assigns relative scores to all nodes in the network based on the principle that connections to nodes having a high score contribute more to the score of the node in question.

Local Bridge: An edge is a local bridge if its endpoints share no common neighbors. Unlike a bridge, a local bridge is contained in a cycle.

Path Length: the distances between pairs of nodes in the network. Average path-length is the average of these distances between all pairs of nodes.

Prestige: In a directed graph prestige is the term used to describe a node's centrality. "Degree Prestige", "Proximity", Prestige", and "Status Prestige" are all measures of Prestige

Radiality: Degree an individual's network reaches out into the network and provides novel information and influence

Reach: The degree any member of a network can reach other members of the network.

Structural Cohesion: The minimum number of members who, if removed from a group, would disconnect the group

Structural Equivalence: Refers to the extent to which nodes have a common set of linkages to other nodes in the system, the nodes don't need to have any ties to each other to be structurally equivalent

Structural Hole: Static holes that can be strategically filled by connecting one or more links to link together other points, linked to ideas of social capital: if you link to two people who are not linked you can control their communication.

ENDNOTES

[1] SNA, Social Network Analysis

[2] We define the embeddedness of an edge in a network to be the number of common neighbors the two endpoints have.

[3] ibid. p. 1360

[4] In 1735 he presented a paper to his colleagues at the Academy of Sciences in St. Petersburg, and a year later, in 1736, he wrote up his solution in his celebrated paper in the *Commentarii Academiae Scientarum Imperialis Petropolitanae* under the title "Solutio problematis ad geometriam situs pertinentis" (The solution of a problem relating to the geometry of position).

[5] Retrieved from http:\\barabasilab.com\networksciencebook

[6] Heavy-tailed degree distribution – real-world networks contain lots of nodes with very small degree, but also a small number of nodes ("hubs") with very high degree.

[7] Retrieved from http://www.santafe.edu/sfi/publications/Bulletins/bulletin-Fall99/workInProgress/smallWorld.html

[8] The giant component is the largest connected (not necessarily strongly connected) sub graph of the undirected graph. The component structure undergoes a phase transition when a graph acquires more and more edges, see: Bollobás, B. (2001) *Random Graphs 2nd Edition*. Cambridge, UK: Cambridge University Press.

9   A simple network example shows centrality measures of *betweenness* (red), *closeness* (light blue), *degree* (green), and *eigenvector* (green).

10   Acyclic networks do not have "loops" (cycles). A loop or cycle is a path that returns to a node previously left. If the arcs correspond to activities that have a time sequence, the network is naturally acyclic. A fixed-degree interconnection networks are called cyclic networks.

11   Nighborhood is the collection of ego and all nodes to whom he is connected at some path length. In SNA, neighborhood always includes only ego and actors directly adjacent.

12   adjusted from: http://bioinformatics.wikidot.com/network-analysis-in-cell-biology (Accessed: 27 July 2011)

13   An early adopter is "an individual or business who uses a new product or technology before others. An early adopter is likely to pay more for the product than later adopters, but accepts this premium if using the product improves efficiency, reduces cost, increases market penetration or simply raises the early adopter's social status. Companies rely on early adopters to provide feedback about product deficiencies, and to cover the cost of the product's research and development." Retreived from http://www.investopedia.com/terms/e/early-adopter.asp

Chapter 5
Data Preparation and Churn Detection

ABSTRACT

This chapter describes data preparation techniques for different churn models. The central topic is data sampling as preparation for building churn models, especially for predictive models. The chapter shows how to construct a data sample that will reflect business reality and show good performance regarding building predictive models. A significant part of the chapter is dedicated to construction of derived variables, which are a direct reflection of expert knowledge used within churn models. Beside data preparation for predictive models, the chapter also describes data preparation techniques for other methods usable for churn modeling like survival models, fuzzy expert systems, K-mean clustering, etc. The attribute relevance analysis chapter described different techniques for attribute importance detection usable in churn modeling. It gave descriptions with examples of how to make an attribute relevance analysis for predictive churn models in case of binomial target variables, as well in case of multinomial target variables. This chapter covers dummy variable construction and profiling techniques based on attribute relevance analysis, as well as logic checks from the perspective of business users.

5.1 DATA PREPARATION FOR PREDICTIVE CHURN MODELING

Predictive churn models are almost synonym for churn modeling. Building predictive churn models are most exploited way in churn solution development.

Aimed outputs from those models are churn probability in defined future period of time.

DOI: 10.4018/978-1-4666-6288-9.ch005

There are few recommended characteristics, which every predictive model should have, and predictive churn models are not exception:

- Reliability
- Usability
- Stability
- Robustness

Reliability in light of churn predictive modeling means, that model should have significant power to predict which customers/consumers/clients will make churn in defined future period (e.g. 6 months). Predictive power could be measured using statistical measures like Kolmogorov Smirnoff test, or ROC curve on test sample. This methodology will be explained in details in following chapter.

Usability means that developed model has integrated business logic, and that it is in line with business perception of existing customer portfolio.

Stability is important characteristic for the models, which should be used periodically, and it implies that model should not contain unstable variables, which could cause instability of the whole model and imprecise probability calculation.

A robustness criterion implies that model is resistant on business environment changes and resistant on market changes. It is unrealistic to expect that it is possible to develop completely resistant model on significant market condition changes, or portfolio structure changes. Robustness means that model will not overreact and will not become unusable in short period of time after market conditions start to change, or portfolio structure start to change.

Each predictive modeling project demands almost 80% of time spending on data preparation. Contrary to rooted belief that data preparation process consists on Extract Transform Load processes, data quality improvement, or data extraction from different data sources only, it is much more broader process.

Data preparation starts with data sample construction planning.

Planning data sample construction for building predictive models is shown in Figure 1.

C- Observation period for active contracts; Od – Observation development point; He – End of outcome period point; Hd – Outcome period for development sample

Origination of data sample construction starts at observation development point (Od). At this point all active contracts/accounts/clients/buyers that started to use our products/services at observation period (C) should be included into data sample. Development data sample should contain socio-demographic data and behavioral characteristics for all active contracts/accounts or clients/buyers. Socio-demographic data are attributes related to client socio-demographic characteristics like age, resi-

Figure 1. Data sample construction for building predictive models

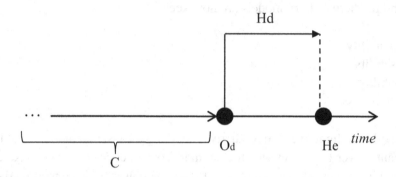

dential status, work details and related stuffs. It is mostly static attributes which values should be determined at observation development point (Od).

Behavioral characteristics are related to contracts/accounts/client/buyer behavior and it usually should be calculated from transactional data. Behavioral attributes for example gives us information (if we talk about telecommunication company) about average call duration in previous three months, number of inbound calls in previous three months, trend of outbound calls in previous three months and similar values.

Experience shows that behavioral attributes are most important variables for churn model construction, and socio-demographic attributes are like a spice which gives flavor to the churn models.

Churn flag (churn = true or false) is generated if client broke or not broke relationship with company within outcome period for development sample (Hd). Length of outcome period should be determined empirically using methods like Cox regression or by experience, or in combination by using both approaches.

Next important topic is data quality check. It consolidates:

- Basic statistical measures, and distribution checking for continuous variables
- Missing value analysis
- Data gap analysis for each attribute
- Logical attribute check
- Business data check and business review of constructed sample

Basic statistical measures are useful for attribute auditing. Mean, standard deviation, quartiles, percentiles applied on continuous variables can give an insight on existing attribute characteristics.

Standard deviation could be useful in finding outliers and extremes within attributes. Sometimes extreme values in variables can be milestones for further investigation regarding churn.

Other important thing in data quality check is missing value analysis. Attributes, which have significant percentage of missing values, are not convenient for model development. Missing value analysis gives information about missing values within attributes. It is not the universal rule that attributes with significant percentage of missing values is not usable for model development. Example for that is situation where client/buyer/contractor does not want to provide some piece of information and that information has great impact on aim variable, like providing residential phone number in fraud detection models.

Unwritten rule is that modeler should use disposable data sample if it is statistically significant for model development. If data sample consists too few attributes, or irrelevant attributes for model development it is important to realize that on time. One scenario in that case could be giving up from model development, and another scenario could be aimed on locating relevant attributes for model development.

Useful technique in data quality check is attributes logical check. This technique controls attribute values by using simple logic checks. Example could be check if working experience is higher than current year minus year of first employment. Another example could be checking how many people within data sample is older than 120 years, or does phone number attributes contains illegal characters.

Business data check and business review of constructed sample are often unduly neglected step during model development process. It implies that in model development process should be included people from the business (model users). Model development is under jurisdiction of modelers, which necessarily do not have business expert knowledge in some specific domains like telecommunication, or insurance. It is important to achieve cooperation between them during model development. Specific information about recent campaigns and market strategy in previous period could be useful, because some findings related to model development could be direct consequence of some specific business policy in near past which could be visible into data sample.

Instead to look at this finding as a significant revelation from perspective of model developers, business user can speed up model development by explaining business decisions and business policies for period covered within data sample. Business users also plays significant role in attribute relevance analysis explanation, because they should logically understand and explain reasons and relations between aim variable and predictor recognized as important for prediction. Created and acceptable data sample from perspective of data quality should be divided into development sample and test sample usually by 80(development): 20% (test) ratio. Model is constructed on development sample, and predictive power is measured on test sample.

Figure 2. Churn prediction with developed model

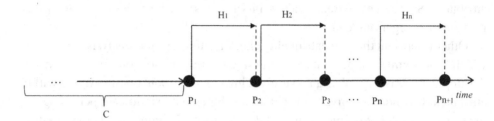

After model development, in practice it could be used after passing certain period of time (e.g. one or two months. Recommendation is to use it in way to avoid significant influence of development sample on new prediction. As it already mentioned behavioral variables plays significant role in qualitative prediction, and often they are calculated by taking in consider past characteristics during defined period of time, e.g. number of inbound calls in previous three months. As time will pass, each contracts/accounts/client/buyer will show new performance characteristics, and predictors will be much more reliable.

Presented example gives an answer why models based on socio-demographic data only, would not be much useful, because those models would depend on mostly static attributes which are mainly unchangeable, or rare unchangeable. That situation does not contribute much to churn prediction, and could be conditionally applicable in dynamic, high penetration markets with lot of new clients/buyers/contractors. From the other hand, socio-demographic data does not give us insight into current customer behavior, and behavior could determine intents.

Variable importance in relation to churn should be calculated, and it is impossible to predict variable importance without attribute relevance analyze. Behavior variables in average have higher relevance as predictors than socio-demographic variables. Predictive churn models justifying their existence in future periods (usually next months), in which they have task to predict future churners.

Principles of churn prediction after model development are shown in Figure 2.

C- Observation period for active contracts; H1, .., Hn – Outcome periods for churn prediction; P1, .., Pn+1 – Predictive points, points which represents prediction for correspondent cycle (1,..,n+1) for correspondent outcome period (H1, .., Hn)

For prediction purposes all active contracts/accounts/clients/buyers that started to use products/services at observation period (C) should be included into data sample. First prediction cycle starts at P1 predictive point. Model should give the answer, will certain contract/account/client/buyer churn or not during H1 outcome period, and with which probability.

Described process could be repeated periodically at equal time intervals, or at various time intervals.

In the meantime it is important to evaluate stability and predictive power of existing model when predicted values became empirical. If model loose in performances it should be redesigned or redeveloped.

As it is visible from the figure, predictive models depend in "long term usable models" category. It means that developed model should be used to make prediction many times in the future, contrary to "short term usable model" category, which is oriented on single time model usage. It also implies that "long term usable models" should be monitored and maintained periodically to keep performances regarding prediction and stability. To achieve mentioned aims, it is important to plan model development taking in consider various aspects which has influence on model stability and predictive power.

5.1.1 Finding Optimal Time Horizon

When we are talking about time horizon from perspective of churn predictive modeling, it refers on observation period and outcome period. For both zones there are no predefined rules how to determine optimal length. They should be determined taking in consider various factors like:

- Intensive churn rate in recent period.
- Competition activities in recent period.
- Changes in business policy at recent period.
- Targeting different market segments than usual in recent period.
- General market conditions and macroeconomics trend in recent period.

Key terms in all factors are always "recent period", because stress is on recent period, for which we would like to understand trends regarding churn. Those trends could be caused by various factors, and churn modeling also has task to understand and confirm or reject hypnotizes regarding consumptions about churn reasons.

Unfortunately companies often decide to invest in churn detection models after churn became too obvious, which means that it became big problem, which decreases income. It means that data sample in recent period covers this period for model development purposes. From the one hand it is right approach, but much better situation would be that churn model was developed in the past. In that case in period of intensive churn trends it is much easier to find out key factors which have greatest influence on churn. From the other hand churn is rare so intensive that it challenges companies within short period of time (e.g. month or two). It often became unobserved, and during significant period of time when it jeopardizes business it became obvious. From this perspective churn detection models also plays role, as early warning system and it could be useful in detecting early trends and churn causes.

Competition for sure could be one of the main factors, which has strong impact on churn rate. Main question is, does competition really cause higher churn rate in our portfolio, how they did it and which customer segments are most sensitive on their activities. Competitor activities cold be trigger for customer/subscriber/buyer churn, but reason also could lay in changing business policies which makes part of existing market segment unsatisfied, even those changes has completely different aim.

Similar situation is when company decide to change strategic focus to some other market segment, other than previously targeted, neglecting unintentionally market segment which generates most of the income for the company. Focus on some other specific market segment could cause less care on primary market segment, and maybe because of assurance that those segment generates profit and it has adequately adopted services or products it is not in primary focus. General market conditions and macroeconomics trend could also be reason of rising churn rate. Unfortunately if a general market condition is bad as well as macroeconomics trends it is hard to find adequate solution for his situation, but it could be somehow mitigated. It is important to understand business environment completely, because it is condition for better model development. Mentioned factors are illustrative examples what can cause rising churn trends, and during data sample preparation and determination of time horizons it is important to have it in mind. Business experts can estimate period when some of the observed factors has strongest impact and it is valuable input for time horizon estimation. Beside estimation from the experts, survival models like Cox regression, or Kaplan Meier model could be useful.

Survival models give an insight on survival rate of existing portfolio as it is visible in Figure 3.

As it is visible from figure, at the beginning of the observation point (let it be Od – Observation development point), there is present 100% of active contracts/ buyers/clients. As time pass (in this example months), survival rate became lower. It is in fact company churn rate observed by months. Survival models give an insight when churn rate was intensive, and when it became stable. It is important to find out period of intensive churn trend to make focus on that period which determines outcome period borders. Period, in which churn rate became stable, is not so interesting for inclusion into outcome period. Logical question is why do we need churn model if churn rate became stable? These techniques are useful if we make churn models for new contracts/buyers/clients, and we would like to evaluate key driven factors of their churn motivation. Additional answer on this question is that stabilization does not necessary means churn rate of zero percent. It means that churn rate in some zones are not so intensive, but it is still present and significant. Com-

Figure 3. Survival models in time horizon determination

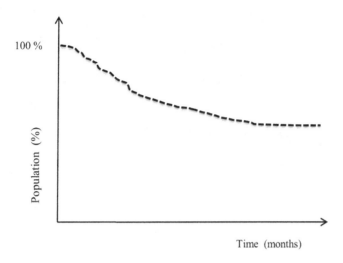

bination of expert knowledge and survival models usage could shape final decision for length of outcome period. Churn model could referee on whole portfolio of existing contracts/buyers/clients, or it could be focused on e.g. new contracts/buyers/clients, which started to work with company in last year. Also, company could decide that churn model will cover only most profitable company contractors/buyers/clients. This decision determines length of observation period for contracts/buyers/clients.

After that decision, remains decision about horizon for behavior variables construction. Will it be unique, e.g. three months, and all behavioral variables will be calculated within tis period, like: "number of inbound calls within three months in history from Od – Observation development point ", or it could be various for each behavior variable.

Relation between time horizons and data table are shown in Figure 4.

Churn indicator is generated by observing contracts/buyers/clients churn status within outcome period (Hd). If contract/buyer/client makes churn within this period, it gives churn flag "1", otherwise "0".

In situation where we have contracts it is easy to realize in which period churn had happened. It is characteristic for insurance business, telecommunication business or banking business. In retail area it is much more complicated to determine when buyer has committed churn.

Churn in insurance, telecommunication or banking is evident when contractor interrupt contract and it is marked in information system, related to existing business procedure in case of voluntary churn. This action is base for churn flag construction

Figure 4. Relation between time horizons and data table

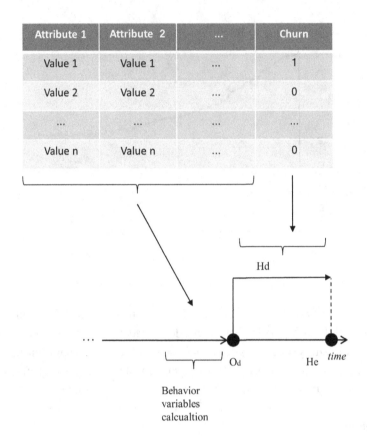

Attribute 1	Attribute 2	...	Churn
Value 1	Value 1	...	1
Value 2	Value 2	...	0
...	...	...	...
Value n	Value n	...	0

Hd

Od

He   *time*

Behavior
variables
calcualtion

within outcome period, and it is precise. In retail business where contract interruption does not exist, because of its nature, it is not so easy to determine when buyer has committed churn. Churn flag in retail area could be determined in way to assign churn flag "1" to all buyers which did not visit shop last three months from observation point. With this kind of definition recommendation is that seasonal periods should be taken in consideration as well as some specifics like specific buyer prefers to buy some specific item, which is on sale in specific period of the year. Precision in this situation could be achieved by analyzing data and behavior for each buyer individually. It means that churn flag will be determined due to individual shopping behavior. It could include fact that specific buyer could have longer delays (longer than e.g. three months), but it behave on that way frequently, and delay longer than three months for this specific buyer does not mean that he has committed churn. One of the rules during time horizon determination is avoiding sample dilution. In few worlds it means avoidance of too long horizon related to behavior variables calculation, and evasion of too long outcome period, which could cause observation point placement deep into history. Sample dilution could cause construction of inadequate data sample, which does not reflect realistic business situation, and further analysis would give inappropriate outputs.

Sample creation process should exclude involuntary churn cases, cases on probationary period for some product or services, fraud cases, and similar cases, which should not be integrated into development, sample for predictive churn model.

Involuntary churn could be initiated by company for the contracts with significant days past due regarding payment obligations or non-activated contracts. It implies that company committed churn, and it has committed because arrangers did not fulfill their obligations to the company. In here we remove non-perspective customers, which shows poor performance regarding their obligation to company. These cases should be removed from the development data sample.

A company often offers using some product or services on probationary period (e.g. 3-6 months). It is well known practice in telecommunication companies. After probationary period, customer could sign contract for further usage, or it can give up. It would be unrealistic to include probationary period sample within development sample for churn prediction modeling.

Fraud cases should also be removed from development sample, and it could be declared as special cases of involuntary churn.

Removing enumerated cases, and cases with similar characteristics from the development sample, increases reliability of the sample. If we would not remove them, it could cause sample dilution. Intensity of that effect is in direct correlation with number of cases, which should be removed. In some extreme situations it could be more than 20% of the original sample, and this volume for sure would have impact on attribute relevance analyses, and at the end on the final churn prediction model. Sample construction should follow business logic. It is obvious that involuntary churn cases, cases on probationary period for some product or services, fraud cases, and similar cases, are not appropriate for churn investigation, and building predictive churn models. It contains different behavior pattern, and different churn reasons, irrelevant in situation where company try to understand and predict churn behavior for perspective customers. By following business logic it should be removed from churn prediction development data sample.

5.1.2 Fixed Outcome Period vs. Stepwise Outcome Period

There are two main techniques for sample construction using existing contracts/buyers/clients:

- Fixed outcome period construction principle.
- Stepwise outcome period construction principle.

Fixed outcome period construction sample principle is used for churn prediction purposes in case of mature portfolio. It implies existence of customers with long-term existing contracts, which are members of company portfolio for a longer period of time. In that case company has significant track record of customer behavior in past. Illustration of fixed outcome period construction sample is shown in Figure 5.

After observation period length determination (e.g. 12 months) and outcome period (e.g. 12 months), sample contains all active contracts during observation period. It also implies that those contracts have at least few months of history as contractors with a company before observation point, because of behavior variable construction purposes. It means if one of behavior variable has definition: "Average number of inbound calls in last three months before observation point", it implies that contracts which was signed two months before observation point will not enter into the sample.

Outcome period is in service of creating churn flag regarding fact did customer committed churn within this period.

Figure 6 shows three cases (let it be three contracts, Case "A", Case "B" and Case "C"). As it is visible from the figure, all three contracts begins their lifecycle during observation period T(a), T(b), T(c), and ends contracts during outcome period T(a1), T(b1), T(c1). Case "A", and case "C" has enough history for behavior variable construction, contrary to case "B". As it is visible, all three cases have different maturity status. It is not usual to use fixed outcome period for immature portfolio. Fixed outcome period construction sample is much appropriate for mature portfolios.

Other criterion for applying fixed outcome period construction sample is portfolio stability, which could be achieved also in mature portfolios. During sample construction for predictive purposes, regarding different nature of long-term existing arrangers, and short-term existing arrangers within portfolio, it is recommenda-

Figure 5. Fixed outcome period construction principle

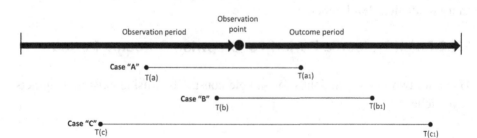

Figure 6. Stepwise outcome period construction principle

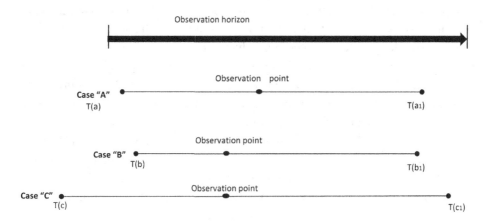

tion to exclude short-term existing arrangers into separate sample, and even they have long enough history for behavior variable construction. With this procedure we improve reliability of future predictive models for churn detection.

It is important to have in mind purpose of the churn model and it determines sample construction, but in generally it is logical to make separate data samples and separate predictive model for those contract categories. Fixed outcome period construction tends in more behavior variable construction with longer horizons for behavior variables that also could be trend oriented (e.g. trend of mobile phone calls abroad between two quarters before observation point). An immature contracts does not have such long history data, and companies do not have opportunity get to know them better through behavior variables. On the other hand, each new contract should pass period of adaption with company, and it requires some time during which contractor are not so stable in way it is mature arrangers.

Contract immaturity, reliance on mostly socio demographic data is characteristic of sample construction for the new arrangers. For this situation is much more convenient sample construction based on stepwise outcome period shown in next figure.

As it is visible from the figure, during observation horizon which is placed in recent period and could be long e.g. 1,5 years, we take into sample all contracts signed during observation horizon period. Case "A" starts with contract within observation period in T(a) point, and case "B" starts with contract within observation period in T(b) point. Case "C" starts with contract outside observation period in T(c) point and it will be excluded from the sample. All three cases end their business activities within observation horizon (if they would not it will have status: "churn"="No"). Observation point is key factor in here, because after observations point all contracts should be observed during defined period of time e.g. 12 months. In this case a contracts which does not have enough time for committing churn because of to short period after observation point will also be removed from the sample. Main reason for this approach lays in avoiding sample dilution with contracts, which does not have enough opportunity to commit churn. In some extreme situations where we would not make exclusion of those arrangers it would be possible to have into sample contracts with lifecycle within company no longer than 2 - 3 months. This contract for sure has less chance to commit churn than contracts with e.g. 12 months lifecycle within company. If contract commit churn after observation point it will have status:" churn="Yes", otherwise it is churn="No". Behavioral variables could improve data sample quality for prediction purposes, but in case when history does not exists, sample could be based on socio demographic data only. It is not perfect solution, but only possible, if we are constructing sample for new arrangers.

Business situation where it should be constructed sample for churn detection based on new contracts could be related to specific campaigns e.g. new prepaid telecom users, for which we would like to develop predictive churn model, for understand their profiles and churn motivators in period when history of product usage does not exist. It is not impossible or wrong to use stepwise outcome period approach of sample construction for long-term arrangers or fixed outcome period approach of sample construction for short-term arrangers. Proposed approach gives good results in practice, and it is presented from those perspectives. It is consumption that long term arrangers which already passed their adoption period with company at observation point after longer lifetime cycle has generally similar characteristic, or they all have similar conditions for committing churn. Same opportunity to commit churn should be given to new arrangers by observation during fixed period of time after observation point within observation horizon. It is main advantage for using stepwise outcome period construction sample principle where newcomers did not pass their adoption period with company and there are unstable. In this case, predetermined length of customized observation period shortly after contracting some product or services will show their characteristics.

5.1.3 Influence of Past Business Activities on Data Sample

Each new campaign contributes in new customers volumes, contributes in portfolio structure changes as well. In perfect market condition with unlimited sources of potential new clients, with consumption that company always targets exactly same market segment, portfolio structure will more- less remain unchanged. Changes would be related to customer lifecycle only. Real business is something completely different, because companies does not have unlimited sources of potential new clients, and depending on business policies and market opportunities, companies can target different market segments through long period of time. On the other hand churn rate changes also portfolio structure. From the one side companies obtain new customers, and from the other side customers broke contracts/relationship with company. This customer input and customer output changes balances in customer portfolio structure. Customer lifecycle also plays significant role in portfolio structure through portfolio maturity stages. Customers with same initial characteristics from some specific market segment could show different behavioral patterns during different stages in lifecycle. Newcomers, for example has less expectation in company discounts than customers, which longer uses same product or service. Market saturation could be example where companies should be creative and flexible in new clients acquisition from the competition, and those strategies include targeting of variety market segments with different characteristics. Described situations and events, cause dynamical changes within portfolio structure, which also has impact on churn rate. Each existing customer/arranger/client within portfolio carries some personal characteristics socio- demographic or behavioral. Attribute relevance analysis phase has task to recognize attributes (characteristics) with strongest impact on churn. Attributes which shows greatest segregation power in relation with churn (churn = "Yes" or "No") by attribute relevance analysis will be selected as best candidates for building predictive churn model. Segregation power could vary in relation with changing portfolio characteristics. For example, we can assume that insurance company starts acquisition of new customers by targeting middle-aged persons, which lives in suburb area for life insurance policy acquisition. After competitor's campaign in which it offers significant discount for real estate insurance policies if they arrange main life insurance policy, insurance company notice raising churn rate. Attribute relevance analysis shows that main attribute which shows greatest segregation power in relation with churn is number of children.

From the business perspective, it does have sense, because potential arranges are middle-aged persons who care about their families, and has better conditions at other insurance company. Regarding that insurance company should promote adequate product to keep existing customers.

After certain period of time insurance company decided to move focus on different market segment –young professionals. They also have campaign, which was focused on life insurance selling activities to young professionals. This campaign was active long period of time and it changed existing portfolio structure (life insurance policy users), after numerous new contracts.

In case of the same competitor's campaign in which it offers significant discount for real estate insurance policies if they arrange main life insurance policy, main attribute which shows greatest segregation power in relation with churn for sure will not be number of children. Reason for that lays in fact that most of the young professionals, which arranged life insurance policy in company, does not have children. This simple illustrative sample shows relation between business actions (decisions) and changes in sample (data) characteristics related to target variable (churn). It is obvious that a business policy does not have immediate influence on sample characteristics, but it become more and more important as time pass by. Quarterly monitoring and predictive power testing of developed predictive model is important because of that phenomenon. In early stages it is important to be aware of existing trends, and it is important to redesign models when noticed trends became key driven factor of churn appearance. As it was previously explained, except input (new contracts), churners also could change portfolio characteristics. In case of high churn rate, during certain period of time churners "caries" their characteristics out from portfolio. Regarding all described situations, events and business decision it is obvious that churn modeling is dynamic analytical task. Developed model should be frequently monitored, and all new observed trends should be explained from perspective of business decisions and market trends. It is important to be aware that all business decisions regarding customer acquisition could have strong impact in near future on churn motivators, causes and reasons. It is impossible to assume which it will be. This task has churn models, but without deeper understanding causes and consequences, which can be revealed during development process by using expert knowledge and analytical techniques, it is hard to develop it. Changes in portfolio structure could be observed by stability index calculation, which will be shown later in text.

5.1.4 Creating Virtual Predictors

Virtual variables in literature also known as derived variables are powerful tool for customer behavior exploration. A virtual variable mainly does not exist within database relation model, and it is constructed based on expert knowledge. Virtual variable construction has a lot in common with methodology of expert system planning, because expert knowledge should be expressed into variables, and experts in process of knowledge elicitation should provide knowledge. For example, experts assume from the past experience that variable purchasing trend in last six months has great impact on churn prediction in future period. If customer decreases purchasing, expert assumes that it is indicator for churn in future period. Analyst in this situation has role as knowledge engineer, and it means precise definition of term "purchasing trend in last six months". It should be clarified, firstly does existing database contain transactional data or other data, which are necessary for variable construction. Also, analyst should clearly define algorithm or formula for variable construction, based on expert definition. Based on presented example, formula for variable construction could be defined as follow:

$$Pt = \sum_{i=1}^{n} \frac{Pa_i}{n} - \sum_{j=1}^{k} \frac{Pa_j}{k} \tag{1}$$

Where Pt is purchasing trend, if it is negative, it means that customer decreases purchasing activities in last six months in comparison with first six months, if it is equal to 0, it means that customer keeps same trend of purchasing,, if it is positive, it means that customer increases purchasing activities in last six months in comparison with first six months:

- i..n represents months indexes in last six month period,
- j..k represents months indexes in first six month period,
- Pa represents monthly purchasing amount expressed in local currency for first six months (i..n), and for last six months (j..k).

For easiest perception, this variable (purchasing trend) could also be expressed by percentages. For this purpose base for percentage calculation could be sum of purchasing amount in first six-month period. In that way on individual client level it is possible to make comparison between existing customers regardless purchasing amounts. Advantage of that approach is related to fact that it is possible to define purchasing decrease as decrease by 40% or more.

This is illustration how same piece of information could be expressed in different ways. Experts should be motivated to propose as much as possible virtual (derived variables), which from their opinions could have an impact on churn prediction. Even it is time consuming and exhausting process, and after attribute relevance analysis most of those variables will not survive for further model construction, it is important to test all possible hypothesis about variable importance. Behavioral variables caries predictive churn models and contributes in model predictive power much more than static socio-demographic variables. Expert knowledge about customer behavior and potentially significant customer behavior as early warning signal of future churn commitment is valuable for building qualitative predictive churn model. In stage of virtual variable construction, experts should not be fettered in consumptions, because their hypothesis will be tested and variables will be reduced in attribute relevance analysis stage. Virtual variable construction stage is often neglected in churn modeling, and it is wrong approach. In this stage important role plays cooperation between analyst (data miners) and people from the business. Attribute relevance analysis gives a confirmation or rejection of the assurances related to churn problematic within company. Good approach for initiation of virtual variable construction is brainstorming process with more than one expert interested or related in churn problematic. Brainstorming process could end with top twenty or top thirty variables selection with consensus between experts, if company would like to optimize resources and development time by project plan.

Socio demographic data analysis provides customer profiles, and behavior data usage and analysis provides behavioral profile and could give answers on questions like:

- Which is typical behavioral pattern of customer, which has intention to commit churn in near future?
- Does stagnation in product usage could be significant warning signal for future churn commitment?
- Does decreasing purchasing trend could be significant warning signal for future churn commitment?
- Does increasing delay shop visiting could be warning signal for future churn commitment?

Answer on those questions, related to defined virtual variables could result in better understanding of churner's behavior and behavioral pattern, which implies churn in near future.

Special case of derived behavioral variable is churn indicator in retail business or similar business where a customer does not sign contracts. In this case there is no precise information about churn commitment and precise time when it happened could be derived from purchasing behavioral characteristics at some point of time. Churn indicator could be determined by behavioral characteristic calculation on customer level. I means that calculation should respect individual behavioral characteristics in conclusion does somebody commit or does not commit churn. It also implies taking recognized seasonal factors (seasonal behavioral characteristics for each client) into account. There are numerous approaches in churn recognition methodology in retail business. By one theory churn commitment could be recognized as no purchasing at defined period of time (e.g. one month). It could be tricky in case if company calculates churn flag in some specific period where part of existing clients behave as they always do and for example does not make any purchasing in longer period of time because there are on vacation.

In that case taking in account seasonal factor could show much more realistic picture. Another approach define churn as "significant decreasing in purchasing at some period of time". That implies purchasing trend calculation between two different time spans. Significant drop in purchasing trend could be defined as churn, and smaller drop in purchasing trend as soft churn. Definition depends on company policy and analytical aims. The easiest way for churn recognition is contract existence and customer obligation to break it if he decides not to use product or service anymore. In that case company has precise date when customer broke contract, and from analytical point of view it is most clear situation.

5.2 DATA PREPARATION SPECIFICS FOR SURVIVAL ANALYSIS, FUZZY EXPERT SYSTEMS, AND OTHER METHODS RELATED TO CHURN MODELING

Data preparation for churn modelling purposes has some specifics, but from perspective of model usage common rules exists during data preparation and they are related to specific models, which are used. Purpose of this part of text is to stress some common important fact related to specific data mining techniques usage, which model developers should have in mind during solution development.

Survival models in comparison to other predictive models or other model types have uniqueness related to using time component as a main part of the model. That implies mandatory interpolation of temporal attribute into data sample along churn indicator attribute. Temporal attribute could be expressed in days, weeks, months, years or other time measures. Churn indicator keeps the same logic in construction as for predictive models If customer committed churn at some observation period, churn indicator assume value ="Yes" or "1" otherwise churn indicator assume value ="No" or "0". Length of observation period in this case should be determined by expert knowledge. These two elements are minimum requirement for carrying out survival analysis. Putting other variables like socio demographic and behavioral one into data sample could do complete analysis. Continuous variables within data sample should be categorized. Categorization could be done by using weight of evidence technique, which will be described in next chapter, or by expert knowledge. Information value measure, which will also be explained in next chapter, can also be useful in number of attribute reduction, especially in situation when data set contains numerous attributes. Information value in this situation has role to find out most significant attributes related to churn, which deserve attention for further analysis. In churn modeling practice, survival analysis is often used for outcome period length optimization for prediction model sample.

Expert systems in general are good choice for churn detection in situation when event that define moment of churn does not exist (e.g. contract termination), or we would like to recognize soft churn. Main advantage of expert systems is ability to explain reasons why do they conclude that some subject commit e.g. soft churn. By personal experience authors prefer to use fuzzy expert systems for this purpose. Data preparation for fuzzy expert systems is based on behavioral variables preparation, mainly from databases. Behavioral variables are defined by expert knowledge and expertise, and it follows methodology, which was previously described as part of virtual variables creation. Variable definitions follow nature of fuzzy expert system. That means if company develop fuzzy expert system for soft churn recognition, expert should define possible behavioral variables, which could help in soft churn detection. Also, if company develops fuzzy expert system for hard churn detection, expert should define possible behavioral variables, which could help in hard churn detection.

Behavior variables recognized as important from problem solving should be precise defined which is first step in recognition does all needed attributes for behavioral variable construction exists into databases. If it does not exists, analysts/ developers can decide to modify definition of problematic behavioral variables to achieve attribute coverage into databases, or some behavioral variables could be rejected or substituted completely with new behavioral variables.

Precise definition of behavior variables implies precise mathematical definition, because descriptive definition could be imprecise, and could cause dilemma during code creation.

Example for this situation could be behavior variable: "average number of calls during workdays."

Logical question for developer, which writes program code, would be:

- Which is measure of time for average calculation?
- Average in which period?
- Does Saturdays should be included in workdays?

Precise definition should avoid misunderstandings and potential mistakes during behavior variable construction phase. Data preparation for fuzzy expert systems after behavior variable definition is concentrated on Extract Transform Load procedures development for each variable, and their consolidation into unique data table, which will be input for fuzzy expert system. There are no unique prescribed methodology and method usage for setting perfect churn solution. Enumerated methods from perspective of data preparation are possible ways for reaching this aim. Beside mentioned data mining methods there are various numbers of other data mining methods, and in context of data preparation for churn purposes, Bayesian networks and clustering will also be mentioned as potentially useful methods. It does not mean that only methods mentioned in this book are only appropriate for churn modeling. Reason for Bayesian networks and clustering methods description from perspective of data preparation lies in fact that it has minor specifics in comparison with e.g. decision trees. Decision trees have also many variations, some of them operate with categorical variables only, some of them with continuous and categorical variables at the same time, and there is no specifics related to churn detection in decision trees usage. Contrary, Bayesian networks universally uses categorical variables only as a part of conditional probability tables. Constructing churn models solution based on Bayesian networks are not exception regarding categorical variables usage. Categorization could be done by using weight of evidence technique, or by expert knowledge. Target variable in this kind of models is churn flag, and that is the reason for weight of evidence technique usage. Bayesian networks in light of churn modeling could be used as predictive models, but also as sensitivity analysis models. Clustering has also many variations. For churn modeling purposes, authors have been used K-means clustering, and Self Organizing Maps. Self-Organizing Maps are not originally declared as clustering techniques, more as type of neural network methodology, but it also could be used for clustering purposes. Common characteristics for both techniques are that data preparation includes attribute normalization process on numeric attributes. All input attributes must be numeric regarding calculation processes based on distance calculations. Attribute normalization is must for highest value attributes influence reduction on clustering formation. Attribute normalization guarantee that variables with highest values into sample like e.g. yearly income or yearly crossed miles with car will not take over their influence to variables like e.g. age in years, or working experience in years. Normalization algorithms all the variables expresses within same scale, for example from 0 to 1. Clustering without normalization would be clustering based on variables with highest values, with neglecting influence of other significant variables with smallest or globally minor values.

A contemporary software solution mostly has incorporated normalization algorithms as part of clustering process. Clustering methods could be useful in churn understanding and churner profiling. Recognized clusters and their characteristic are good starting point for understanding churner motivators and basic profiles. As it was already mentioned, described specifics are not only related to churn modeling, it is common for e.g. fraud modeling, best next offer modeling purposes, etc. from perspective of data mining techniques usage. Reason for emphasizing those specifics is in their usability and importance to have it in mind during churn solution development.

REFERENCES

Berry, M., & Linhoff, G. (2004). Data Mining Techniques for Marketing Sales and Customer Support. Wiley.

Buckinx, & Van den Poel. (2005). Customer base analysis: Partial defection of behaviourally loyal clients in a noncontractual. *Europeaz Journal of Operational Research, 164*, 252-268, 296.

Chandar, L. K. (2006). Modeling churn behavior of bank customers using predictive data mining techniques. Institute for Development and Research in Banking Technology(IDRBT).

Chu, B., Tsai, M., & Ho, T. (2007). Toward a hybrid data mining model for customer retention. *Knowledge-Based Systems, 20,* 703–718. doi:10.1016/j.knosys.2006.10.003

Coussement, B., Benoit, D. F., & Van den Poel, D. (2010). Improved marketing decision making in a customer churn prediction context using generalized additive models. *Expert Systems with Applications, 37*(3), 2132–2143. doi:10.1016/j.eswa.2009.07.029

De Bock, K., & Van den Poel, D. (2010). Ensembles of Probability Estimation Trees for Customer Churn Prediction, Trends In Applied Intelligent Systems, Pt Ii. *Lecture Notes in Artificial Intelligence, 6097,* 57–66.

Hwang, T., & Suh, E. (2004). An LTV model and customer segmentation based on customer value: A case study on the wireless telecommunication industry. *Expert Systems with Applications, 26*(2), 181–188. doi:10.1016/S0957-4174(03)00133-7

Morik, K., & Opcke, H. (2004). Analyzing Customer Churn in Insurance Data. In *Proceedings of Knowledge Discovery in Databases* (LNCS) (vol. 3202, pp. 325-336). Berlin: Springer. doi: 10.1007/978-3-540-30116-5_31

Osei-Bryson, K. (2004). Evaluation of decision trees: A multi-criteria approach. *Computers & Operations Research, 31*(11), 1933–1945. doi:10.1016/S0305-0548(03)00156-4

Popović, D., & Dalbelo Bašić, B. (2009). Churn Prediction Model in Retail Banking Using Fuzzy C-Means Algorithm. *Faculty of Electrical Engineering and Computing, 33,* 243–247.

SPSS Inc. (2007). *Clementine 12.0 Algorithms Guide.* Author.

Tsai, C., & Chen, M. (2010). Variable selection by association rules for customer churn prediction of multimedia on demand. *Expert Systems with Applications, 37*(3), 2006–2015. doi:10.1016/j.eswa.2009.06.076

Tsai, C., & Lu, Y. (2009). Customer churn prediction by hybrid neural networks. *Expert Systems with Applications, 36*(10), 12547–12553. doi:10.1016/j.eswa.2009.05.032

KEY TERMS AND DEFINITIONS

Derived Variable: Variable calculated from database, and which originally does not exist within database.

Observation Period: Time horizon before observation point.

Pre-Processing: Data transformation for modelling or other purposes.

Time Point: Point which divides observation from outcome period.

Chapter 6
Churn Analysis Using Selected Structured Analytic Techniques

ABSTRACT

After explaining how to prepare data, an introduction to structured analytic techniques is covered in this chapter. The importance of structured techniques comes from their simplicity and wide usage, making them fast to use and efficient to structure in even complex environments. For further explanation of how those techniques could be applied in the business environment, analysts (readers) should look closer into the case studies in last chapter of this book. Besides the ability to structure logic problems, analysts (readers) also needs to be aware of the different motivators influencing market conditions, especially from the customers' perspective. The chapter ends with a brief introduction of consumer behavior, making it part of the churn topic.

6.1 SIMPLE HYPOTHESIS

A hypothesis is, widely, potential explanation or conclusion which is tested by collecting and presenting evidences (Heuer, Pherson, 2010.). It is s statement which was not confirmed to be true or, in other words, temporary explanation based on observation which has to be confirmed or rejected. A hypothesis has to fulfill following terms:

DOI: 10.4018/978-1-4666-6288-9.ch006

- To be written as clear statement, not question,
- To be based on observation and knowledge,
- It can be confirmed or rejected,
- It clearly predicts expectable results,
- It contains dependent and non-dependent variable.

While using hypotheses, common question is which hypothesis is true or most probable. Analyst will choose most probable answer using intuition and then will look for hypothesis confirmation using available data. By using hypotheses, analyst must be aware of wider perspective, avoiding to be focused only on one hypothesis and always looking for approval and alternatives. Hypothesis testing is used in situations:

- When we need to analyze all alternatives in details,
- When we have large number of variables,
- When there is uncertainty regarding final outcome,
- When analysts or decision maker do not have same perception for same problem.

In order to generate hypotheses, different techniques are used like brainstorming, scenario analysis, quadrant crunching or Delphi method. Also, for purpose of hypotheses development, techniques like simple hypothesis, multiple hypotheses generator, quadrant hypothesis generation (Heuer, Pherson, 2010.).

While using hypothesis testing analyst can efficiently avoid several common problems:

- Rushing into conclusions,
- To be blinded with first impression,
- To be misled with first answer which looks good enough,
- To focus on limited alternatives rather than full project scope,
- To use answer suitable for most target audience,
  To use certain answers in order to protect him from error.

6.2 ACH (COMPETITIVE HYPOTHESES ANALYSIS)

While hypothesis is a form of a statement yet to be confirmed, its trueness has to be confirmed using evidence. If we knew that any statement is true, it won't be named hypothesis (Heuer, Pherson, 2010.).

Hypotheses plays key role in analysis because of its capability to narrow down number/area of results, very efficient characteristic for understanding and managing complex environment. Although narrowing of problem space can be efficient in order to focus on important rather than everything, it can be a limitation if not used with caution. It is up to analyst to choose several hypotheses and then to look for most appropriate one(s) in order to analyze consequences. ACH (competitive hypotheses analysis) is simple and efficient model which helps in solving complex problems especially useful when many alternatives need to be evaluated in past, present and future. This technique helps analyst to overcome or to minimize some of common cognitive limitations by creating proofs and hypothesis matrix layout in order to visualize problem structure and understand correlations between complex environment parts. At the same time matrix allows us to record process steps towards solution.

ACH can be very effective in collaboration between analyses since it can avoid subjective influence to analysis process. Visualization matrix can be used to present areas of disagreement between analyses, if any.

In its process ACH is looking for hypothesis with less number if inconsistent proofs instead of looking for highest number of consistent ones. By looking for consistency analyst can easily be misled by many hypotheses, while only inconsistency have true value for proofing certain hypothesis credibility. So, idea is to stress test every hypothesis by trying to make it wrong and the best one will be one with less probability to be turned down.

There are four key differences between ACH and conventional analysis based on intuition:

- Analysis starts with brainstorming in order to identify whole group of alternative hypotheses and to avoid trap of going for most likely one, this approach include similar perspective for every hypotheses including those less likely but possible,
- Analysis identify and points out several standalone proofs and assumptions with highest diagnostically value used for ranking of hypotheses value, this is performed by evaluating every single evidence testing it with every hypothesis for consistency,
- ACH follows elementary rule of scientific methodology for confirming or declining hypothesis and usage of only those which cannot be declined, most likely hypothese with less declining evidences is ranked higher that one with most any positive approval from evidences,
- Using ACH software analyst is able to classify and compare evidences in different ways (diagnostic value, relevance, date and source characteristics, timeline), therefore time factor can be used as well (something what is normal today can be less normal in future)

6.3 METHOD 180 DEGREES

Method 180 degrees consider using stress test opposite of analysis goal. For example if we would like to increase number of customers we need to find answers to question "what we need to do to lose all customers". It is similar to stress test or reverse stress test methods widely used in finance industry and can be valuable in expanding analyst's way of thinking.

Ability to take a look at problem scope from different angle (180 degrees turn) can be surprisingly efficient because it can reveal not only real base of our problem but also directly identify problem cause.

6.4 INDICATOR BASED METHODS

Indicator validation (Heuer, Pherson, 2010.) is simple tool used to evaluate diagnostic indicator value also used in hypotheses and scenario analysis. After analyst generates different scenario alternatives for future, indicators for every scenario should be created. Different scenarios can have same indicators however those indicators don't have value for diagnostic purpose and can't be treated as reliable. Ideal indicator is one significantly consistent with scenario or significantly inconsistent with scenario. By using indicator it is possible to increase quality of analysis so their usage is advisable if possible.

Indicators are phenomenon which can easily be seen. Indicators allow events to be monitored, allows similar trends to be noticed, can warn on abnormalities and can be revised over time. Indicators can be monitored on tactical, operational and strategic level. Their usage in prediction and early warning systems is widely known no matter if we are using predictive or descriptive ones. By creating list of indicators one can be able to efficiently manage wide areas simply ba following change in important factors.

In order to be efficient, while we are creating indicator list we have to be aware of its characteristics and limitations. Therefore indicator should be:

- Visible, based on rational expectation that something can happen,
- Relevant, in terms of relevance of indicator to express a state that analyst is looking for,
- Reliable, in terms of consistency even when different methods and approaches are used,
- Stabile, indicator have to be useful over time period in order to compare its values and change over time,

- Unique, it has to measure only one event focused only on single phenomenon which is linked to.

While using or choosing from large number of indicators technique known as indicator validation should be performed in order to evaluate diagnostical probability for every indicator to show up in specific scenario analysis.

6.5 HOW TO USE STRUCTURED ANALYTIC TECHNIQUES IN CHURN ANALYSIS

Any research is always starting with structuring problem space. Even though analysts have to be able to think in structured way as part of their work, it is important to also understand wider perspective of different structured techniques available in order to combine them with other methods.

For summary of this chapter we will move through illustrative case in textile retail. As it is known global economic crisis hits global markets hard in 2008. therefore it is more complex to evaluate and estimate market conditions in years after 2008. However, crisis hits markets generally so environment is more-less changed for all participants in same way. Of course, some participants have different market strategy or were able to adopt faster.

In order to illustrate usage of analytic techniques selected for this chapter we will take a look at situation with following characteristics:

- We are looking at sales trend from one retail store in downtown area,
- Store is performing with negative trend in past seasons,
- Economy is having negative trend in past seasons,
- Market competition is heavily increasing in area, city, region and country,
- Store is hardly following in store quality (sales personnel, in store visual merchandising, stock delivered on time).
- Store is facing fast development of visual merchandising on market in general (shop windows, overall marketing and brand presence).

It is easy and logical how to create simple hypotheses for this simplified scenario. Figures 1 and 2 show hypotheses inconsistency analysis provided by PARC ACH tool[1] showing how easily we can remove hypotheses with high weighted inconsistency score and focus on ones which can improve our business.

By combination of indicators, simple hypotheses and ACH analysis we create powerful and useful model for business analysis. By combining our hypothesis with 180 method we can simulate all needed factors in order to decrease turnover,

Figure 1. PARC ACH tool, example table

		Type	Credibility	Relevance	H: 1	H: 2	H: 3	H: 4	H: 5
					Problem in store	Problem outside store, surroundings	Problem in region	Problem in economy	Problem with competition
	Weighted Inconsistency Score ⇨				-1,414	-4,242	-1,414	-1,414	-2,828
	Enter Evidence								
E4	Rasing trend for cost of goods	HIGH	MEDIUM		I	I I	C	C C	I I
E3	Negative trend in margin volume	HIGH	MEDIUM		C	I	I	I	C
E2	Negative trend in sales quantity	MEDIUM	MEDIUM		C C	C	C	C	C
E1	Negative trend in sales turnover	MEDIUM	MEDIUM		C C	C C	C	C	C C

profit and number of customers having quality structured portfolio of tasks worth taking care.

Finally, as spice to traditional attributes, analyst has to be aware of behavioral ones as well. At the end, that whole book is not only about mathematics but about modeling and understanding. Behavioral attributes are base for every customer analysis and has to be combines with other attributes while looking for answers. Different types of behavioral attributes can be aggregated during different phases of project making them crucial additional value for final model differentiation and usability. Behavioral attributes, its value and usage will be explained in more details in other chapters of this book.

Before we move on and regarding behavioral attributes, we need to introduce consumer behavior as process. In 1970's marketing science became more and more important and researchers and practitioners are starting to explore market influencers and rules. In short period of time general conclusion was made that market drivers are consumers and their behavior so in order to be effective one need to understand needs and changes in that process. Term „consumer behavior" means consumer market activities and it include process of product/service buying and usage. It also includes post sales processes like valuation (product/service but from the other side consumer as well) and post sales behavior (sharing experience). For research to be more effective, individuals are grouped into segments (like family, company, men, women etc.) Market segments or groups became more and more important over time. Up to date analysis shows that women in countries with higher BDP are responsible for almost 80% of all buying decisions (Poslovni Dnevnik, 2008). Also, women are influencing all buying decisions related to consumer electronics in approximately 66% cases, related to family car purchase 60%, women own 89% of all bank accounts and 27% married women influences decisions regarding home (house or flat) purchases (Majer, 2009; GFK, n.d.) (Figure 3).

Figure 2. PARC ACH tool, example graph

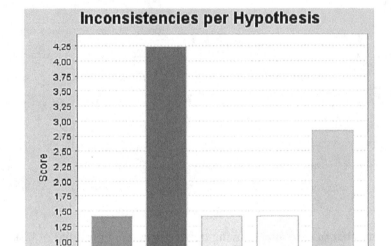

Looking from the company perspective, it is always a question how to manage relationship with customers, to whom we will push our best offers and shall we approach only loyal or also temporary customers. One of interesting authors, Seth Godin, provide a simple but reasonable explanation: it is always important to be able to extend product/service to next level of improvement because it is hard to imagine that first version will be perfect for all. At the same time Godin pointed out that „even worst offer can create great experience if we found efficient way to communicate with customer (Godin, 2008, pp. 72-73).

We will end this chapter with customer loyalty issue. While in the first, loyalty was related to special offers in modern markets those offer became more and more aggressive (like Groupon or similar services) while loyalty became more like membership to certain group sometimes without real tangible benefits. It is more like identification of someone's lifestyle to specific group, related to specific way of life. It is important for company to understand their customers and to find best way to identify product/service with target group (Noize, 2015).

Figure 3. Consumer behavior model (Engel et al, 1995, 53)

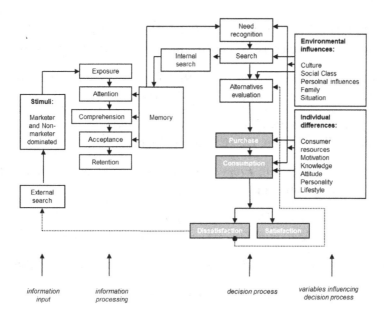

As a kind of conclusion or introductory to behavioral attributes explained in next chapter we will notice best practice key facts regarding customer retention (Cooper, 2011).

- Provide long term satisfaction through customer care,
- Keep connection with customer active,
- Reward customer activity/loyalty,
- Deeply understand customer needs,
- Look for response from customer especially regarding quality of product/ service,
- Make relationship personal as much as possible,
- Provide long term quality assurance (customer 50th visit to store should be same experience as 1st one),
- Provide permanent education of own personnel,
- Deeply understand competition and their campaigns,
- Occasionally surprise client with something new

For effective analysis and especially churn analysis, deep understanding od customers is one of crucial things. In next chapters you will find way how to value and monitor bahaviuor dana and how to create indicators needed for churn analysis and early warning systems.

REFERENCES

Cooper, C. (2011). *10 Tips for Retaining Loyal Guests*. Retrieved from http://www. hotelnewsnow.com/Articles.aspx/6068/10-tips-for-retaining-loyal-guests

GFK. (n.d.). *Stats report Croatia 1995-2010*. Retreived from http://www.gfk.hr/ public_relations/press/press_articles/006398/index.hr.html

Heuer, R. J., & Pherson, R. H. (2010). *Structured Analytic Techniques for Intelligence Analysis*. Washington, DC: CW Press College.

Majer, A. (2009). *The Selling Process*. Institut prodaje/Seles Institute. Retreived from http://kakoprodavati.com

Noize, V. (2015). *Financial. The Pro & Con of Groupon*. Retrieved from http://www. evancarmichael.com/Marketing/3973/The-Pro--Con-of-Groupon.html

Pavlek, Z. (2008). *Marketing: Važne rodne razlike*. Poslovni dnevnik/Business daily.

Dnevnik, P. (2008). *Marketing: Važne rodne razlike*. Author.

KEY TERMS AND DEFINITIONS

ACH: Provides an unbiased methodology for evaluating multiple competing hypotheses for observed data.
Hypothesis: Proposed explanation for a phenomenon.
PARC: *Palo Alto Research Center.*

ENDNOTES

[1]   PARC ACH tool, version 2.0.5.

Chapter 7
Attribute Relevance Analysis

ABSTRACT

Structured problems need to be quantified by relevance, and that is explained in this chapter. The most common methods of relevance analysis and different strength and sensitivity measures are explained in a way that practitioners can easily use them and start experimenting. Contrary to the belief that powerful hardware and sophisticated software can substitute for attribute relevance analysis, attribute relevance analysis is an important part of each analysis that operates with the target variable. Recognition of the most important variables, those with the greatest impact on the target variable, reduces redundancy and uncertainty at the model development process stage. It provides robustness of the model and model reliability. Attribute relevance analysis also evaluates attribute characteristics. Attribute characteristics evaluation includes measuring attribute values' impact on target variables. It helps in understanding relations and logic between the most important predictors and the target variable and understanding relations and logic between the most important predictors from the target variable perspective. Making models relevant and being able to proof them is relevant and almost as important as the ability to build them. After completing this chapter, analysts (readers) are ready to start projects.

DOI: 10.4018/978-1-4666-6288-9.ch007

7.1 INTRODUCTION AND BASIC CONCEPTS

A robust and stable predictive model has few attributes incorporated into model. It could be 6-10 of most predictive attributes. As it is evident initial data sample could contain more than hundreds of potential predictors. Some of them are original variables from databases as socio demographic values assigned to each customer, and other has behavioral characteristics defined by experts and extracted from existing transactional data.

Attribute relevance analysis has two important functions:

- Recognition of most important variables which has greatest impact on target variable.
- Understanding relations and logic between most important predictor and target variable, and understanding relations and logic between most important predictors from target variable perspective.

Contrary to assurance that powerful hardware and sophisticated software can substitute need for attribute relevance analysis, attribute relevance analysis is important part of each analysis, which operates with target variable. Recognition of most important variables, which has greatest impact on target variable, reduces redundancy and uncertainty at model development process stage. It provides robustness of the model and model reliability. Attribute relevance analysis besides importance measuring, evaluates attribute characteristics. Attribute characteristics evaluation includes measuring attribute values impact on target variables. It helps on understanding relations and logic between most important predictors and target variable, and understanding relations and logic between most important predictors from target variable perspective. After attribute relevance analysis stage, analyst has initial picture about churner profile and behavior. This stage often opens many additional questions related to reveled relations and sometimes induces construction of new behavioral (derived) variables, which also should pass attribute relevance analysis process.

From perspective of predictive churn modeling there are two basic data sample types for predictive churn model development:

- Data sample with binomial target variable
- Data sample with multinomial target variable

7.2 BINOMIAL TARGET VARIABLE VERSUS MULTINOMIAL TARGET VARIABLE

Data sample with binomial target variable contains target variable with two finite states. In churn problematic this states could be marked as: "Yes" or "No". "Yes" or "No" states determines churn commitment within some period (outcome period). It also could be marked differently (as numeric values) into data sample e.g. with "1" and "0". Data sample with binomial target variable is most common one in predictive churn modeling, and it is mostly used for hard churn modeling in situation where we have proven that customer has committed churn based on interrupted contract. In situation where we do not operate with contracts, as it was already presented, criteria for churn should be defined, and if customer reached defined criteria, he or she could be marked within data sample with churn status = "Yes". It is situation where contract does not exist like in retail. Data sample with multinomial target variable contains target variable with more than two finite states.

In churn problematic this states could be marked e.g. as: "Yes", "No", "Soft Churn", "Unknown etc. Enumerated states determine churn status within some period (outcome period). It also could be marked differently (as numeric values) into data sample e.g. with "1", "0", "2","3" etc.

Data sample with multinomial target variable is used in situation when company would like to determine not only who will or will not commit churn, but also would like to determine e.g. who will commit soft churn, and it is unclear does customer committed some kind of churn or not (situation where contracts does not exist and e.g. reason for customer inactivity could be seasonal factors within short period of time). Data sample with multinomial target variable for churn predictive modeling purposes is less used methodology than data sample with binomial target variable. Reason for that will be explained later in details. Attribute relevance analysis process is next big step after sample construction and data quality, consistency, logic checks that could not be avoided. This process gives first qualitative and quantitative insight into potential churn causes (if we are talking about churn prediction models), and churner profiles. Attribute relevance analysis techniques for binomial target variable data sets, and attribute relevance analysis techniques for multinomial target variable data sets will be presented and illustrated on practical examples in following text.

7.3 ATTRIBUTE RELEVANCE ANALYSIS IN CASE OF BINOMIAL TARGET VARIABLE

7.3.1 Weight of Evidence Calculation and Information Value Calculation

Prerequisite for attribute relevance analyze is existence of single table with prepared data. Data must be prepared in way that there are no doubts about data quality, without open questions about business logic for any variable contained into final table, for model construction. Table contains socio demographic and derived (variables) as potential predictors, and target variable, as it is shown in Table 1.

In this stage it is desirable to have as much as possible potential predictors, because in that case there is higher opportunity for adequate predictor selection. Attribute relevance analysis process has task to find best predictors, which goes into following churn model building stage. It is expected that most of the attributes will be removed from the sample as predictors, because of poor predictive power in relation with churn flag. Before attribute relevance analysis starts, data sample should be divided in two parts, development sample and test sample usually on 80%: 20% ratio. Dividing should be done randomly e.g. by using linear congruence generator. Development sample is used for model development, and test sample are used for predictive power testing. In case of attribute relevance analysis Information value and Weight of Evidence measure could be used.

Formulas for weight of evidence calculation and information value calculation are shown below:

$$WoE = \ln\left(\frac{D_{nc}}{D_c}\right)$$

$$IV = \left(D_{nc_i} - D_{c_i}\right) * \ln\left(\frac{D_{nc_i}}{D_{c_i}}\right)$$

(1)

Table 1. Sample data structure and binomial target variable

Attribute 1	Attribute 2	Attribute ...	Attribute n	Churn
Value	Value	...	Value	yes
Value	Value	...	Value	no
Value	Value	...	Value	no

Weight of evidence is calculated as a natural logarithm of ratio between distribution of non-churners (D_{nc}) and churners (D_c) in distribution spans. Information value is calculated as sum of differences between distribution of non-churners and churners in distribution spans and product of corresponding weight of evidence.

Weight of evidence calculation will be illustrated on attribute Monthly average number of long distance calls in last 6 months. This attribute is derived from existing transactional calls history data. Before calculation process, continuous variable should be fine classed (grouped) on 5%-10% classes, and corresponded percentages in relation to churn status yes or no should be calculated, as it is visible in Table 2. On given percentages previous formulas for weight of evidence and information value should be applied.

It is important to include missing values category in calculation (if any exists) as stand alone bin, otherwise (regarding to nature of calculation), results could be imprecise. Business logic check for observed variable could be easily done by presenting weight of evidence values on graph, as it is visible in Figure 1.

Positive weight of evidence value implies low churn expectation in these zones. Regarding that, for subscribers that do not have long distance calls in 6 months we

Table 2. Fine classing and WoE calculation for continuous variable

		Churn			
		Yes	No		
		Column N %	Column N %	WoE	IV
Average number of long distance calls in 6 months	0	0.0030%	2.5096%	6.73	0.17
	0-5	0.0265%	4.7414%	5.19	0.24
	5 - 10	0.0796%	4.8615%	4.11	0.20
	10 - 15	0.0265%	1.9017%	4.27	0.08
	15 - 25	0.0796%	3.7121%	3.84	0.14
	25 - 30	0.2387%	4.2712%	2.88	0.12
	30 - 35	0.1857%	4.6328%	3.22	0.14
	35 - 40	0.1326%	2.4633%	2.92	0.07
	40 - 45	0.2653%	6.0609%	3.13	0.18
	45 - 50	0.6366%	5.7536%	2.20	0.11
	50 - 55	0.7692%	3.6908%	1.57	0.05
	55 - 60	5.0504%	5.2840%	0.05	0.00
	60- 65	22.6260%	16.1170%	-0.34	0.02
	65 - 70	35.8355%	21.0000%	-0.53	0.08
	70+	34.0477%	13.0000%	-0.96	0.20
	Total	100.0%	100.0%		1.80

Figure 1. Weight of evidence values for average numbers of long distance calls in 6 months

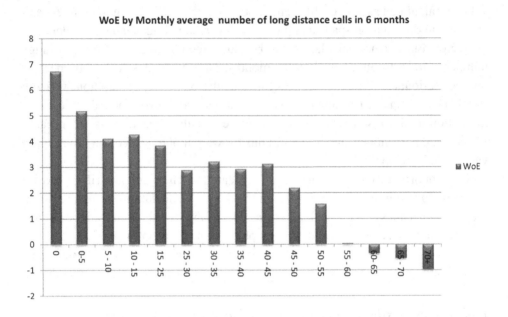

do not expect significant churn rate. As number of calls goes up, churn expectation rise. Break point is at 55-60 long distance calls in 6 months, after this point subscriber has high propensity to churn. Most risky subscribers from perspective of churn are subscribers with more than 60 long distance calls in 6 months. Business logic behind this variable lies in fact that more long distance calls in 6 months implies higher churn risk. Alarming point is at 60 calls, because after that point regarding negative Woe, those subscribers will commit churn.

From the business perspective, churn has some connection with long distance calls, and subscribers, which makes often long distance calls. Is it too expensive in comparison to competitors, or maybe problem lays in infrastructure, or service usage conditions? Information value, which is 1.8, implies that this variable has high importance from churn perspective. For orientation, attributes with information value close to 0 do not have significant importance in relation with aim variable. Information values from 0.2 to 0.6 should be observed as potentially good predictors, and variables with information values above 0.6 are good predictors. Information value above 1 should be reconsidered as correlated variable. That implies reconsideration of this variable as well in real analytical projects. For sake of simplicity we will neglect this facts.

Attribute Relevance Analysis

As it was already mentioned missed values should be also included into calculation. Missing values could provide good directions on customer behavior understanding. For example, if customer does not have intention to realize long term relationship with company and it use some product on probation period only, or it use some product or service with intent to break relationship with company in short period of time it does not provide most of the personal data which are not mandatory for making contracts. One of the reasons could be avoiding further direct mails or campaigns, because he or she is not interested in it. Non-existence of some data could also be milestone for making hypothesis during weight of evidence calculation. After fine classing and attribute relevance analyze, attributes with higher information values should be selected. Another criteria for variable rejection, even it has high information value could be lack of business logic within variable. This step assures robust and interpretable final modeling solution.

Attributes which survives selection process goes into coarse class process, as it visible in Table 3.

Table 3. Coarse classing

		Churn				Churn			
		Yes	No			Yes (G)	No (G)		
		Column N %	Column N %	WoE	IV	Column N %	Column N %	WoE (G)	IV (G)
	0	0.0030%	2.5096%	6.73	0.17	0.0030%	2.5096%	6.73	0.17
	0-5	0.0265%	4.7414%	5.19	0.24	0.0265%	4.7414%	5.19	0.24
	5 - 10	0.0796%	4.8615%	4.11	0.20	0.1857%	10.4753%	4.03	0.41
	10 - 15	0.0265%	1.9017%	4.27	0.08				
	15 - 25	0.0796%	3.7121%	3.84	0.14				
	25 - 30	0.2387%	4.2712%	2.88	0.12	0.8223%	17.4282%	3.05	0.51
Average number of long distance calls in 6 months	30 - 35	0.1857%	4.6328%	3.22	0.14				
	35 - 40	0.1326%	2.4633%	2.92	0.07				
	40 - 45	0.2653%	6.0609%	3.13	0.18				
	45 - 50	0.6366%	5.7536%	2.20	0.11	0.6366%	5.7536%	2.20	0.11
	50 - 55	0.7692%	3.6908%	1.57	0.05	0.7692%	3.6908%	1.57	0.05
	55 - 60	5.0504%	5.2840%	0.05	0.00	5.0504%	5.2840%	0.05	0.00
	60- 65	22.6260%	16.1170%	-0.34	0.02	22.6260%	16.1170%	-0.34	0.02
	65 - 70	35.8355%	21.0000%	-0.53	0.08	35.8355%	21.0000%	-0.53	0.08
	70+	34.0477%	13.0000%	-0.96	0.20	34.0477%	13.0000%	-0.96	0.20
	Total	100.0%	100.0%		1.80	100.0%	100.0%		0.46

Coarse classing process has task to unite parts of observed variables into subgroups based on weight of evidence values. Basic idea behind that lies in fact that bins with similar weight of evidence values provides similar value of information in relation to target variable.

Table shows zones with similar weight of evidence values, which are grouped into larger classes. This variable is potentially unstable and should be reconsidered for usage in model, because there is significant shift in information value after coarse classing. That implies instability, and these kinds of variables are not advisable for building models, which should be usable in certain period of time. Main disadvantage of using this kind of variables are instability of the whole model in near future, and performance drop, which can cause often model redesign.

Business logic should not lie on linear dependencies only. Business logic can be represented by "U" shape weight of evidence, where e.g. younger and older population behaves in the same way (has less propensity on churn), and middle-aged population has higher propensity on churn. Data mining is discipline, which reveals new hidden patterns from the data, and critics could say that this approach is not in line with basic data mining idea. Contrary to that, to be in line with business understanding and expectation does not mean to limit data mining methodology, it means to have deeper understanding of trends within data and which is key churn factors. It also helps in hypothesis creation, which is a basic for deeper investigation and for finding better understanding of existing portfolio.

In case of categorical variables, attribute relevance analysis is the same, without fine classing part. Coarse classing could be done on same principles with sorting categories by weight of evidence values, and making coarse classes by similarity principles. Main goal of attribute relevance analysis is attribute reduction by predictive power criteria. Other important function is profiling and causes and consequences recognition in relations with churn. Deeper investigation based on weight of evidence calculation could be good starting point for better understanding churn nature within specific portfolio. It sometimes could be sufficient for reaching crucial conclusions about churn causes. Mostly it is good starting point for creating hypothesis, which should be additionally investigated. Weight of evidence calculation for example could provide information that subscribers from eastern region, younger and middle aged persons, which usually makes long distance calls, and makes phone calls more often during weekends has higher propensity to make churn. Regarding revealed profile and behavior, company could assume that in eastern region exists competitors with lower prices for long distance calls, and younger and middle aged persons are more flexible in changing telecommunication company than older persons from the same region. On the other hand, higher propensity of making churn for persons which calls more often during weekends could be also motivated with better/higher discounts at other company.

All those conclusions are hypothesis, which should be tested, and it helps for deeper understanding nature of churn within observed portfolio. In this stage brainstorming are welcomed. New derived variable creation could be also result of brainstorming, and their role is hypothesis rejection or acceptance. Hypothesis rejection or acceptance could be based on weight of evidence and information value calculation, or usage of data mining techniques on data sample together with newly derived variable by using e.g. decision tree or Bayesian networks.

Experience in specific business is important for setting right and qualitative hypothesis. For example let suppose that car company interviewed former car buyers to find out key churn factors. They made classic phone call interview on former car buyer's sample. One of the questions is: "Does Break Assistant has often been activated in your car." Offered answers could be:

- Never
- No
- Yes
- I do not know what Break Assistant is
- I do not have Break Assistant
- I do not know

Let suppose that about 25% of interviewed persons selected "I do not know" as answer. If Break Assistant is not part of the standard car equipment, it tells something about that population. If more of that population, which selected "I do not know" as answer, bought another car at another company, it talks something about their profile. Maybe it is not persons, which care about safety; maybe it is persons, which does not have enough information about additional car equipment. Also it could be careful drivers, which drives slowly and this part of equipment is not in their focus. From the other hand main question is why do they choose another company for buying another car?

Maybe campaigns were not adopted for that population. Making hypothesis based on one attribute does not have much sense, but it illustrates way of thinking and making conclusions based on interesting findings. Same answers could also be interested for insurance company; their perspective could be little bit different. In case when they have significant number of churners, which answer is mostly "Yes" on question "Does Break Assistant has often been activated in your car." Probably insurance company would not much regret for those clients. Reason for that is higher risk, which implies higher costs for insurance company. Often new volumes into insurance company portfolio could cause loss if new clients are riskier.

Privilege for constructing derived variables based on behavioral characteristic does not have all business areas equally. A business, which has more interactions with subscribers/buyers or clients, has more opportunities for derived variables construction. It means that those business areas could be much more precise and much more successful in churn prediction and mitigation. One of the much more privileged business area from those perspective is telecommunication business. From the one hand they have clear picture when subscriber starts and stop using product and services, and from the other hand their customers has daily activities related with company. It is wealth source for derived variable construction. Financial institutions are also in similar position depending on product and services usage. Retail from this perspective is somewhere in the middle, because, interaction with customers could be random without clear notification about beginning and the end of relationship, with possible longer inactivity periods which could be (by mistake) interpreted as churn. Insurance business from this perspective is in worst position. They have information when client starts and stop using products or services, but they do not have, or have rare interactions with client during service or product usage. It is very unfavorable situation for derived variable construction.

Higher degree of interactivity with clients/buyers/customers, recorded within databases provides higher opportunities for adequate derived variable construction in relation with churn. It provides possibility for variables creation, which also has role as early warning signals. Static / inactive portfolio (from perspective of inbound data flow during customer lifetime cycle) is vulnerable and with higher risk of stopping using product and services. Companies, which offers product and services with frequent interaction with users, also has opportunity to manage with customer loyalty and customer prospective customer value. Lack of information often means potential uncontrolled customer loss. One of possible technique for vaulting lack of information is more frequent cross selling activities, which also could be aimed on data collection. Data collection in process of cross selling and giving offers could be valuable for early warning signals detections. It is not perfect technique, but in case like insurance business (e.g. car insurance) it assures some source of information, which could be valuable for churn mitigation purposes.

7.3.2 How to Create "Dummy" Variables

One of the common techniques for predictive model building is creating dummy variables, based on formed coarse classes. Coarse classes are created regarding similar weight of evidence values, and dummy variables are copies of constructed coarse classes. Each dummy variable represents one coarse class, and if observed case has attribute value within coarse class, dummy variable has value "1" otherwise "0". It is simple remapping procedure, which contribute in data set adoption for applying data mining methods like neural networks, or logistic regression. For illustration, let assume that data set contains attribute age. After attribute relevance analysis, three coarse classes were created. Age less than eighteen, from eighteen to forty, and higher than frothy. Dummy variables based on existing coarse classes could be declared as "dummy_LT_18", "dummy_18_40", "dummy_GT_40". If member of specific case is thirty five years old, dummy variable "dummy_18_40" will get value "1", and other dummy variables will get value "0". For coarse classes, which have weight of evidence close to 0, dummy variables should not be created, because those variables will not increase model predictive performance.

Correlation analysis also should be part of building churn predictive model. Correlation should be calculated between all created dummy variables, and dummy variables, which has correlation factor greater than 0.3, should be removed from the sample. Another criterion for dummy variable selection when correlation exists is weight of evidence value. If two dummy variables are correlated, dummy variables with lower weight of evidence should be removed from the sample. Final sample for churn predictive model building in case when described technique contains only values with "0" and "1". The same values contains target variable (churn) as well.

Described techniques, in combination with binary output in churn target variable, showed good performance in practice. Main advantage of described sample preparation methodology is ability to understand relations between target variable and potential predictors and business logic check. From technical point of view, data mining techniques like neural networks, and logistic regression by the nature of their algorithms, prefers to operate with values between 0 and 1. Dummy variables could be interpreted as membership declaration with 0 and 1 values. If some value belongs into specific class represented as dummy variable, it is true and dummy variable has value "1" otherwise "0".

Contrary to predictive model development in area of credit scoring, which is origin of described methodology, creating churn predictive models does not have limitations in way of taking in consider additional rules specific for banking industry. Applying those rules could result in additional rejection of existing dummy variables, and even attributes. Churn modeling from perspective of dummy variables creation have task to build high performance predictive model. Variables, which are part of predictive models, should contain strong business logic approved and checked with people from business practice. Approved and checked business logic assure also trust into developed model, because business users also on quantitative models looks as on black boxes, especially when it is complex as it is the case with churn models. Understanding inputs and logic of those inputs, which is in line with their perception of their problem area could result on better cooperation and better results in efforts for churn mitigation and churn reduction.

7.4 MULTINOMIAL TARGET VARIABLE ATTRIBUTE RELEVANCE ANALYSIS

Predictive modeling is commonly focused in developing models with binary target variable. Roots for this approach lay in fact, that usual task for predictive model development is finding out who would and who would not commit churn in certain future period with probability evaluation. Sometimes churn models could have more than two states into target variable. Target variable with more than two states could be used in situation where it is not clear did customer commit churn or not based on his previous behavior (situation in retail for buyers which could be categorized as soft churners or we would like to extend target variable with state "soft churn"). In that case same model has role to recognize future churners, non-churners, and soft churners.

Advantage of models, which uses multinomial target variable, is in their predictive power for more than two categories. Disadvantage is that attribute relevance analysis is not such transparent as in case when two states in target variable exists. It does not mean that methods as Info Gain could not produce qualitative evaluation of predictive power for potential predictors. It works well, but problem is in finding clear interpretable relations between target variable and predictor's state values. In case when we have two states like churn = "Yes" or churn="No", in attribute relevance analysis process it is easy to find relations between those two states and e.g. variable "Age". With weight of evidence measure, it is possible to find out who is riskiest for committing churn younger customers, or older customers. In situation where more than two states exists into target variable like churn = "Yes" or churn = "No" or churn = "Soft", or churn="Unknown", methods like Info Gain, or Relief does not have answer how to find out similar relations for multinomial target variables which is preparation for dummy variable creation. Final stage in attribute relevance analysis (binary target variable) is dummy variables creation. In case of multinomial target variable it is impossible to create dummy variables on similar way, because dummy variables are based on binary relations, which exists in binary target variable. Usage of multinomial target variables implies potential overleaping between predictor zones in relation with multinomial target states, which is hard to express through dummy variables. Measures like Info Gain, or Relief provides info about variable predictive power and could be useful for churn model development in case of multinomial target variable.

Fact that multinomial target variable is limiting factor for dummy variable creation, and churner profiling in way as it is possible to do in case of binary target variable, is not limiting factor for churn model development.

Main limitation is harder churner profiling due to fact of several states into target variable and not such clear interpretation and understanding relations between target variable and predictors, especially into created model. In situation where should be operated with more than two state variables within aim variable, and when it is important to have clear explanation about profiles and relations between them solution exists. It implies developing separate models for each state within target variable in way to create binary states. Binary states refers on currently observed state and "other states" as one group, which could be declared as "not member of currently observed state".

For example, if target variable "Churn" consists of four states:

- "Yes"
- "No"
- "Soft"
- "Undefined"

Described methodology implies developing separate predictive models with binary target variables.

Next examples illustrate possible solutions for binary target variable construction.

First model could have target variable with states churn="Yes" and churn="No", where churn="No" category consolidates all other states ("No", "Soft", "Undefined").

Second model could have target variable with states churn="Soft" and churn="No", where churn="No" category consolidates all other states ("Yes", "Soft", "Undefined").

Third model could have target variable with states churn="Undefined" and churn="No", where churn="No" category consolidates all other states ("Yes", "Soft", "No").

Fourth model could have target variable with states churn="No" and churn="Other", where churn="Other" category consolidates all other states ("Yes", "Soft", "Undefined").

Binary target variable construction should follow business logic; it implies some state exclusion from the sample if it better reflect business needs for model development. Illustration for that could be exclusion of "Undefined" category from the fourth model, or "Soft" category from the first model.

There are no predefined rules how to develop binomial target variables from multinomial target variable, basic idea is variable construction based on business needs.

Described methodology gives solution how to make control on each category within multinomial target variable. Presented methodology has advantage in data sample control, and possible category exclusions in "not member of currently observed state", which could be useful tool for adoption to business needs. Clear and simple, often linear dependent explanation of relations, and possibility of designing dummy variables with more control on developed model is advantage of using weight of evidence calculation for multinomial target variable by transformation multinomial target variable into binomial target variables.

7.5 WHY DO WE NEED ATTRIBUTE RELEVANCE ANALYSIS?

Attribute relevance analysis is key process in model development. It assures right variable selection and avoids model building with irrelevant attributes, which can cause with unpredictable outputs, unusable in churn prediction. Beside mentioned function, attribute relevance analysis has important role in understanding of key churn factors. It does not mean that this stage in modeling will provide all the answers important for churn understanding, but it for sure raises right questions and opens horizons in understanding of churn nature for specific portfolio. Regarding that, using weight of evidence measures and redesigning multinomial variables as binomial helps in better understanding of relations between target variables and predictors. From the business side it could be milestones for generating hypothesis about churn causes, if it is not evident on the first sight. If for example weight of evidence shows relation that number of complains via call center has strong impact on churn rate, and churn probability raises with numbers of complains via call center it is milestone for deeper investigation and making some hypothesis. Hypothesis could be related with introducing some new product and inadequate technical support for them. For proving hypothesis, additional data from call center database should be analyzed for finding out does churners has been complained in previous period in connection with potential technical or other problems with new product. If it is true, it could be half way for finding solution.

Sometimes important relation and patterns could be found in attribute relevance analysis stage.

Often churn reasons are not so obvious, but combination of several reveled relations could be good direction for getting idea where is the root of the problem. Developed predictive model could have high predictive power, but it does not mean that company fully understands reasons why churn had happened. Unfortunately further investigation about churn nature often stops, after predictive churn model has been done, and it is mistake, because, company in that case only has probability calculator for churn without deeper understanding what is actually going on. By using predictive churn models as churn probability calculator it is possible to recognize who will commit churn, but without deeper understanding of causes it is impossible to make good strategy for churn prevention. That is the reason why churn model development should not be only aim of churn prevention/mitigation projects. Data mining methodology also implies ad hoc analysis based upon expert hypothesis. Illustration for that situation could be predictive churn model in retail, which contains variables: Age, County, buying trend in previous three months, changes in buying habits, and respond on campaigns in last six months. Attribute relevance analysis could show that most risky buyers are middle-aged buyers, which lives in some specific county, and have been changed their buying habits and did not respond on campaigns in last six months. Based upon recognized relations in data, it is easy to develop predictive model for probability calculation who will probably churn in near future. Taking in consider all reveled knowledge, it is hard to make strategic plan how to decrease churn rates. First step is to find adequate questions like: Why middle aged buyers, which lives in some specific county, and have been changed their buying habits and did not respond on campaigns in last six months are most riskiest buyers? Which factor is leading factor for committing churn: age, county, changes in buying habits, or responding on campaigns?

This is an "obvious" question derived from attribute relevance analysis results. Less obvious question should be questioned from the experts by their experience like: Is our assortment fully adapted to market segments? Was our campaign good enough from perspective of targeting segments?

Did our campaigns miss some facts in relations with middle-aged buyers, which live in specific counties, and it was trigger for churn? As it is shown, attribute relevance analysis even it could be aimed firstly on predictive model development, it is also groundwork for further analysis and deeper investigation. Parallel with predictive model development, after hypothesis creation, other data mining methods could be used for hypothesis confirmation or rejection. All those processes are in service of understanding churn reasons and causes. Churn predictive model as churn probability calculator, and clear picture what had happened that churn occurred are two elements with which churn problems could be solved. With the first element it is possible to calculate who will commit churn in near future period. With the second element it is possible to design strategy for retaining customers/buyers/clients. If any of those two elements is missing, project will for sure fail. On first sight it is unusual why all those themes are topics in attribute analysis part. It is only on first sight, because part of understanding churns reasons in churn projects are often neglected, and churn projects often became churn probability calculator projects. Churn modeling for predictive models after attribute relevance analysis part should be split after attribute relevance analysis in predictive model development and churn causes investigation (modeling).

REFERENCES

Ahn, J. H., Han, S. P., & Lee, Y. S. (2006). Customer churn analysis: Churn determinants and mediation effects of partial defection in the Korean mobile telecommunications service industry. *Telecommunications Policy*, *30*(10-11), 552–568. doi:10.1016/j.telpol.2006.09.006

Berry, M., & Linhoff, G. (2004). Data Mining Techniques for Marketing Sales and Customer Support. Wiley.

Chu, B., Tsai, M., & Ho, T. (2007). Toward a hybrid data mining model for customer retention. *Knowledge-Based Systems*, *20*(8), 703–718. doi:10.1016/j.knosys.2006.10.003

Hadden, J., Ashtoush, T., Rajkumar, R., & Ruta, D. (2006). Churn Prediction: Does Technology Matter? *International Journal of Electrical and Computer Engineering*, *1*, 6.

Lazarov, V., & Capota, M. (2010). *Churn Prediction*. Retrieved from http://home.in.tum.de/~lazarov/files/research/papers/churn-prediction.pdf

Osei-Bryson, K. (2004). Evaluation of decision trees: A multi-criteria approach. *Computers & Operations Research*, *31*(11), 1933–1945. doi:10.1016/S0305-0548(03)00156-4

Rashid, T. (2010). Classification of Churn and non-Churn Customers for Telecommunication Companies. *International Journal of Biometrics and Bioinformatics, 3*(5).

Soeini, R., & Rodpysh, K. (2012). Evaluations of Data Mining Methods in Order to Provide the Optimum Method for Customer Churn Prediction: Case Study Insurance Industry. In *Proceedings of 2012 International Conference on Information and Computer Applications* (ICICA 2012). ICICA.

SPSS Inc. (2007). *Clementine 12.0 Algorithms Guide*. Author.

Tsai, C., & Chen, M. (2010). Variable selection by association rules for customer churn prediction of multimedia on demand. *Expert Systems with Applications*, *37*(3), 2006–2015. doi:10.1016/j.eswa.2009.06.076

Tsai, C., & Lu, Y. (2009). Customer churn prediction by hybrid neural networks. *Expert Systems with Applications*, *36*(10), 12547–12553. doi:10.1016/j.eswa.2009.05.032

KEY TERMS AND DEFINITIONS

Attribute Relevance Analysis: Process of finding attributes which has predictive power regarding aim variable.

Binominal Variable: Variable which has two states.

Coarse Classing: Making groups within variable regarding results of attribute relevance analysis (Weight of Evidence, WoE).

Dummy Variable: Derived variable, which has two states, 0 or 1.

Multinomial Variable: Variable which has more than two states.

Chapter 8
From Churn Models to Churn Solution

ABSTRACT

This chapter explains churn model classification, describes techniques for developing predictive churn models, and describes how to build churn segmentation models, churn time-dependent models, and expert models for churn reduction. Analysts (readers) are shown a holistic picture for churn modeling and presented an analytical method with techniques described as elements that could be used for building a final churn solution depending on current business problems and expected outputs. There are numerous ways for designing final churn models (solutions). The first criteria is to find solutions that will be in line with business needs. The problem is not applying some data mining technique; the problem is in choosing and preparing appropriate data sets. Applied techniques should show holistic solution pictures for churn, which are explainable and understandable for making decisions, which will help in churn understanding and churn mitigation.

8.1 INTRODUCTION

Classification of churn models is easy task in way of classifying it by functionality in situation of observing specific model for itself, which should solve some specific task in domain of churn. In that case models could be aimed (classified) as churn prediction models, survival models, profiling models, segmentation models etc. In practice it is very rare situation in which only one type of model is convenient for

DOI: 10.4018/978-1-4666-6288-9.ch008

designing final churn solution. It is often solution, which demands chaining various model types depending on specific situation.

Generally speaking appropriate classification of churn model is by their dominant characteristics. A real life churn project uses several methods, but they usually have one central point/task around which whole solution is build. It implies situation where company has need for predictive churn solution, and during solution development process, additional analysis related to churner profiling and customer life period could be done. In general it is still predictive churn model, but it also contains additional values important for decision support. It is not always possible to make classification taking in consider one aspect. Precise classification could be done taking in consider different aspects.

Regarding dominant characteristics basic churn model classification is:

- Predictive churn models
- Time dependent churn models (survival, seasonal)
- Segmentation churn models
- Profiling churn models

A predictive churn model gives assessment about churn probability in future period of time. They calculate probability that certain subscriber/buyer will commit churn in determined future period of time. These types of models are often widely accepted synonym for churn models.

Time dependent churn models contains time component, which is crucial for the final model construction. In this category belongs a survival model, which calculates survival rates, or models, which primarily analyze temporal subscribers/buyers data and produce time dependent patterns (seasonal regularities, temporal patterns, events related to temporal appearance.) A segmentation churn model has lot in common with regular segmentation models, with one significant characteristic that it makes segmentation on churner data sample. It implies that segmentation churn models try to find mutual characteristics into samples divided by segmentation algorithm. This approach could be extremely useful, because it assume that within churners exists differentiation. Revelation of dominant characteristics within different segments, and existence of segments within churner population could be key for finding solution for churn mitigation. Existence of unique population without possible differentiation also provides useful information for making adequate churn mitigation policy. It could not be determined in advance does segments exists or not, but conscious about their existence could also have influence on further solution development. For example, in case where segments within churner population exist, it is possible to decide to make different predictive churn models for each segment. It depends on analytical aims and project task related to churn.

Profiling churn models on first sight could be wrongly identified as segmentation churn models. They have common points but it is different type of models. Profiling models gives holistic picture of typical churner as member of churner population or as a member of the segment recognized thought segmentation process. Profiling models does not lay on social demographic data only; they also could be constructed by using behavioral and temporal characteristics. Profiling models could provide information how different is for example members of each segments recognized thought segmentation process. It could be trigger for decision about churn mitigation policy, or further analysis processes. Profiling analysis could include variety of data mining techniques.

Regarding determination about churn commitment classification could be done by:

- Soft churn models
- Hard churn models

Soft churn models are related to situation within portfolio where buyer/user/subscribers start to stagnate in product/services usage. It is not always easy to define what stagnation is, especially in situation where it uses more than one product/service, or it is seasonally related. However after definition what is stagnation in usage of product and services in situation where buyer/user/subscribers still uses product/services churn models are applied for finding causes or calculation probabilities or finding mutual patterns for those clients.

Contracts existence is one of dominant consumption for determination of hard churn commitment. If client/buyer/user broke contract it is hard churn. It is different situation, which is usual in retail business, and other similar business where contracts does not exists, and churn could be assumed only on customer behavior. In this situation variety models could be applied for finding causes of churn, or dominant patterns, or segments and profiles as well.

Both, soft or hard churn generates costs to company, and "advantage" in hard churn is that churners are recognized and their characteristics could be used for making analytical models without calculation does he or she committed churn or not. From the business perspective it is worst situation than soft churn, because it is harder to return clients/users/customers, which committed hard churn than to motivate soft churner to stop stagnate usage of products or services. From the other hand, it is harder to realize who real soft churner is, because soft churn sometimes could be caused by expected customer behavior and it needs which stagnates in certain period of time or it could be caused by seasonal factors. Regarding that it is high probability to make impropriate analytical sample for applying data mining methods by fact of imprecise determination who is soft churner.

Regarding determination about churn models nature, classification could be done by:

- Models for churn prevention
- Models for churn preparation
- Models for churn mitigation

Churn prevention models are type of models which should help in situation where churn is not still obvious or mayor problem in company, but it could became obvious or mayor problem because of market condition changes. It has role in possible scenario analysis and preventions regarding possible market threats. Those models are often developed without specific information about future market conditions and it could be based on educated guesses and real consumptions regarding expected market movement.

Models for churn preparation are applied in situation where companies are aware of some specific market scenario, often in situation where it expects penetration of competitor into market. It has some information about competitors, their target groups, competitor's business policies etc. and company wants to create defending strategy against raising churn. In that situation it is important to realize own weak points, opportunities, strength. In that situation it is important for company to find out which are most valuable customers/buyers/users for spending disposable budget on it. Churn defending strategy should be adapted to most valuable customers/buyers/users profiles. Fact is that in this situation it is unrealistic to expect that nobody will not churn, but having as much control over those process as it is possible on given condition is must.

Calculation of prospective customer value, as well as retrospective customer value is useful strategy. With this movement company could focus itself on most valuable customers. Practice often shows Paretto effect, in which about 20% of customers generate about 80% of profit, and about 80% of customers generate about 20% of profit. Finding out right 20% worth for spending budget for keeping it into portfolio is good strategy. Finding their profiles, segments, motivators and probabilities to stop using services or products is half way to keeping most of them into portfolio. Usually in situation where competition enters into market it has attractive offers, which for sure will cause (it is evident in retail industry) short term increasing churn rate. That means that buyers attracted with interesting campaigns which include low prices and fact about new store in town will for sure going to visit competitor's store. It is not unusual in practice, and it could be declared as soft churn. Tools for deeper analysis of that appearance could be survival analysis which could give answer to company what is time period of that effect, and which buyer profile is most sensitive on it. Of course, it is possible to include other analytical methods in described situation, and using survival analysis is one option for finding answers. Acting on most valuable customers and spending budget on them to keeping it into portfolio is possible scenario for described market situation. How to spend budget regarding existing segments, values, expectation is question of results after using additional analytical techniques conducted on most valuable customer population.

Models for churn mitigation are models, which is developed and applied mostly in situation where churn became obvious and big problem within company. Churn mitigation models could rely on predictive churn models, segmentation models, churn profiling, it could be time dependent. Churn mitigation could be aimed on soft or hard churn. Even it is common assurance and fact, that hard churn is bigger problem than soft churn, soft churn could be also dangerous appearance. Often soft churn at certain period of time became hard churn. On the other hand, sometimes expenses in some specific business area for single customer could be higher than profit. In that case even customer did not commit churn, from the company perspective it would be better that it committed churn. As it is visible it is not easy to make unique classification of churn models. It could be classified by different criteria, and there is lot of overlapping situations and common characteristics between defined classes. Churn problematic is complex, and it implies taking in consider various aspect for making churn models classification.

8.2 USING DATA MINING METHODS AS A PUZZLE FOR CHURN SOLUTION

As it was shown, churn models could not be recognized or classified through used data mining techniques. Keeping on mind business needs and business logic should develop churn solution. It demands chaining of various data mining models for achieving final churn solution. For illustration as it was shown in case of models for churn preparation, prospective customer value and retrospective customer value calculation could be solved by using fuzzy expert systems. After recognition by prospective customer value and retrospective customer value calculation, which is most valuable customers, on reduced data sets (most valuable customers only) other data mining techniques could be applied. If company would like to know which is probability that those customers will churn in certain period of time, predictive data mining techniques for designing predictive models could be used. It could be neural networks and/or logistic regression and/or decision tree and/or support vector machines etc. In case that company would like to find out typical churn profiles by potential churner segments, segmentation methods like K-mean clustering or Self-organizing maps could be applied. On recognized segment for profiling methods like market basket analysis and decision trees could also be applied.

There are numerous ways for designing final churn model (solution). First criteria are finding solution, which will be in line with business needs. It is not problem to apply some data mining technique; problem is on which data set (it could be original or reduced due to business requirements and it should follow business logic). Applied techniques should show holistic solution picture for churn, which is explainable and understandable for making decisions, which will helps in, churn understanding and churn mitigation.

It is important to keep in mind that data preparation process takes almost 80% of time in modeling. Churn is not exceptions in that. Data preparation on the other hand contains business logic. Sampling process and data preparation process follows business needs. It could manifest as requests for unprofitable customers rejection, exclusions of some categories from the sample or inclusion of other categories into data sample is in direct connection with business way of thinking. Data sample construction is one way of integrating business logic within models. Other disposable way for integrating business requirements within churn solution is tweaking data mining techniques by chaining methods, or input data modification. Applying some of the data mining method is about 20% of all work on designing final churn solution. There are numerous ways how to apply it, and two different modelers could reach satisfying results on totally different ways. It implies that puzzles could be connected on different ways for reaching same aims.

Following methods will not be presented as a final solution cookbook. It will be presented, as a part with which is possible to create holistic churn solution, by combining it depending on specific situation. Each method will be presented as an element, which makes final solution with situation in which it is suitable for usage with some technical details and their possible interpretation.

Figure 1, it shows churn solution modeling areas and correspondent data mining techniques.

8.2.1 How to Build Predictive Model

Predictive modeling is one of the most common approaches in churn modeling. Basic idea is to calculate churn probabilities in near future period for each client/user/subscriber. After data sampling, attribute relevance analysis, coarse classing, fine classing, dummy variable creation before applying any of data mining techniques for building predictive models correlation analysis should be done. One of the common used methods for correlation calculation is Pearson Correlation (Pearson Product Moment Correlation), which shows the linear relationship between two variables. Correlation should be calculated between dummy variables, and in case that correlation coefficient between variables is high (e.g. less than -0.35 or higher than 0.35), one of the dummy variables from this pair should be removed. A criterion

Figure 1. Churn solution modeling areas and data mining techniques

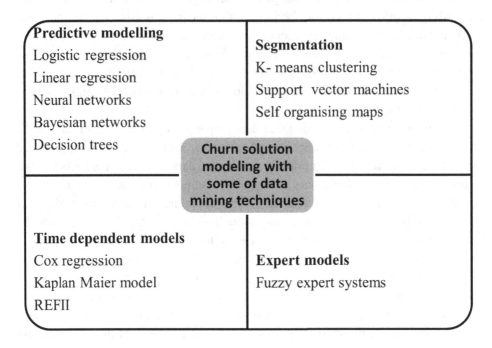

for removing is weight of evidence and/or expert judgment about stability or other business related criteria. It means if two of the dummy variables are correlated, dummy variable with lower weight of evidence should be removed. Sometimes dummy variable with higher weight of evidence could be removed if it is unstable (high volatility after coarse classing). Criteria for removing cold also be achieving as higher as possible predictive power in way of churners predictions, which could imply removing correlated dummy variable with positive weight of evidence value if other dummy variable has negative weight of evidence value. This technique insures much more precise stratification of churners with predictive model. It could imply in extreme cases undefined probability distributions through probability scale (e.g. uniform) for non-churners, but it gains better probability distributions through probability scale for churners. As company is interested to find out churner probabilities and to concentrate on them, this approach has justification for applying.

Correlation calculation process and different approaches to correlation problematic also has significant impact on final model. Regarding business requirements and analytical priorities it is possible to choose methodology, which will adequate, fit in into business needs. Calculating correlations is final stage before applying specific data mining technique for building predictive churn model. Presented methodology regarding attribute relevance analysis and dummy variable creation, correlation analysis as well is appropriate for applying on data sets with binomial target variables.

Some data mining techniques, which could be applied for building predictive models on this data set, are:

- Linear regression
- Logistic regression
- Neural networks
- Bayesian networks
- Decision trees

Illustration of building predictive models will be explained by usage of logistic regression, which is one of often choices for building predictive churn models. Model is built on development sample, and tested on test sample.

Let zi (i = 1, 2, ..., n) be empirical values of a churn, which can take only the values 0 for non-churners and for churners 1.

A logistic regression model calculates probabilities that churn occur in different subpopulation.

$$\pi_i = P\left(Z_i = 1\right) \; for \; i = 1, 2, 3, \ldots, n \tag{1}$$

Logistic regression model for churn probability calculation specifies that an appropriate function of the fitted probability of the event within linear function of the variables recognized in process of attribute relevance analysis in form:

$$log\left[\frac{\pi_i}{1 - \pi_i}\right] = b + a_1 x_{i1} + a_2 x_{i2} + .. + a_m x_{im} \tag{2}$$

As a result we have probability that some subscriber will become churner or non-churner in certain period of time.

By inverting the definition of the logit function, we obtain:

$$\pi_i = \frac{e^{b + a_1 x_{i1} + a_2 x_{i2} + .. + a_m x_{im}}}{1 - e^{b + a_1 x_{i1} + a_2 x_{i2} + .. + a_m x_{im}}} \tag{3}$$

After applying model on empirical data, score bands were created based on probability calculation for

$$P\left(Z_i = 1\left(\text{to became churner}\right)\right) \ for \ i = 1, 2, 3, \ldots, n \ .$$

In practice more than one model (using different data mining techniques) should be built. Model which shows better performance (predictive power) is used for prediction. Using ROC curves, Kolmogorov Smirnov test and similar measures could do predictive power measurement for built predictive model. The area under ROC curve measures discrimination. That is the ability to correctly classify those, which are churners, and those that is not churners. The Kolmogorov–Smirnov statistic quantifies a distance between the empirical distribution function of the sample and the cumulative distribution function of the reference distribution, or between the empirical distribution functions of two samples. Developed predictive churn model calculates churn probabilities, and for the part of portfolio with high churn probability (e.g. churn probability higher than 0.6) churn mitigation strategy should be created. Taking in consider fact that process of attribute relevance analysis with weight of evidence gives essential information regarding churner profiles and behavior, this information could be used for churn mitigation strategy creation. Also, it is important to stress that usage of predictive models should not be only element of churn solution. It contributes to churn solution, but using them, as only element of churn solution could be mistake. Reason for that is that with them company knows who will probably churn in near future period, it knows basic profile and churners behavior, but many aspects still could remain unraveled, if we rely only on predictive models. Temporal dependency, seasonal effects, existing segments, additional profiles information related to churn could stay hidden and uncovered if we capture only one aspect, in this case churn prediction. In line with statement that building churn models are like stacking puzzles, it is only one (important) puzzle, which does not provide whole picture. As it was already mentioned it is possible to apply variety of the data mining techniques for predictive churn models building. Enumerated methods are convenient for building predictive churn models in case of binomial and multinomial target variable within data sample. As weight of evidence measure has significant advantage in comparison to other techniques, because it provides additional information about profiles and churner behavior, it is possible to use it on multinomial target variable within data sample. For this purposes more than one model should be developed in way of applying predictive data mining technique on data sample with binary target variables which were created from target variable with more than two states as it was previously explained in attribute relevance analysis part. Using binary target variables for predictive modeling is not must. Mentioned data mining techniques operates with binomial and multinomial target variables. Regarding arguments mentioned in attributer relevance analysis and advantages of weight of evidence measure usage, recommendation is to adopt data samples with multinomial target variables into several data samples with binomial target variables by keeping business logic.

In case of multinomial target variables usage for predictive modeling purpose, same models will also provide valid results, but it will calculate probabilities for more than two states, and understanding of relations between more than two target states could make difficulties in model interpretation and understanding profiles and churner's behavior. Linear regression, logistic regression and neural networks as methods from perspective of predictive model building and by neglecting specifics for each of them (nature and learning process of linear regression, logistic regression and neural networks) they are pretty similar regarding modeling. Each of them learns parameters from empirical data and build model, which provides probability calculation.

Decision trees as a predictive models, also learn from the empirical data sample and provides rules with belonging probabilities. Their learning process is based on recursive entropy calculation within given empirical data sample. In comparison to other methods, due to fact about their learning process it is pretty unstable model in comparison to other models and it is recommendation to avoid it in for usage as a "long term models", because of that.

Bayesian networks are based on conditional probabilities, and they also provide probability calculation based on conditional probabilities contained within conditional probability tables. Their specifics lays in fact that in it could be integrated parts of the expert knowledge in way what has influence on what. For example, assumption that rises of prices for some specific items will cause decrease in shop visit, and it will cause higher churn rate could be integral part of Bayesian model. That relationship dependency description and influence integration is one of advantages of using Bayesian networks as predictive models. This value addition in way of expert relationship and knowledge integration within models could cause in better prediction.

Mentioned data mining techniques are not only techniques, which could be applied for predictive modeling, but it is widely used for churn predictive modeling purposes.

Fuzzy expert systems, support vector machines and other unmentioned techniques also could be used for predictive modeling, but in light of weight of evidence measure usage, described methods are much more convenient for modeling.

8.2.2 How to Build Segmentation Model

Data mining techniques for segmentation are mostly recognized as the methods applicable in domain of targeting market segment and new products acquisitions. Segmentation is useful in finding sub segments within base population with mutual characteristics. Regarding that fact it could also be applicable on churner population for finding out sub segments within churner population with dominant mutual characteristics. During predictive models development sub segments recognition of churner populations are not in scope, and whole population is observed as differentiation sample. There are possibilities that churner population shows variations regarding some factors. After predictive model development (or before) appliance of segmentation could give addition information about possible existing churners segments. Depending on analysis aims recognized segments (if they are interesting from the business perspective) could become one of predictors for which can be examined attribute relevance, and they can be part of the predictive model. Some of data mining techniques with which segmentation on churner population could be done are K- means clustering, hierarchical clustering self-organizing maps. There are numerous data mining techniques for clustering, and nay of them could be suitable for churner's segmentation. Clustering methods are not the only data mining methods appropriate for finding segments, it also could be used methods which is not related to making clusters like decision trees, or Bayesian networks, but in here is aim to find segments as a sub segments within base churners population with mutual characteristics. In this way clustering methods are much more convenient than other type of the methods.

Segmentation process on churner population could be done on wider data sample than on most predictive variables only after attribute relevance analysis, which should be done for predictive modeling purposes. If we concentrate on clustering methods, their nature as an unsupervised learning method does not demand attribute relevance analysis and including additional attributes in clustering process could be on help for building reliable model. Depending on analysis aims, clustering could be done not only on churners population, it could be done on whole sample, non-churner population and regarding that it is good strategy for trying to find out some conclusions about churners population specifics. Even on segmentation process it is visible in how much different ways in searching for patterns segmentation could be done for churn analysis purposes. Possible analytical scenario for churner's segmentation could be applying clustering (self-organizing maps or K-means clustering) on churner sub population only. Next step could be, applying clustering (self-organizing maps or K-means clustering) on whole population (churners and non-churners). For clustering processes it should not be limitation about attribute usage. Samples could contain behavioral and socio-demographic variables. Variables only should be transformed in way for applying clustering algorithms. It should be transformed into numeric values and normalized usually on scale from 0-1. After clustering process and cluster recognition by clustering algorithms additional analysis should be done for finding out dominant characteristics for each cluster. For this purposes data mining techniques like decision trees could be used. Dominant characteristic cluster analysis should give an answer does it exist some dominant characteristics within observed population which is specific and could be a milestone for further investigation and churn understanding. For example, potentially recognized sub population of churners in telecommunication company which prefer to be prepaid users and makes calls with no more than 3-10 persons could stay uncovered during attribute relevance analysis, because of their absolute size in comparison to whole population. On the other hand, even relatively small in size those profile could be significant role player in future churn trends. It does not mean that each cluster carries dramatic information usable in churn stopping policies creation. There could be few interesting clusters (segment), but from business point of view significant for churn understanding and as a base for creating churn mitigation policies. Applying clustering on churner sub population, and whole sample (churners and non-churners), could give an answer about diversity about clusters between churners only and whole portfolio population. Another strategy could be aimed on creating clusters within non-churners population only and churner population only. On that way it is possible to compare main diversification on recognized segments between those two populations.

Figure 2 provides a graphical representation how clustering strategies could be applied for finding dominant churners characteristics and their sub segments.

Members of churn segments recognized as potentially valuable could be additionally analyzed, not only for finding their dominant characteristics. It could be also analyzed from temporal perspective (temporal behavior of recognized segment, is there any temporal characteristic related to churn, or similar staffs). Segmentation is valuable and important brick in wall called churn solution. It could be used or not. It depends on vision of possible final churn solution and business needs. It could be used in combination with predictive modeling, but they do not depend on each other. They complement each other in way that recognized membership to segment could be expressed as potential predictor for predictive model. It also should pass attribute relevance analyze as significant predictor to be included into predictive model. On the other hand calculated churn probability from predictive model could be included as an attribute for segmentation (clustering process). All that implies that there is no rule what to apply first: segmentation or predictive model design or some other method. Same aim, depending on data sample will give different results. Recommendation is to use different approaches during search for appropriate solution. In case of inclusions other methods beside predictive models

Figure 2. Clustering strategies and dominant churners characteristics

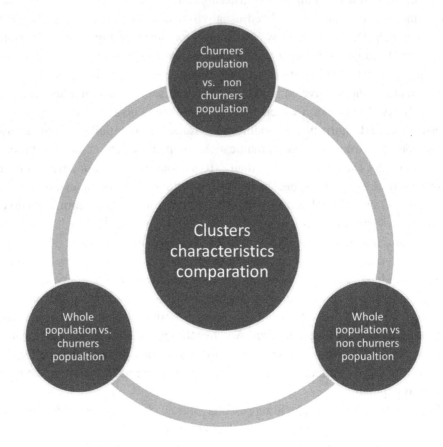

and clustering for developing churn model, things became more complex, especially taking in consider facts that exists sub variants of methods which can be applied for the same purpose.

Clustering as a segmentation tools in churn analysis area has variety of advantages, but also some of disadvantages due to fact that for applying algorithms like K-Mean clustering, analyst should determine in advance numbers of clusters. This could be problem because there is no objective ways to make assumptions about number of future clusters. Numbers of the clusters should be determined in iterative processes and by repeating algorithm on same data sample.

Self-organizing maps suffers from the same problem, because size of self-organizing map should be determined in advance. Regarding that, oversized map or to small map, could cause hiding significant patterns. That implies also iterative processes for finding optimal self-organizing map model. Methods like decision trees, which could be applied, as a toll for segmentation does not have similar characteristics like clustering methods, because it demands target variable. Due to fact that calculation of entropy as a toll fort the next split which has lot in common with attribute analysis process, would not provide results as a clustering methods. Clustering methods are based on distance (similarity) calculation and takes in account all disposable attributes in each calculation for each step. They do not need target variable in clustering process. However, decision tree is a great tool for finding dominant characteristics between clusters, and it often could be combined with clustering as a toll for finding it. Beside decision tree as a tool for finding dominant characteristics between clusters standards statistical methods could be used as well, often as additional toll after decision tree usage.

8.2.3 How to Build Time Dependent Models

Time component in churn solution development plays significant role. Previously described methods have very weak or insignificant connection dependent on time because they use snapshot situation at one specific point in time. This point has references to previous period (if we talk about observation period), or future (if we are talking about outcome period), but this element basically gives snapshot at specific period of time. Same thing is with the behavioral variables, which takes in consider specific behavior at specific time lag, but it is snapshot at specific period of time- observation point. By introducing time component into solution, it is possible to get much more realistic and precise picture what had happened, at which time and why at this specific time point or period. By observing outcome period in finding which clients committed churn during process of sample construction for predictive modeling we do no know does churn was intensive at beginning of outcome period, or it was more intensive at the end of outcome period. On the other hand answers on questions why it was intensive at some period even if we know when churn was higher or lower still stays unrevealed.

Time depending churn analytical models could be used for survival analysis purposes, or for temporal pattern recognition. Survival models give information about survival rates (of churners) during observed period of time, with their dominant factors. Cox regression and Kaplan Maier model are two commonly used methods for this purpose. Survival models are useful in length of outcome period determination, because it shows expected survival churners population rate before stability achievement. Higher churn rate than in stable zone for selected population is important because it implies deviations from the expected rates, which could be caused by some factors, which should be discovered. Spreading observation period deeper into stable zone could cause sample dilution. On the other hand survival models offer the answers which churner characteristics have strongest impact on survival rates.

Temporal pattern recognition relies on time series data mining methods. Time series data mining (temporal data mining) provides information about existing repetitive patterns within time series, seasonal oscillations, temporal patterns caused by clients/buyers/subscribers behavior and similar phenomenon. Recognition of repetitive patterns within time series, which could be related to customer buying habits (and putting it into relation with churn), could be element for better understanding nature of churn into existing portfolio. Often in churn modeling recognized types of customer behavior during period of time could be declared with some specific names like "weekend shoppers", "undecided TV watchers", "late evening buyers", "night callers" etc. Those declarations could be useful for profiling, and it also could be elements for attribute relevance calculation. Time variable/variables in comparison to static one demand additional analysis for finding patterns through declared period of time, and recognizes patterns could became elements for e.g. building predictive models. Time series also could be useful in customer segmentation by temporal characteristics, where recognized segments could be elements into predictive or other type of churn models.

Seasonal factors could also be valuable information in relation with customer habits.

For example, recognition that into retail portfolio exists buyers which into specific period of time stops buying activities because it goes to holidays, with relative precise evaluation about length of their buying inactivity could save company from wrong conclusion that they committed churn. It is especially important if we are talking about churn modeling for retail business and churn recognition in retail business. Time component is often neglected during in churn model development. It has great role on better understanding on churn nature. Fact is that customers could behave in different ways in different period of times regarding changes in conditions of service usage or changes on market. Recognition of key fact, which has strongest influence on customer behavior, is task of temporal data mining, as repetitive behavior at same periods of time or seasons as well. Behavioral variables could not be absolute substitute for temporal analysis, because behavior variables covers shorter time spans, and it is constructed by predefined hypothesis. Predefined hypothesis means that e.g. average duration of night calls in last six months is potentially important variable for churn detection. This approach sets time limits in given example on six month, and makes hypothesis about significant numbers of "night callers". Temporal data mining gives different opportunities. It searches for interesting temporal patterns, and it could be intensive weekend callers or buyers. Those patterns could be found on longer time series. It does not mean that usage of temporal data mining techniques exclude behavioral variables construction. It should complement each other and usage of temporal data mining could also be one of the elements, which could inspire construction of behavior variables. There is no guarantee that patterns will be find with usage of temporal data mining techniques within specific time series. In case of finding some interesting regularity it could be used as an element for profiling, or element for behavior variable construction. As it will be shown in one case study related to telecommunication case study into case study chapter, time series analysis could provide additional valuable information usable for profiling and for predictive model development. There is no prescribed way how to do that, it depends on current situation related to churn, and problem which we should solve. There are many different techniques for time series data mining. For time series data mining authors recommend usage of REFII model (Klepac, 2014).

REFII model is an authorial mathematical model for time series data mining. The main purpose of that model is to automate time series analysis, through a unique transformation model of time series. An advantage of this approach of time series analysis is the linkage of different methods for time series analysis, linking traditional data mining tools in time series, and constructing new algorithms for analyzing time series. It is worth mentioning that REFII model is not a closed system, which means that we have a finite set of methods. At first, this is a model for transformation of values of time series, which prepares data used by different sets of methods based on the same model of transformation in a domain of problem space. REFII model gives a new approach in time series analysis based on a unique model of transformation, which is a base for all kind of time series analysis. The advantage of REFII model in comparison with traditional time series mining is a possibility of analytical method chaining, direct usage of traditional data mining methods on time series, and constructing of new algorithms for non-standard problems in domain of time series data mining.

REFII model is also applicable in many different areas such as finance, medicine, voice recognition, face recognition and text mining. Idea of REFII model and some analytical possibilities will be shortly introduced within case study chapter.

8.2.4 How to Build Expert System

Expert systems for the churn modeling purposes are commonly used in situation when we want to calculate prospective customer value before applying other methods on most valuable customers and for the soft churn prediction. It also could be used in situations where we want to determine did customer committed or not hard churn in situation where we do not have contracts like in retail business. Usage of expert systems are not limited only on this topics, it could be valuable for early warning churn system development and other purposes related to churn where we should apply expert knowledge on some data. Prospective customer value calculation plays significant role in churn modeling. It assure concentration in modeling phase on most valuable customers and sample construction for predictive or segmentation purposes on most valuable customers only. This approach has variety of advantages. Let assume that thirty percent of customers contribute in eighty percent of profit and seventy percent of customers contribute in twenty percent of profit. If we have limited budget (and it is often the case) for churn mitigation purposes, it is logical that company want to spend those budget on most valuable customers. In presented hypothetical example focusing on most valuable customers with existing customers would be better strategy than spending it on whole portfolio, because efficiency from perspective of profitability will be worst. No one could make evaluation about those ratios before making calculation about prospective customer value, and one of disposable ways to make that calculation is usage of expert systems. One of described case studies in case study section gives detailed insight how to make expert system for prospective value calculation. After recognition which are the most valuable customers within portfolio, it is logical to concentrate only on them e.g. for predictive churn model development, because company is much more interested to keep them into portfolio, because it generates most of the profit. Form the other hand, taking in consider whole portfolio for predictive modeling purposes would cause in sample dilution, where because of higher number of less profitable, their characteristics could be recognized as significant for predictive churn model development. At the end in that case model could have great predictive power, and they would recognize potential future churner but mostly unprofitable one. Profitable customer characteristic in that case could become insignificant into model in comparison with unprofitable one because of their potential size. From this perspective prospective value calculation are extremely, often neglected step in process of modeling churn solution.

Soft churn detection is also area where expert systems could be usable. In situation where there is no exact indicator did churn had happened; it could be realized only on expert evaluation (knowledge). It is common situation in retail industry, when based on expert consumptions could be determined did customer committed churn (soft or hard) or not. If we are talking about using puzzles as a metaphor for building churn solution in that case piece of a puzzle could be using time series data mining to discover seasonal oscillations. Knowledge about seasonal decreasing in goods and services usage could be integrated into expert system on customer level for better prediction about churn in retail industry.

Expert systems also plays central role in churn early warning system development. It could be identified with soft churn detection models, but they have much wider scope than soft churn detection models. Sometimes they could have mutual characteristics of prospective value calculation, soft churn detectors, riskiness evaluator and other characteristics. Depending on which aspect is more interesting for the company, they have much of those characteristics. It means that early warning systems with primary scope on soft churn detection could also calculate prospective customer value, evaluates riskiness for each customer and calculates opportunity costs for each customer. For example if company sells paints, varnishes and supplies to car body painters it can evaluate customer value for each car body painter, does he committed or not soft churn, which is his riskiness regarding payments, and regarding existing grades does he ordered expected amount of supplies regarding ordered paint.

With this tool company could make segments e.g. customers with high prospective value, with low risk, high opportunity costs and high suspicious rate regarding soft churn, or customers with low prospective value, with low risk, low opportunity costs and middle suspicious rate regarding soft churn etc. For each segment company could apply different churn strategy or different marketing strategy.

Type of expert system which authors prefer for described purposes is fuzzy expert systems. Instead of expert systems usage for some purposes like early warning systems, soft churn detection, and Bayesian networks could also be used. Bayesian networks are not expert systems, but it allowed combining conditional probabilities (which could be extracted from the data or on expert way) with expert knowledge regarding influences between categories.

8.3 FINDING OPTIMAL CHURN SOLUTION

"All the ways leads to Rome", it is the same for finding optimal churn solution. There are many ways how to achieve aims regarding final churn solution and there is no prescribed cookbook for each situation because there is to many situations and variations of the situations, which cannot be covered within any book. Presented data mining techniques are pieces of the puzzles which analyst should apply depending on current situation, disposable data sources and company specifics. Finding out that usage of some method as a part of final solution does not give the right answer, or it should not be done in that way is not failure. It should be observed as cognition that it is not appropriate way for making that specific churn solution. That implies finding another solution, which will be applicable for defined targets. Presented data mining methods should not be percept as only methods appropriate for building churn solutions. They are presented regarding authors experience. Also, way how the methods are ordered within text, or were used through some example should not be an only way for their usage. Each project is challenge for itself and same method could be used in many different ways for achieving aim, depending on industry, disposable data, company specifics and other factors.

REFERENCES

Berson, Smith, & Therling. (1999). *Building data mining applications for CRM*. New York: McGraw-Hill.

Corr, J. (2008). *Why could 'frustration churn' be costing you over 15% of the potential value of your business?* London, UK: Close Quarter Limited.

Kim, P., Park, M.-C., & Jeong, D.-H. (2004). The effects of customer satisfaction and switching barriers on customer loyalty in Korean mobile telecommunication services. *Telecommunications Policy, 28*(2), 145–159. doi:10.1016/j.telpol.2003.12.003

Klepac, G. (2014). Data Mining Models as a Tool for Churn Reduction and Custom Product Development in Telecommunication Industries. In P. M. Vasant (Ed.), *Handbook of Research on Novel Soft Computing Intelligent Algorithms: Theory and Practical Applications*. Hershey, PA: IGI Global.

Klepac, G., & Panian, Ž. (2005). *Poslovna inteligencija*. Masmedia Zagreb.

Madden, Savage, & Coble-Neal. (1999). Subscriber churn in the Australian ISP market. *Information Economics and Policy, 11*(2), 195–207.

Parks Associates. (2003). *US Mobile Market Intelligence August*. Author.

Silber. (1997). Combating the churn phenomenon. *Telecommunications, 31*(10), 77–81.

Tsiptsis, K., & Chorianopoulos, A. (2010). *Data Mining Techniquies in CRM: Inside Customer Segmentation*. Wiley. doi:10.1002/9780470685815

Whitten, I. H., & Frank, T. (2005). Data Mining. Elsevier.

KEY TERMS AND DEFINITIONS

Churn Solution: Holistic solution for solving churn problems, which can contain numerous different data mining techniques.

Expert Models: Model based on expert knowledge. It is mostly expert system.

Predictive Models: Models, which has task to predict future, state of aim variable regarding values on input variables.

Time Dependent Models: Models that are time related, or has task to predict some state regarding temporal component.

Chapter 9
Measuring Predictive Power

ABSTRACT

This chapter explains common methods in evaluating model predictive power. If the goal is defined as finding the most important/risky customers, there are many different ways using the available resources. Analysts measure accuracy and look for answers. It is obvious that two different analysts would provide different models; however, what both are looking for is an adequate level of accuracy. That means that analysts have freedom while looking for models, but the final model needs to be accurate and usable for decision making. No matter what the final model is, the most important factors before the final results are confirmed are the model relevance tests. One can, for example, create several models with the same goal but using different methods or methodologies. The one with highest accuracy level is the best one. It is important to point out that models do not have to be based only on one method but can combine several methods at the same time.

9.1 PRINCIPLE 80:20

Looking for ideal environment for prediction, aim is not to deal with individuals but to form a foundation able to deals with groups or behavior in wider perspective. In the light of any individual memory of previous events, prediction models have to deal with wide number of attributes in databases which are related to specific group or segment and are created by combining data from individuals. We can say that

DOI: 10.4018/978-1-4666-6288-9.ch009

environment for prediction, and also churn, is really a collective „memory" created from processed data patterns and „conclusions" made with appliance of analytical methods. While creating and using model, analyst is trying to mimic human cognitive processes. We can use simple equation to express this:

Knowledge = Memory + Intelligence (1)

In order to discover knowledge, we need history (data, memory) and intelligence based on methods and models. While using methods with historic data, we gain knowledge which will be further used in business practice. For any model but especially more complex ones, it is always a question how efficiently we can predict future events by looking at the past ones. Researches so far shows that, especially in modern fast changing economy, historic data has to be used (we need to learn from past) however with constant re-evaluation of added value research is bringing to table for prediction of the future. We can explain process of modeling by looking into future using analytical rear-view made of databases and intelligent computational methods.

Not like traditional history analysis, analytic modelling is also based on iterative process of building models known as iterative or spiral approach. Usage of this approach, allows constant model improvement and development together with errors minimization using back propagation principle. Right after first prediction, future became past and system can learn on its errors, understanding problems in previous predictions and making every new iteration step more accurate and efficient.

If we are analyzing these kind of models and its capabilities understanding its own errors, we need to point out that human help is still dominant factor for efficiency because although those systems are more and more advanced every day, they are still no table to completely auto adapt and autocorrect on their own. Historic data are not useful only for prediction but also when we want to analyze market segments or specific clients.

Historic data can help us in situations when we are looking for answers on questions like:

- Why sales trend is decreasing?
- What causes decreasing trend?
- What to do to improve sales?
- What to do to decrease cost level?
- If we decrease price on specific product, can we improve its sales volume?
- Which customers are most likely to end relationship and move for competitor's offer?

If we take a look at those questions, we can find that human cognitive process also look for historic data while looking for conclusions. In churn analysis we are looking for same methodology. It is obvious that using analytical methods we can find answers for many questions, for process to be efficient those question needs to be structured in very clear way. Problem needs to be defined very precisely while question needs to be structured in a way which will give clear and undoubtful guidelines to analyst who will build final model. We can illustrate this with simple question quiz: what is 25=? Possible solutions are illustrated in Table 1.

Table is showing several of many possible solutions, however it is important to understand that all of those are correct. With mathematical expression 25=? as goal, that goal can be achieved in many, many ways. So, even we have very precisely and clear goal we are still facing indefinite number of possible correct solutions. Unlike simple math, business problems are sometimes harder to express in similar simple way however we can illustrate an example.

If we define our goal with question „*who are our most risky customers and why?*" there are *n* different ways towards answers using available resources. Analyst is starting from goal and is building analytical models, is measuring accuracy and is looking for answers. It is obvious that two different analysts would provide different models, however what both are looking for is adequate level of accuracy. That means that analysts have freedom while looking for model but final model needs to be accurate and usable for decision making. Over time analysts are developing unique styles how any of them is building a model based on knowledge, experience, and field of research. No matter of final model, most important factor before final results are confirmed is model relevance tests. We can, for example, create several models with same goal but using different methods or methodologies. As best one, we will use one with highest accuracy level. It is important to point out that models do not have to be based only on one method but can combine several methods at the same time. Therefore, we need to manage ways to measure accuracy and control data

Table 1. Ways to calculate 25

25=?
5*5
5+20
10+15
27-2
(3+2)*5
0.1+24.9
...

Figure 1. Models evaluation chart (Sayad, 2014)

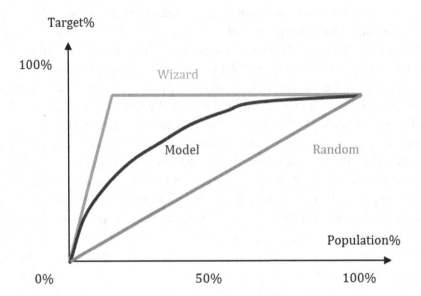

samples if available sources very big. No matter if used for simplifying or accuracy test, sampling is crucial and needs deep understanding (Figure 1).

After model is developed by learning on historic data used to train model, testing is implemented on different sample from same source used only to test accuarcy of new model. It is common that original data sample is partitioned in 80%: 20% ratio while 80% part is used to train model and remaining 20% are used to test model accuracy.

Very popular method to train model accuracy (classification, prediction models) is cumulative Gains curve which clearly shows model accuracy. Gain or lift is a measure of the effectiveness of a classification model calculated as the ratio between the results obtained with and without the model. Gain and lift charts are visual aids for evaluating performance of classification models. Gain or lift chart evaluates model performance in a portion of the population (Sayad, 2014) (Figure 2).

In simple words, if we are estimating accuracy level of prediction model by building decision tree to find out which customers will follow defined goal. Decision tree was built on 80% part of data sample and trained for results. To establish accuracy level, remaining 20% of data sample was used to look for all buyers who should buy product A.

The lift chart shows how much more likely we are to receive positive responses than if we contact a random sample of customers. For example, by contacting only

Measuring Predictive Power

Figure 2. Gain chart, prediction model accuracy (Sayad, 2014)

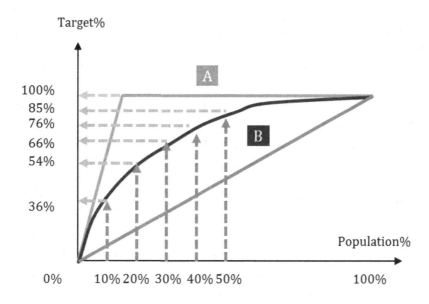

10% of customers based on the predictive model we will reach 3 times as many respondents, as if we use no model (Figure 3).

Role of manager in this process is to monitor process and goals. If we don't structure goals in right way, aligned with business practice and company strategy, we can't expect any improvement but only waste of time and resources. Generally,

Figure 3. Lift chart, prediction model accuracy (Sayad, 2014)

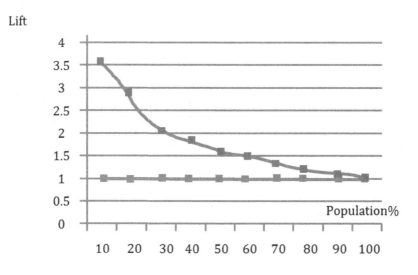

we can conclude that with structured and understandable goals business intelligence can reach answers very easily unlike daily business without any analytics. However, we need to be careful and follow best practice step by step to avoid stepping into dead ends (Figure 4).

Looking in terms of churn management us sholud look for efficiency and time consumig issues of complex data mining. While using data mining methods for business purposes we always have to sacrifice some data by choosing adequate level of aggregation. Therefore, certain amount of data will always be excluded therefore we always need to understand how not to excule important data. In similar way we need to be very aware of time consuming factor. To prepare, execute and sometimes combine methods it takes significant time. By choosing the right questions instead of looking for answers we should move towards efficient resource utilization.

Other thing that had to be pointed out is working with groups and samples. It this book churn analysis is explained in all its details together with sampling technique no matter if it was used to simplify available customer data or to create groups of customers with similar characteristics in order to execute more efficient analysis. While sung sampling techniques, we should pay attention of how samples are extracted. Most popular software packages have automatized procedures how to separate data and use different samples for analysis and model accuracy test. Analyst should always be aware, even while using out-of-the-box functions in software packages, of data quality, size and possible limitations of data and samples (for example, some dominant values can significantly change sample characteristic).

Figure 4. Corresponding data for gain and lift chart (Sayad, 2014)

Score Table			Sorted by Score			Gain Table			Lift Table	
Target	**Score**		**Target**	**Score**		**Count%**	**Target%**		**Count%**	**Lift**
0	235		1	880		10	36		10	3.6
1	724		1	724		20	54		20	2.7
1	556		1	676		30	66		30	2.2
0	345		1	556		40	76		40	1.9
0	480		0	480		50	85		50	1.7
1	676		0	368		60	90		60	1.5
0	195		0	345		70	94		70	1.3
1	880		0	235		80	98		80	1.2
0	368		0	195		90	100		90	1.1
...	...		...	...		100	100		100	1

9.2 ROC CHART

The ROC chart is similar to the gain or lift charts in that they provide a means of comparison between classification models (UNMC, n.d.). The ROC chart shows false positive rate (1-specificity) on X-axis, the probability of target=1 when its true value is 0, against true positive rate (sensitivity) on Y-axis, the probability of target=1 when its true value is 1. Ideally, the curve will climb quickly toward the top-left meaning the model correctly predicted the cases. The diagonal red line is for a random model. This type of graph is called a Receiver Operating Characteristic curve (or ROC curve.) In other words we can explain it as a plot of the true positive rate against the false positive rate for the different possible cut points of a scenario.

An ROC curve demonstrates several points (UNMC, n.d.):

- It shows the tradeoff between sensitivity and specificity (any increase in sensitivity will be accompanied by a decrease in specificity),
- The closer the curve follows the left-hand border and then the top border of the ROC space, the more accurate the test,
- The closer the curve comes to the 45-degree diagonal of the ROC space, the less accurate the test,
- The slope of the tangent line at a cut point gives the likelihood ratio (LR) for that value of the test,
- The area under the curve is a measure of text accuracy (Figure 5).

While using this type of analysis, accuracy of the test depends on how well the test separates the group being tested into those with and without increasing likehood to churn. Accuracy is measured by the area under the ROC curve.

At this point, you may be wondering what this area number really means and how it is computed. The area measures discrimination, that is, the ability of the test to correctly classify those with and without likehood to churn. Consider the situation in which customers are already correctly classified into two groups. You randomly pick one from first group and one from the second group and do the test on both. The customer with the more abnormal test result should be the one from the group likely to churn. The area under the curve is the percentage of randomly drawn pairs for which this is true (that is, the test correctly classifies the two customers in the random pair).

Area under ROC curve is often used as a measure of quality of the classification models. A random classifier has an area under the curve of 0.5, while AUC for a perfect classifier is equal to 1. In practice, most of the classification models have an AUC between 0.5 and 1 (Figure 6).

Figure 5. ROC chart, example (Sayad, 2014)

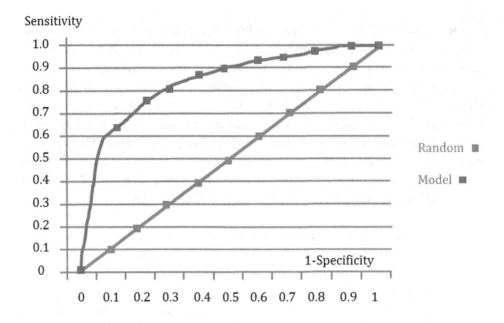

Figure 6. Area Under the Curve (AUC), example (Sayad, 2014)

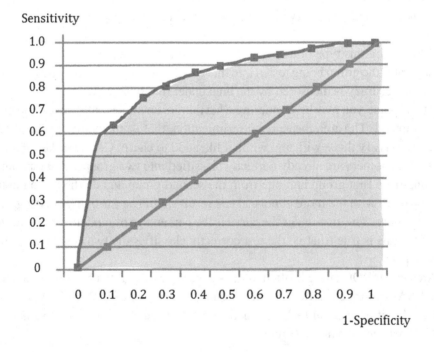

An area under the ROC curve of 0.8, for example, means that a randomly selected case from the group with the target equals 1 has a score larger than that for a randomly chosen case from the group with the target equals 0 in 80% of the time. When a classifier cannot distinguish between the two groups, the area will be equal to 0.5 (the ROC curve will coincide with the diagonal). When there is a perfect separation of the two groups, i.e., no overlapping of the distributions, the area under the ROC curve reaches to 1 (the ROC curve will reach the upper left corner of the plot). Simply put, the area under the curve (AUC) of a receiver operating characteristic (ROC) curve is a way to reduce ROC performance to a single value representing expected performance.

To explain with a little more detail, a ROC curve plots the true positives (sensitivity) vs. false positives (1 − specificity), for a binary classifier system as its discrimination threshold is varied. Since, a random method describes a horizontal curve through the unit interval, it has an AUC of 0.5. Minimally, classifiers should perform better than this, and the extent to which they score higher than one another (meaning the area under the ROC curve is larger), they have better expected performance.

You may be wondering where the name "Receiver Operating Characteristic" came from. ROC analysis is part of a field called "Signal Detection Theory" developed during World War II for the analysis of radar images. Radar operators had to decide whether a blip on the screen represented an enemy target, a friendly ship, or just noise. Signal detection theory measures the ability of radar receiver operators to make these important distinctions. Their ability to do so was called the Receiver Operating Characteristics. It was not until the 1970's that signal detection theory was recognized as useful for interpreting medical test results (Taper, 1999).

9.3 KOLMOGOROV-SMIRNOV CHART

The Kolmogorov-Smirnov test (KS-test) tries to determine if two datasets differ significantly (CSBSJU, n.d.). The KS-test has the advantage of making no assumption about the distribution of data. Note however, that this generality comes at some cost: other tests (for example Student's t-test) may be more sensitive if the data meet the requirements of the test. In a typical experiment, data collected in one situation (let's call this the „non like to churn" group) is compared to data collected in a different situation (let's call this the „churned" group) with the aim of seeing if the first situation produces different results from the second situation. If the outcomes for the treatment situation are "the same" as outcomes in the control situation, we assume that our activities in fact causes no effect. Rarely are the outcomes of the two groups identical, so the question arises, how different must the outcomes be?

Statistics aim to assign numbers to the test results, reject the null hypothesis if probability is "small".

Kolmogorov-Smirnov chart measures performance of classification models. More accurately, K-S is a measure of the degree of separation between the positive and negative distributions. The K-S is 100 if the scores partition the population into two separate groups in which one group contains all the positives and the other all the negatives. On the other hand, If the model cannot differentiate between positives and negatives, then it is as if the model selects cases randomly from the population. The K-S would be 0. In most classification models the K-S will fall between 0 and 100, and that the higher the value the better the model is at separating the positive from negative cases.

The following example shows the results from a classification model. The model assigns a score between 0-1000 to each positive (target) and negative (non-target) outcome (Figure 7, Figure 8).

The process of assigning numbers to results is not straightforward. There is no fairy god simple way to tell if results are evidence for or against an effective activity. One simple strategy you might have thought of is surely wrong, try lots of different statistics and picks the one that reports want you want. Every statistical test makes "mistakes", tells you the action is effective when it isn't or tells you the treat-

Figure 7. K-S chart, example (Sayad, 2014)

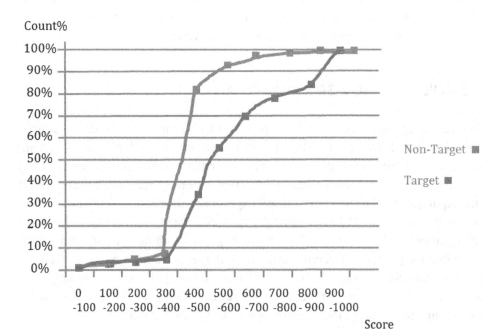

Figure 8. Corresponding data for K-S chart (Sayad, 2014)

Score Range		Count		Cumulative Count		
Lower	Upper	Target	Non-Target	Target	Non-Target	K-S
0	100	3	62	0.5%	0.8%	0.3%
100	200	0	23	0.5%	1.1%	0.6%
200	300	1	66	0.7%	2.9%	1.3%
300	400	7	434	2.0%	7.7%	5.7%
400	500	181	5627	34.3%	81.7%	47.4%
500	600	112	886	54.3%	93.3%	39.0%
600	700	83	332	69.1%	97.7%	28.6%
700	800	45	63	77.1%	98.5%	21.4%
800	900	29	37	82.3%	99.0%	16.7%
900	1000	99	77	100.0%	100.0%	0.0%

K-S

K(0.95) = 6.0%
K(0.99) = 7.1%

ment is not effective when it is effective. These mistakes are not user-errors, rather the statistical tool (properly used and applied to real data) simply lies some small fraction (say a few percent) of the time. Therefore if you apply many different statistical tests you are very likely to get at least one wrong answer (CSBSJU, n.d.).

Statisticians, of course, try to make statistics that only rarely (say 5% of the time) lie. In doing this they tune their tests to be particularly good at detecting differences in common situations. Used in those situations the tests may be the best possible tests. Used in different situations the tests may lie outrageously. This is important because users of statistical tests often do not know if their dataset meets the criteria intended by the creator of the statistical test (CSBSJU, n.d.).

9.4 STABILITY INDEX

Any random variable, by definition, has a distribution, which might be discrete or continuous based on the set of values it admits and independent copies mean independent draws from the distribution of X, i.e. X1, X2... Fx. Stable distributions are called so because a sum such as the one you described, leaves the shape of the distribution unchanged (Feller, 1971).

In probability theory, the stability of a random variable is the property that a linear combination of two independent copies of the variable has the same distribution, up to location and scale parameters. The distributions of random variables having this property are said to be "stable distributions". Results available in probability theory show that all possible distributions having this property are members of a four-parameter family of distributions. The importance in probability theory of "stability" and of the stable family of probability distributions is that they are "attractors" for properly normed sums of independent and identically distributed random variables. Important special cases of stable distributions are the normal distribution, the Cauchy distribution and the Lévy distribution.

The central limit theorem and infinite divisibility are properties associated with the normal distribution. The stable distributions extend family of distributions to other distributions that have the infinite divisibility property and a limit theorem called the stable law. Convergence of averages to the normal distribution requires certain properties of the random variables. For illustration, we shall just consider the simple case where the random variables are independent and identically distributed. In that case the central limit theorem holds under mild conditions. First, the variance must exist and, second, any moment slightly higher than the 2nd moment must exist. Now distributions that do not have a finite variance and even some that don't have a finite mean will still have their independent sums properly normalized converge to one of the stable distributions. The stable distributions are indexed by a parameter alpha that can be >0 but <=2. The index 2 corresponds to the normal distribution.

For churn analysis purposes we have to be aware of stability related to understanding of data sample that is available. Analyst needs to know more of specific field and widely understand business implications on history (of company, of data sample) but also present in order to efficiently predict future (Nolan, 2000).

REFERENCES

CSBSJU. (n.d.). Retrieved from http://www.physics.csbsju.edu/stats/KS-test.html

Heuer, R. J., & Pherson, R. H. (2010). *Structured Analytic Techniques for Intelligence Analysis*. Washington, DC: CW Press College.

Kirkman, T. W. (1996). *Statistics to Use*. Retrieved from http://www.physics.csbsju.edu/stats/KS-test.html

Larose, D. T. (2005). *Discovering Knowledge in Data: An Introduction to Data Mining*. New York: John Wiley &Sons Inc. doi:10.1002/0471687545

Larose, D. T. (2006). *Data mining methods and models*. New York: John Wiley &Sons Inc.

Mannila, H., & Hand, D. (2001). *Principles of Data Mining*. The MIT press.

Mršić, L. (2005). *Appliance of data mining methods in textile retail.* (Master of Science Thesis). Faculty of Economic and Business, Zagreb, Croatia.

Mršić, L. (2012). *Decision support model in retail based on unique time transformation method (REFII) and Bayesian logic.* (Doctoral Thesis). Faculty of Humanities and Social Sciences, Zagreb, Croatia.

Nolan, J. (2000). *Information on Stable Distributrions.* Retrieved from http://academic2.american.edu/~jpnolan/stable/stable.html

Sayad, S. (2014). *Model Evaluation – Classification.* Retrieved from http://www.saedsayad.com/model_evaluation_c.htm

Taper, T. G. (1999). *Interpreting Diagnostic Tests.* University of Nebraska Medical Center. Retrieved from http://gim.unmc.edu/dxtests/roc3.htm

UNMC. (n.d.). Retrieved from http://gim.unmc.edu/dxtests/Default.htm

KEY TERMS AND DEFINITIONS

Gain Chart/Lift Chart: *Gain* and lift *charts* are visual aids for evaluating performance of classification models.

Kolmogorov-Smirnov (K-S) Chart/Test: Nonparametric test for the equality of continuous, one-dimensional probability distributions that can be used to compare a sample with a reference probability distribution (one-sample K–S test), or to compare two samples (two-sample K–S test), Kolmogorov–Smirnov statistic quantifies a distance between the empirical distribution function of the sample and the cumulative distribution function of the reference distribution, or between the empirical distribution functions of two samples.

ROC Curve/ROC Chart: Receiver Operating Characteristic curve (or ROC curve) is a plot of the true positive rate against the false positive rate for the different possible cutpoints of a diagnostic test.

Stability Index: Index which shows degree of stability within some system.

Chapter 10
Churn Model Development, Monitoring, and Adjustment

ABSTRACT

This chapter is based on the fact that the finalization of the model building stage is the beginning of the periodic monitoring and redesigning stage. The churn solution should be adopted by market changes, internal company policy changes, portfolio structure changes, and other factors. The chapter gives answers about monitoring frequency and techniques with which the company could realize when to change into the existing churn solution. Another important topic covered in this chapter is "what if" analysis techniques, how to make scenarios for future churn trends regarding planned changes while taking in consideration the current state of the existing portfolio. The chapter ends with business strategy creation based on revealed knowledge from the churn solution and explains the importance of cooperation between business sectors and analysts in all stages of churn solution development from planning and realization to usage.

DOI: 10.4018/978-1-4666-6288-9.ch010

10.1 CHURN MODEL DEVELOPMENT

Developed churn solution is a result of current portfolio state. It is unrealistic to expect that developed solution will be usable, predictive or reliable without periodical redesign. Changes in market conditions, implies changes on developed churn solution. To achieve this aim it is prescribed to make periodic validation of existing solution, and in case that it shows poor performance it should be recalibrated or redesigned. Due to different potential changes in the market, competitor's movement, macroeconomic changes or other factors, developed churn solution could become inappropriate for function for which it was made. To be aware is developed churn solution is still valid or it needs recalibration or redevelopment, it should be periodically validated. There is no rule how often validation should be done, but there is simple rule that turbulent markets needs more frequent checks on developed models than steady markets. This trend became obvious in situation when new competitor enters into market, and churn solution is one of the instruments for having control what is going on into existing portfolio due to amended market condition, where changes could be very often and invisible without deeper data analysis.

Each type of the developed data mining models, which makes final churn solution, could be stricken by market changes. Predictive models could lose their predictive power due to fact that some other type of customers and their behavior became more risky than at the previous period. It simply could be explained with the fact that competitors could target different market segments from company portfolio as a result of changing its market strategy. Changes in competitor's strategy will not cause loss of predictive power in predictive models immediately; it will be relatively long process. It is important to realize those trends in early stage, which could give an opportunity to company which is threatened with those strategy to make right decisions on time and to calibrate and redesign existing churn models. If model validation is performed very often (e.g. monthly), these trends will not be so explicit, than if model validation is performed less often. Frequent validation performing assures early warning systems recognition. Changing in competitors strategy could also affect on developed segmentation models, prospective customer values and all other developed models, which are integral part of, churn solution. Regarding all that facts it is important to perform periodic validation process, which assures solution, which is applicable for current market situation.

Frequent validation process is welcomed, but problem is that within short time spans there could be too few sample elements for analysis, which will capture new trends into portfolio. One of the technique is using part of period on which model was developed (most recent one) to achieve reliable data sample. This technique has a weakness, because it does not captures real recent sample only, it combines it with part of the sample on which mode was developed. Mitigating circumstance is that it takes most recent on periods and it shows real picture in current portfolio state. As mentioned before, some of the tools which analyst has in performing validation process (mostly for predictive models) are:

- ROC curve
- Kolmogorov- Smirnov test
- Stability index

With applying ROC curve and Kolmogorov-Smirnov test on recent sample for existing predictive models it is possible to realize does model lost in predictive power or not. Also, it is possible to monitoring trends of the model in predictive power, does it loose it power as time goes by or it is evident some different type of trend. Continuous losing in predictive power of the model implies evident changes in churner's portfolio structure. It could be early warning signal for significant changes in market which could be caused by competitors activities or because some other reasons. It does not mean that predictive model should lose it predictive power in way that it is unusable. Predictive model could still have great predictive power, but fact that it continuously loses its power implies that obviously some other characteristics of churners became much more significant. For finding out what is the reason for that, it is recommended to repeat attribute relevance analysis (Weight of evidence, Information Value). Regarding satisfying predictive power, for sure it would not be dramatically changes in results, but indications of rising trends which causes predictive power drop will be visible. Regarding those trends, company can make or redesign churn strategy for further period. It also can put focus on revealed (now relatively weak) indicators, especially on periodic validations to reject or accept some hypothesis about market changes, competitor's new strategy, or macroeconomic influence on existing portfolio. Usage of Weight of evidence and Information Value measures, could also be useful during validation process, even churn solution does not contain predictive model. By applying described methods, company could recognize mentioned trends, churners profile, their motivators, behavior, and changes in them.

Stability index is another great tool for recognizing changes in portfolio structure (churners structure). It could be used in combination with predictive models, where some classification regarding churn probability exists, and portfolio is categorized within churn probability by binned probability scales. In that case it is common way how stability index could be applied. In case where predictive model is not part of the churn solution, stability index could be applied on some other categories/groups like clusters from self-organizing maps, or prospective customer values expressed as categories from e.g. fuzzy expert system. Stability index shows potential layering within recent sample (most fresh one) and existing portfolio.

It is important to mention few very important facts, which could cause misunderstanding during validation process and potentially wrong conclusions:

- New clients attracted with the new campaigns could have great influence on stability, especially if company changes in marketing strategy and it can have influence on predictive models power drop. This possibility also should be examined during validation process.
- New clients attracted by recent campaigns by default has less probability to commit churn, or churn can be motivated by other factors (finishing probation period etc.). It is important to examine which new volume of the new clients should be included into validation process.
- It is important to keep logic as it was applied during model development for the sample construction (especially for predictive models), because it guarantees continuity and same logic for validation process, as for development process. In case of breaking continuity of sample development, and model construction, it is potentially danger that company will make comparison between two different concepts, which can cause wrong conclusions.
- It is important to keep in mind that churn models are used, developed and applied with one main purpose, to stop it as much as possible. Regarding that fact company acts on existing portfolio, and sometimes predictive power drop could be result on company active churn stopping policy. One of the possible solutions regarding that fact is statistically significant subsample exclusion, on which company will not try to minimize churn rate. Predictive power measurement could be performed on this sample. By applying described methods, company could have clear picture about model reliability.
- Survival models are great tools for monitoring churn trends and their characteristics. It should be mandatory part of each validation process, because it can show trends and main characteristics, which has influence on those trends.

There are numerous techniques for the validation sample construction. If we are talking about predictive model validation, window-slicing technique could be applied for outcome period determination and observation period as well. The art is to find optimal frequency of the validation with data sample, which will be enough representatives for showing changes into existing portfolio from perspective of the churn.

10.2 HOW MUCH MONITORING AND ADJUSTMENT IS ENOUGH?

As it was already mentioned, there is no prescribed frequency for monitoring and adjustment existing churn solution. It depends on market instability, changes in company strategies regarding marketing penetration, or competitors market activities. On extremely turbulent markets, monitoring should be done almost monthly, and some expectable frequency for monitoring on average turbulent markets is quarterly monitoring. Depending on current results and observe trends in last period company could make decision about more or less frequent need for monitoring of existing churn solution. Signal that something is going on the market and that there is need for deeper investigation and most frequent monitoring could be comprehended on results from survival analysis, stability index calculation and predictive power calculation. Company expects falling trend in churn rate, or at least stabile same trend as it was in previous period. Rising trend after applying churn solution and after business decision, which should mitigate or stop this trend, is worrisome. It is reason for alarm that demands deeper investigation.

Survival models can give an instant answer on churn trend and which factor has the greatest influence on this trend. It should be always first element for monitoring churn trend. Losing predictive power in predictive model (if churn solution contains one) is not big problem, because models could be calibrated and predictive power could not be lost in short period that predictive model is useless. Continuous loss of predictive power shows on going changes within portfolio and changes in churner's population. If predictive power loosing is in correlation with falling churner rate l it could be good sign, because implies good trends regarding churn for the company. Worst-case scenario could be predictive power losing in combination with rising churn trend. It implies some unpredictable situations within portfolio/market.

Most effective way for realizing structural changes within churner and portfolio structure is stability index calculation. In situation where predictive model exists, it could be applied on probability bins, which is based on probability scale. It also could be applied on variables which were recognized as most predictive during attribute relevance analysis process, customer prospective value categories, segments which were recognized by clustering algorithms or similar results which is integral part of the churn solution.

Stability index is calculated as it is shown in following formula:

$$Si = \sum_{i=1}^{n} \left(\%Actual\_curn_i - \%Expected\_churn_i \right) * \ln\left(\frac{\%Actual\_churn_i}{\%Expected\_churn_i} \right) \tag{1}$$

where S_i is stability index, index i...n represents observed categories (e.g. probability bins based on probability scale or other categories). Actual churn percentage represents churn percentage for observed period (current quarter or current month). Expected churn percentage, represents expected churn percentage based on previous periods (previous quarter or previous month).

Stable population has stability index less than 0,1. Values of stability index from 0,1 to 0,25 imply changes, which should be observed and analyzed (medium changes). Values of stability index greater than 0,25 implies significant changes within observed population. Table 1 gives an example of stability index calculation.

As it is visible from stability index value of 0.0619, it is stable population.

For the stable population especially when there is no drop in predictive power (if churn solution contains one), there is no need for further investigation, and only churn rate for which is expected that it is less than in previous period should be checked. Stress in here is on business side, which should decide about further activities and disposable budget, and survival rate of customers with highest prospective customer values. If churn rate remains the same like in last period, it should be observe some other churn mitigation policy, more adequate for the current churner characteristics. Medium changes within churner's population, demands deeper investigation, which factors caused those movements. It could be announcement for necessity of churn stopping strategy change. For this purpose it is important to understand does few factors or more than few caused those trend. Are they in line with existing company policy regarding churn, and is their rising trend, which will cause greater instability in next period.

It is important to understand that strategy for churn stopping is made for portfolio in same state, where recognized churn factors and discovered relations implies finding adequate solutions throughout business decision and strategy. In situation

Table 1. Stability index calculation

Churn Probability Category	% Actual	% Expected	Actual-Expected	Actual/Expected	ln(A/E)	Index
A	7%	10%	-3%	0.70000	-0.356674944	0.010700248
B	19%	15%	4%	1.26667	0.236388778	0.009455551
C	21%	24%	-3%	0.87500	-0.133531393	0.004005942
D	33%	23%	10%	1.43478	0.361013346	0.036101335
E	38%	40%	-2%	0.95000	-0.051293294	0.001025866
F	59%	61%	-2%	0.96721	-0.03333642	0.000666728
Stability index	0.06195567					

where there is announcement of changes in recognized factors and relations, it is important to be aware of that fact and to see dominant directions in which those factors can go or can be replaced. Due to that fact it is important to prepare adequate new strategy or to have prepared strategy for period when it will became reality.

Significant changes within churner population demands deeper investigation, and readiness for significant changes into existing churn solution. It is not always the case, but significant changes in population could be important sign for evaluation of existing solution, as well as company policy regarding churn. Unstable population do not imply predictive power drop into predictive model if churn solution contain it. It can imply changes within churner structure, or even successful anti churns policy. But fact is that "something significantly changed" within churner population, and it demands deeper investigation and company anti churn policy evaluation due to fact of observed changes. Significant changes within population sometimes can leave existing churn solution unchanged after evaluation, but sometimes it can be trigger for thorough changes. It also can depend which methods were used for constructing final churn solutions. Some methods, which are very sensitive regarding portfolio structural changes like decision trees will always demand, redesign in case of population instability. More robust methods will be much more resistant on these changes.

Monitoring frequency and model adjustment is only one part of the story. All those activities should be supported and done in cooperation with business. It can have great influence on business strategy for churn reduction. Different market segments regarding different motivators, demands different approaches in convincing and motivation. Churn rate could be reduced, but for example it can show better results on clients with lower prospective customer value, and worst result on clients with higher prospective customer value. From rough analytical perspective solution shows good performance. If monitoring is done correctly it will show those facts, and it will imply changes in business strategy.

10.3 "WHAT IF" ANALYSIS

As it was already shown, it is important to realize what had happened in previous period regarding changes into portfolio from perspective of churn. On that way it is possible to create right strategy for churn reduction. Most advanced approach in churn reduction is advanced planning and scenario analysis. It means that company in advance regarding current state tries to predict future trend and regarding it analyze causes and effect for different scenarios. It puts in focus not only churn reduction but also future campaign planning with accumulated knowledge and projections how will future customers will behave regarding churn.

Portfolio observation could be done based on present or past portfolio state, in which we take in consideration real present or past portfolio situation. This approach could not give us an opportunity to do *what if* analysis. It is important for the business to evaluate consequences of present business decisions in the future. It means that managers should have an opportunity to decrease uncertainty during decision-making process. Uncertainty could be decreased by analyzing current and past portfolio state, but much more precise approach for that purpose is applying *what if* analysis on portfolio. This could be done by using weights on current portfolio. Weights have influence on portfolio volume and portfolio structure change. In case we discovered several crucial factors (during process of attribute relevance analysis) which have a great influence on portfolio risk we could do *what if* scenarios using weights. This means that we could virtually increase portfolio volume with portfolio members, which have riskiest characteristic. We could also make *what if* scenarios by changing portfolio structure in which risky parameters have greater influence on the same portfolio volume. Those two approaches depend on final aim of the analysis /business decision. If we would like to know, for example in case of new marketing campaign in which we would like to attract new portfolio members (customers) from some district, and our aim is to increase portfolio volume for 5%, how churn parameters will change in the future if we will have great devaluation, we will use weights which will virtually increase portfolio volume for 5% with increasing portfolio members which have described characteristics. If we would like to know for example how different portfolio structure in the same portfolio volume would have influence on churn (e.g. dominant younger population with from specific districts) we will use weights for changing portfolio structure.

Originally, weighting techniques were used for correcting survey errors, when respondent sample does not represent population well (Sarraf & Chen, 2007). Basic idea is to represent projected portfolio population in the future as population in surveys, which leads us to implying weighting techniques. For the mentioned purposes we could use two types of weighting techniques (Sarraf & Chen, 2007), (Maletta, 2006):

Scale weight calculation

$$w_i = \frac{P_i}{R_i} \tag{2}$$

where w_i is scale weight

P_i is population subgroup count regarding i
R_i is respondent subgroup count regarding i

i is subgroup index

Proportional weight calculation

$$w_p = \frac{Percent\_of\_population}{Percent\_of\_respondents} = \frac{\dfrac{P_i}{P_{total}}}{\dfrac{R_i}{R_{total}}} \tag{3}$$

where

w_p is proportional weight
P_i is population subgroup count regarding i
R_i is respondent subgroup count regarding i
P_{total} is total number of members in population
R_{total} is total number of respondents
i is subgroup index

Scale weight will be used in case when we would like to measure effects of structural and volume changes in portfolio.

Proportional weight will be used in cases when we would like to measure effects of structural changes on same portfolio volume.

Weighting could be applied in cases when we would like to monitor changes in portfolio caused by changes in a few critical variables. In case we would like to monitor changes in portfolio caused by changes in more than a few variables (e.g. five or more), it is very hard to create scenario analysis using weighting. It is possible, but very inconvenient and hard. In that case we can use Bayesian networks. From the experience point, described weighting techniques could be sufficient for those purposes of applying what if analysis, because we already know through attribute relevance analysis which variables have the biggest influence on portfolio credit risk. It is often not more than four variables, which could be covered by proposed weighting model. Sometimes, if we would like to construct complex model, which integrates numerous additional variables with key variables recognized through attribute relevance analysis, it is better to use Bayesian networks. Reasons for that lays in fact that Bayesian network are much more powerful to following synergy between variables than logistic regression, and Bayesian network models has modules for sensitivity analyze when we changes probability states of several variables.

Using Bayesian networks for what if analysis demands additional deeper analysis and using expert knowledge for creating qualitative *what if* churn models.

Table 2. Cross tabulation on data sample by district and age

		District			
		A	**B**	**C**	**D**
		Count	**Count**	**Count**	**Count**
Age	<= 35,0	68	28	85	27
	36,0 - 65,0	74	79	460	217
	66,0+	64	59	63	1

Typical scenario for *what if* analysis from the churn perspective is interest e.g. what will happened regarding churn rate if portfolio expands for 7% with middle aged population which lives in X district. Attribute relevance analysis shows which attributes are the most relevant for churn prediction. This implies that significant changes in portfolio structure regarding attributes with highest information values would surely have a reflection on churn rate. Let's suppose that two most significant attributes in observed portfolio are age and district. Let's suppose that we would like to investigate our portfolio regarding two most significant attributes, which have the biggest influence on churn. Using cross tabulation between mentioned variables regarding recognized significant subgroups within variables could do it. Result of the conducted analysis is visible in Table 2.

Let's suppose that we plan an acquisition of new customers and we would like to target potential customers taking into consideration increasing overall volume of portfolio, but also increasing number of members of observed subgroups in portfolio. As we know that district and age in our hypothetical case have the biggest influence on churn, we could make an assumption of portfolio volume increasing for approximately 55%. We would like to know whether churn rate in portfolio will be lower or higher if marketing campaign would be targeted on specific segments (see bold values in table 10.3, bold values mean changes in portfolio). Bold values in table 10.3 mean planned new values in portfolio segments. It is important to have in mind that we calculate churn rate risk on period, which is used in observation window, and it is usually one year. It means that we make a simulation to give an answer to the question: "Will new clients churn during one year (length of observation period) which became members of portfolio today" (Table 3).

If we would like to give an answer on that question we have to make weights on existing data sample (portfolio). In case we are interested in measuring risk parameters after increasing portfolio volume with altered portfolio structure we calculate scale weights. Using formula for weighting on table *scale weights* and table *proportional weights* we could calculate scale weights presented in Table 4.

Table 3. Cross tabulation on aimed population by district and age

		District			
		A	**B**	**C**	**D**
		Count	**Count**	**Count**	**Count**
Age	<= 35,0	68	56	85	54
	36,0 - 65,0	74	237	920	217
	66,0+	64	59	63	4

Table 4. Scale weights

		District			
		A	**B**	**C**	**D**
Age	<= 35,0	1	2	1	2
	36,0 - 65,0	1	3	2	1
	66,0+	1	1	1	4

In case we are interested in measuring churn parameters without increasing portfolio volume, and we would like to know if the portfolio credit risk will increase with the same volume, but with different portfolio structure we calculate scale weights. We could also calculate proportional weights presented in Table 5.

Churn rate calculation was made before and after each weighting (e.g. using created predictive churn model). Results are shown in Table 6.

Table 6 shows that if we increase portfolio with targeted segments, churn rate will decrease for 1%. Churn risk would fall by 1% in case we increase portfolio members with targeted characteristic (scale weights). Churn risk would fall by 1% in case that we have altered portfolio structure with targeted segments without increasing portfolio volume. For complete picture, it is important to take in consider other factors like expected prospective customer value for increasing portfolio, and expected profitability. In case of low profitability segment or expected low customer value

Table 5. Proportional weights

		District			
		A	**B**	**C**	**D**
Age	<= 35,0	0.644398	1.288795371	0.644397685	1.288795371
	36,0 - 65,0	0.644398	1.933193056	1.288795371	0.644397685
	66,0+	0.644398	0.644397685	0.644397685	2.577590742

market segment lower churn rate is not such successful business strategy if we are expect low income from those segment. Proposed methodology could be helpful for future portfolio risk planning. Depending on chosen strategy, given methodology gives an opportunity to simulate consequences of potential business decisions. Regarding that, it is possible to evaluate potential future portfolio risk, which is directly caused by planned future portfolio structure, or potential changes in market (altered macroeconomic conditions). Instead of an educated guess proposed model offers decreasing uncertainty for business decision purposes. Methodology based on weighting operates only with several most significant variables. It is sufficient for that kind of simulation and planning. Weighting methodology can be applicable for including microeconomic and macroeconomic variables into the model. Planning process can be completed with profitability parameters calculation while including market parameters as base for qualitative business decision. Depending on strategy and given calculation it is possible to find an optimal solution for risky but more profitable portfolio which can cover potential planned losses, or less risky, but less profitable portfolio if we prefer the conservative approach. When including more than several parameters into the model, Bayesian networks should be used. Bayesian networks can operate with numerous variables. Form perspective of practical experience, methodology based on weighting techniques can be sufficient for qualitative analysis, because this methodology puts focus on factors, which mostly contribute to portfolio churn sensitivity.

10.4 HOW TO EFFICIENTLY FOLLOW BUSINESS STRATEGY

Initial churn solution development is beginning of repetitive monitoring process for developed solution, with one scope, adequate and useful tool for churn reduction. Churn solution should be in line with business requirements and strategic aims. It also could be changed, not because of predictive power drop but because of changed business strategy. It means that existing solution could have good performance from perspective of predictive power or customer prospective value calculation, but due

Table 6. Churn rates before and after portfolio weighting

Churn rate (Original Portfolio)	Churn Rate (Weighted Portfolio) –Scale Weights	Change in Churn Rate– Scale Weights	Churn Rate (Weighted Portfolio) – Proportional Weights	Change in Churn Rate– Proportional Weights
26.4%	25.4%	-1%	25.4%	-1%

to strategic changes where some other market segments starts to became more in focus, existing solution should be adopted.

It is wrong approach where churn problematic is observed chiefly from perspective of data mining usage. Business needs are key factor in developing churn solution, and data mining methods should be instrumentality for achieving primary aim regarding churn reduction and detection. From the first sight it looks little bit strange that there could be more than unique aim in business churn modeling. Main goal always is to reduce churn rate. Things became more complicated when we are talking about environment and industry and market conditions in which we should achieve that primary goal.

It is not the same do we want to reduce churn rate in turbulent market, or stabile market. It is not the same do we prepare our company for forthcoming competition, or existing competitors became more aggressive on market, which has an influence on our churn rate. Also, it is important which client we want to keep, regarding their value and our budget for churn reducing activities. Specifics in different industries also plays crucial role in churn solution development. Different industries and different type of business has users with specifics, which should be taken into account during churn solution development. All those facts, conditions and changes leads us to conclusion that developed churn solution should be adopted due to current state of many factors. Existing solution monitoring is one of the ways for orientation what is the current situation (taking in consider all enumerated facts and more) regarding potential churners and is current solution adequate for the current market and other conditions.

Churn solutions based on data mining models does not offers instant solution how to reduce churn, it is a tool for decision makers which provides directions for churn solutions and reduce uncertainty in decision making. It is important due to those facts that those tools are adopted regarding current market conditions and in line with company strategic directions.

REFERENCES

Carrington, P. J., Scott, J., & Wasserman, S. (Eds.). (2005). *Models and Methods in Social Network Analysis*. Cambridge, UK: Cambridge University Press. doi:10.1017/CBO9780511811395

Coser, L. A. (1977). Masters of Sociological Thought: Ideas in Historical and Social Context (2nd ed.). New York, NY: Harcourt.

Engel, F. J., Blackwell, D. R., & Miniard, W. P. (1995). *Consumer Behavior*. The Dryden Press.

Feller, W. (1971). *An Introduction to Probability Theory and Its Applications* (Vol. 2). Wiley.

Freeman, L. C. (2004). *The Development of Social Network Analysis: A Study in The Sociology of Science*. Empirical Press Vancouver.

Godin, S. (2008, June 26). Loš stol. *Livingstone Magazine Croatia*, 72-73.

Klepac, G. (2010). Preparing for New Competition in the Retail Industry. In A. Syvajarvi, & J. Stenvall (Eds.), *Data Mining in Public and Private Sectors: Organizational and Government Applications* (pp. 245–266). Hershey, PA: Information Science Reference. doi:10.4018/978-1-60566-906-9.ch013

Klepac, G. (2013). Risk Evaluation in the Insurance Company Using REFII Model. In S. Dehuri, M. Patra, B. Misra, & A. Jagadev (Eds.), *Intelligent Techniques in Recommendation Systems: Contextual Advancements and New Methods* (pp. 84–104). Hershey, PA: Information Science Reference.

Klepac, G. (2014). Data Mining Models as a Tool for Churn Reduction and Custom Product Development in Telecommunication Industries. In P. M. Vasant (Ed.), *Handbook of Research on Novel Soft Computing Intelligent Algorithms: Theory and Practical Applications*. Hershey, PA: IGI Global.

Maletta, H. (2006). *Weighting*. Retreieved from Rayland Levesque's website: http://www.spsstools.net/Tutorials/weighting.pdf

Moreno, J. L. (1951). *Sociometry, Experimental Method, and the Science of Society*. Ambler, PA: Beacon House.

Sarraf, S., & Chen, D. (2007). *Creating weights to improve survey population estimates*. Paper presented at the INAIR 21st Annual Conference. Bloomington, IN.

Scott, J. (1987). *Social Network Analysis: A Handbook*. London: Sage Publications.

Simmel, G. (1971). How is Society Possible?. In *On Individuality and Social Forms*. Chicago, IL: University of Chicago Press.

Zhang, M. (2010). Social Network Analysis: History, Concepts, and Research. In *Handbook of Social Network Technologies and Applications*. New York, NY: Springer. doi:10.1007/978-1-4419-7142-5_1

KEY TERMS AND DEFINITIONS

Simulation: Process, which shows results after changing parameters into some system.

Stability Index: Index which shows degree of stability within some system.

Projection: Evaluation of system state after changing parameters or condition changing.

Weighting: Process of assigning weights.

Chapter 11
Churn Case Studies

ABSTRACT

This case study chapter brings two business cases in the domain of churn, both unique in many ways, combining almost all the topics covered inside book. The first business case presents a retail company facing new competitors and consequently preparing a customer-retention strategy. The case introduces the business environment in which the company was operating prior to the arrival of new competitors while the model is being devised for the purpose of preventing or at least buffering the churn trend as a reaction to the new competition. Development of an early warning indicator system based on data mining methods is also described as a support to the management in the early detection of both market opportunities and threats. The second business case describes the situation in a telecommunication company in the domain of churn prediction and churn mitigation. The churn project was divided into a few stages and is fully described in the chapter. The case explains how the company can decrease the churn rate and gives directions for better understanding of customer needs and behaviors.

11.1 INTRODUCTION

Churn modeling is complex process, which demands combination and chaining many data mining methods and cooperation with business for reaching analytical aims. Churn problem solving depends on current company market position, competitor's strength, customer's perception on company, future and current competitor's activities

DOI: 10.4018/978-1-4666-6288-9.ch011

and many other factors. It is rare situation that usage of one data mining model for churn solving problems will be enough. Fortunately/unfortunately today's existing data mining oriented software packages gives power to the user to make analysis on instant way. In that situation, it is enough from perspective of inexperienced user to connect input data table with some method, and some model for sure will be produced. This model will have "some plausible" predictive power and formally (if it is predictive churn model) that is all what should be done. Reality is different, because software a package often does not care about, attribute relevance analysis and other important things mentioned within book. From the user perspective it should not be done because "software and infrastructure is strong enough to operate with numerous attributes and data records". Final result of that approach is that nobody could approve that input data sample is adequate to business needs and aims. From the other hand it is hard to explain model background and does all relevant attributes entered into model, and does some attributes because of it strong correlation took control over the model. Model stability in near future is questionable as well as model usability. From inexperienced user perspective, everything is perfect, and first problems will be visible in next period when it will be late for corrections.

Right approach implies good understanding of business problem background. Those understanding leads to finding strategy for optimal solution by combining not only data mining methods but also making specific data preprocessing and derived variables creation for achieving best results. Often it is repeating process with two steps forward and one step backward until reaching optimal solution. Solution includes taking care and integrates stability into models, especially for "long term models", and reflection of business needs with referencing on portfolio, or part of portfolio, which is under examination. Automatic solutions, which could be realized through data mining oriented software packages, do not have answers on optimization of outcome and observation period and optimal sample construction. It is more business related problem, which is basis for qualitative model solution. Following two complex real case studies shows different business environment and different business needs related to churn problematic and their solutions. One case study is from retail business area, and another is from telecommunication business area. Both of them have churn problematic in common, but business needs and churn problematic has different character, as expectations from developed solution, which were used as input for business decisions. These two case studies explain importance of creativity and understanding business problems in different domains. Churn modeling is not only model development based on some data mining technique which has some input and output values, it should be custom made based upon specific business needs. It often demands careful data preparation and sampling, method chaining, and active inclusion persons involved in core business. Churn modeling is art of integration business needs, common sense, information technology and data mining methods for reaching optimal solution usable in churn mitigation and churn interruption.

Following two complex real case studies will illustrate that process.

11.2 CASE STUDY 1: PREPARING FOR NEW COMPETITION IN THE RETAIL INDUSTRY

A business case presents a retail company facing new competitors and consequently preparing a customer retention strategy. The business environment in which the company was operating prior to the arrival of new competitors can be described as a stable market. Bearing in mind the plans and marketing activities of a competitor retail chain and making use of the data mining methods a system is being devised for the purpose of preventing or at least buffering the churn trend. Development of an early warning indicator system based on data mining methods is also being described as a support to the management in early detection of both market opportunities and threats. Research in data mining could also be concentrated on applying existing data mining techniques to find the best solution regarding practical business problems in the public or private sector. Knowledge regarding how some business cases were solved using data mining techniques could contribute in a better understanding of the nature or data mining nature and help solve specific business issues (Klepac, 2010).

11.2.1 How to Fight with Competition

Trgovina is a wholesale and retail business, owning approximately thirty retail stores (supermarkets) across Croatia, as well as three wholesale stores whose main purpose is to provide goods to the retail stores, but also to sell goods to other legal persons in the retail and wholesale business. Trgovina deals in consumer goods and it owns a central transactional database (Oracle) system, integrating all stores. The main transactional data stored in the information system consist of data sets from each filled out invoice related to codes of goods sold (categorized in the system), quantities bought, time of issuing the invoice and all other legally relevant elements necessary for creating a turnover book. Two years ago, the aforementioned company started a loyalty cards program. Within the program, customers collected points and, having collected a certain number of points, they earned the right to buy products at discount prices and periodically they were awarded gifts depending on the number of points collected.

The customers were obliged to provide the following data into the loyalty card application form:

- Name and surname
- Full address
- Year of birth
- Family status (married or not)
- Number of children
- Education level
- Categorized hobbies (sport, arts…).

As a response to one competitor's plans to increase the number of its retail stores in a substantial number of regions where Trgovina's retail stores are present, the company has to increase the loyalty of existing customers and acquire new ones with the tendency of keeping them even in conditions when competition starts operating in the neighborhood of some of the existing Trgovina retail stores. The company is well aware of the fact that the initial strategy of its competitors to acquire business in a certain region involves attracting as many customers as possible and ensuring their long -term loyalty. It is expected that, in order to achieve this goal, the competition will be willing to invest a certain amount of money, resulting in very low and competitive prices, other benefits and a strategy aimed at targeted market segments. Based on the previous analyses, Trgovina has segmented its market and performed an analysis of typical profiles and behavior models for each market segment at the regional level. Since the onset of fierce market competition is inevitable, during which the competition will try to acquire and keep as many customers of other retail stores as possible, it is necessary to devise a strategy for keeping as many existing customers in given circumstances. On the one hand, it is obvious that Trgovina will have certain costs related to accomplishing this goal. In all probability, a number of customers will defect to the competition. It is of vital importance to distinguish which customers will go to the competition, i.e. it is crucial that the resources spent in keeping the existing customers are invested to keep the most important customers. The competition probably counts on the attractiveness factor which, multiplied by curiosity, is certainly on their side. Regardless of the loyalty level, it is very probable that a great number of customers loyal to Trgovina will make a certain number of purchases in the competitor's store, but the aim is to bring back as many customers as possible. This fact will probably significantly decrease Trgovina's income during the estimated maximum period of two months where competitors stake their ground in a new region. After the two months, a period of stabilization is expected mostly due to the planned analysis. An additional latent danger present in the described situation is the threat of potential long-term loss of customers; in this kind of a new market situation there is a continued danger of customer attrition. Such loss may be caused by well positioned competitors campaigns geared towards acquiring customers from the other retailers. On the other hand, the loss may be caused by the increase in the numbers of existing customers, which are dissatisfied with service provided, or the extreme differences in prices of some or most of the products offered on the shelves.

Due to this reason, it is necessary to develop a monitoring system primarily responsible for recording customer churn or stagnation of sales amount. Furthermore, it is necessary to make an estimated profile of a typical customer prone to buying Trgovina goods and to conduct the analysis prior to the opening of the competitors store as well as two months after the competitors store had been opened. With regard to the comparatively stable situation in the market over the last five years, the estimation of churn based on data from the previous period may be questionable, especially given that in most of the regions where Trgovina stores are located, no other large stores opened, with the exception of small shops which posed no competitive danger. In order to make a precise estimation of churn probability, it is possible to conduct classical market research on a sample of Trgovina's customers with the purpose of getting a clearer picture of possible churns after the opening of a competitor store.

11.2.2 Analysis Goals

The goals of the analysis have to be in line with the strategic goals. The main strategic goal is to retain existing customers, primarily the high quality ones. In accordance with this objective, certain activities will be planned with the purpose of motivating all customers (especially the highest quality customers) to increase their loyalty level and continue buying in the Trgovina store. A further strategic goal, observed from the defensive point of view, is to monitor the customers with the purpose of preventing long-term churn trends. These goals are common for data mining projects (Dresner 2008) (Berry 2000) (Berry 1997) (Faulkner (2003).

In accordance with the strategic goals, the first step of the analysis should encompass the evaluation of customers and their classification in a number of categories, in order to estimate the importance of customer to the company by segment. It was decided that only customers with loyalty cards would be included in the evaluation model, because they comprise 85% of all customers. Customers having no loyalty card are impossible to identify based on past transactions only. The obtained results shall yield the customer structure classified on the basis of their importance for the company. Taking into account the results, the following steps will be considering further analytical procedures with the aim of increasing customer loyalty and monitoring the customers during the period of entry of competition into the region with the purpose of maintaining the market share. The monitoring should serve as a decision support system for the decision makers in conditions when the competition exercises a more aggressive market approach. Since retail stores are dispersed throughout Croatia, the analyses shall encompass micro segments, i.e. the market shall be analyzed from the regional perspective. The idea is to keep as many existing customers, especially those who are of vital importance for the company, to acquire new customers if possible, and to prepare for the first wave of competitive campaigns using customer-related monitoring systems with the possibility of ad hoc analyses in case of massive customer churn that would serve as means of preventing those trends. Once the market has stabilized, the aims of analysis may have a proactive structure and be aimed at acquiring competitor's customers.

11.2.3 Conceptual Target Model Development

In literature there are numerous solution regarding churn analysis (Berry 2000) (Berry, 1997) (Namid, 2004). The presented case is specific because of expected churn trends, and the fact that it describes a different approach to problem solution. Firstly we need to recognize customers with high perceived customer value, and after that we should develop a churn monitoring system. The conceptual solution model consists of two basic segments. The first segment should evaluate customers on a regional basis using the scoring model. Customers from each region should be evaluated in several categories based on expert knowledge. In this manner better insight into customer behavior based on their importance to the company should be gained.

Since the goal of the company is to retain as many clients as possible (especially the most important ones) a strategy shall be devised based on the results of the analysis with the purpose of increasing customer loyalty. The competition will inevitably attract a certain number of customers, so the second segment of the solution model will focus on monitoring customer churn or stagnation of sales Trgovina retail stores. With regard to the stable market conditions in the past and almost negligible percentage of customer churn, which makes the analysis more difficult, a classical market research should be performed in the beginning with the aid of a market research agency. This research should provide answers to questions such as which market segments of existing customers of Trgovina stores on a regional basis would be prone to start buying from competition and under which conditions. As well as what would be their prime reasons for continuous buying in competitor's stores and what would motivate them to continue buying from the Trgovina retail stores.

All the aforementioned information could serve as a basis for devising a strategy for successful resistance during the period of competitor's intense and aggressive advertising campaigns at the time of their entering the market and to their attempts to win over the customers. Since it is almost certain that the competition shall constantly and suddenly undertake advertising activities with the aim of taking over a number of customers, a system of permanent monitoring should be developed with the purpose of early diagnosis of churn trends in certain market segments, with the possibility of analyzing their dominant characteristics. To this aim, the so-called survival models would be implemented. Having in mind that each future aggressive advertising campaign of the competition poses a threat of losing a number of customers, one should also note that this present an opportunity for conducting additional analyses which would help the Trgovina company to recognize the behavior of its customers and promptly react to reduce the consequences of future market actions of the competition. For example, if a sudden competitor's advertising campaign manages to win over a portion of customers having a common attribute, it is an outcome which Trgovina may use to its advantage in order to aim its own campaign towards winning those customers back (with respect to motivating factors of that market segment) and, if possible, attracts competitor's customers. For the purposes of future analyses, it is possible to store the data related to competitor's campaigns and their main attributes, as shown in (Table 1).

If the data from such tables are paired with the results obtained using the survival models, which can provide us with common attributes of customers who churned or decreased the cooperation, it is possible to obtain additional information related to the character of competitor's campaigns. Based on the accumulated knowledge of possible motivators of a certain market segment, Trgovina may plan its own campaigns at a regional level. For instance, if a decrease is observed in purchases made by male clients (data known from loyalty cards), which are regular customers with relatively high turnover per invoice in previous transactions, and if that stagnation of sales amount correlates with the period of competitor's promotion of new assortment of tools, this data can be very useful for planning a campaign aimed at returning the customers and attracting new ones. First of all, it is important to conduct the analysis of the new tool selection. Is buying those tools a matter of prestige, or are the tools sold at a very good price but their quality is not guaranteed, or are these the high quality tools, with good price, but their purchasing is not a matter of prestige... Taking into account all the variables, it is possible to launch a campaign with the goal of returning churned customers. One must always bear in mind that it is much cheaper to prevent situations of possible customer churn, than

Table 1. A proposition of table for monitoring the promotional activities

Date of the Campaign	Character of the Campaign	Accent is On	Duration of the Campaign
05.05.2006	Discount Sale	Consumer goods	7 days
10.06.2006	Regular campaign	Gardening tools	14 days
10.07.2006	Promotion of new products	Tools	14 days

to try and win customers back. Concerning fierce market competition, it is advisable to develop an action plan for such situations as well. Conceptual solution models are idea generators and present a beginning of any serious analysis. They also serve as a recapitulation of goals, primarily from the perspective of available methodology and data. Conceptual solution models mostly do not represent the final model solutions which may be considered as a finished project task, because the flow of analysis itself and the obtained results guide further analytical processes, while the goals of the analysis are clearly defined. Having developed the conceptual solution model, where the methodology of conducting the analysis is clearly profiled, the following step is to select software for performing the needed analyses and creating the analytical models.

11.2.4 Scoring Model Development

There are two dominant planned types of analysis in this case – the scoring analysis and the customer churn analysis. The scoring model may be developed with the aid of fuzzy expert systems, based on the rules resulting from expert knowledge. Since the goal of the first step of the analysis is the evaluation of customers based on the scoring model at the level of each region, it is necessary to define the possible sub-goals of analysis, which are defined, in this business case, as measuring the level of client loyalty. In the development of scoring models based on fuzzy logic, it is crucial to hire business experts as team members who are active in the development (Aracil 2000) (Pedrycz 1998) (Siler 2005). The work of the team is coordinated by an analyst or consultant who is at the same time in charge of the entire project. The Trgovina team consisted of a consultant, sales executive and his assistant, marketing executive and chief information system architect. The consultant's task was to coordinate and lead the team and to develop the scoring model. The sales executive and his assistant worked with the marketing executive and they were in charge of creating business rules and defining the key indicators for scoring (with the help of the consultant). The chief information system architect of Trgovina gave suggestions and opinions related to the existence of the data in the database based on the defined key indicators. He was also in charge of creating the documentation used for subsequent pre-processing of the data for the needs of the scoring model. During the final stage of the project, the chief information system architect worked with the consultant to create the solution for the integration of the scoring model into the existing information system. Alongside the mentioned team members, a certain number of programmers also worked on the project. They developed the ETL solutions for the scoring model based on the specification and took part in the operative segment of the integration of the scoring model into the existing information system based on the documentation created.

11.2.4.1 User Interviews

Successful interviewing of users is one of the crucial factors on which the overall success of scoring projects based on fuzzy expert systems depends. During the user interviews it is essential to have in mind the desired goal of scoring. In the case of Trgovina, it is the evaluation of customers in retail stores. The consultant or the person in charge of the development of the model itself conducts the interviews.

It is crucial to ask the questions that will be used to recognize the key indicators and categories relevant for scoring. Based on the interviews, we obtain a clearer picture of the users' perception of a problem we want to solve, i.e. in this case to model it using the fuzzy expert systems.

Some of the questions put to the Trgovina were:

- Name at least three categories (e.g. promising, profitable, loyal...) based on which you can evaluate each of your customers.
- Is loyalty as category relevant for the evaluation of customers (scoring) in your company?
- On which grounds (which procedures, behavior models) may loyalty of a customer be evaluated within your company?
- Which indicators (e.g. turnover, difference in turnover per invoice, campaign costs...) are relevant for estimation of customer profitability within your company?

The questions listed here are just an example of questions put to the auditorium during the brainstorming process, the goal of which was to recognize the key categories and indicators for building a scoring model. In this business case, as well as in all other business cases where scoring models are developed, the consultant (or person in charge of the development of the scoring model) plays a key role in conducting the interview in the right manner. During the interview, this person obtains key information relevant for establishing a basic version of the model.

The described business case defines a situation typical in cases where some team members belong to a business and other to a technical sector. Team members belonging to the business sector made their suggestions disregarding the fact that some suggested indicators would take a long time to preprocess regarding the scope of the data and complexity of the procedure of algorithm processing. The presence of the chief information system architect was very useful here, since he suggested considering other solution modalities. On the other hand, the chief information system architect questioned the suggestions made by team members belonging to the business sector related to using indicators which were important in their opinion but were stored in databases other than the main one. The consultant had a prominent role in the motivation of team members to reach a compromise acceptable from the perspective of model development which does not diminish its plausibility, at the same time having respect of the technical limitations and difficulties resulting from the database architecture.

11.2.4.2 Key Indicators Development

The primary goal of the interviewing process was to define key indicators and basic categories as structural elements of a fuzzy expert system. Key indicators may be defined as basic variables, which provide input to a fuzzy expert system (Aracil, 2000) (Pedrycz, 1998) (Siler, 2005). The categories consist of more abstract notions defined using the key indicators. For example, key indicators are sales revenue, campaign costs, duration of business relationship. Based on these key indicators, a category of profitability is defined and limited with a set of rules.

Based on business experience and with the help of the consultant, Trgovina recognized during the interview the three main categories, which had an immediate influence on the client scoring:

- Client profitability
- Client loyalty
- Client outlook

Each of the categories should be defined using key indicators, developed on the grounds of available databases. These indicators are input parameters for a fuzzy expert system model. As a result of brainstorming during the interview, the key indicators for each category (at the customer level) are defined as illustrated in Table 2.

Having finished the brainstorming session, the expert team agreed that the selected indicators best describe the chosen categories. Since the internal company experts know their customers the best, based on their expert knowledge, they estimate which indicators in the databases are the best to describe the chosen categories further used for evaluation of scoring. The consultant's task during the brainstorming (as it was the case in this example) is to guide the experts to select the most significant indicators describing the chosen categories. During this process, the number of key indicators defining a category must be taken into account. Sometimes this involves the additional selection of the most important indicators among the important ones in order to keep a number of indicators allocated to a category under four or five. The reason for such a reduction of indicators stems from limited human perception. Each indicator comprises a body of a rule. When more than five indicators comprising the rule conditions are present (and each indicator may have a number of subcategories), the process of defining rules is often burdened with more

Table 2. Key indicators

Client profitability
Total sales price difference in the last six months
Total promotion expenses based on the loyalty card program (gifts) within the last six months
Total expenses based on the advertising campaigns within the last six months
Client loyalty
Frequency of purchasing within the last six months (number of visits)
Response to campaigns aimed at loyalty card holders within last six months
Number of points on the loyalty card
Client outlook
Purchasing trends within the last two quarters
Tendency of purchasing new brands in the store within the last year
Cross selling trends within the last two quarters

than five conditions in addition to the inevitable, often large number of rules. Under such circumstances, it is extremely hard to define the rules. If more than five indicators must inevitably be used, it is possible to introduce more categories into the system. This simplifies the process of defining the rules by the experts, and the expert system itself becomes more transparent and easier-to-survey.

11.2.4.3 Pre-Processing Algorithms Development

In most cases, it is necessary to deduce the defined key indicators serving as an entrance to the fuzzy expert system model on the basis of the available data, because they do not exist in the transactional database in a form defined as entry into a fuzzy expert system. For example, in order to obtain a key indicator number of visits within the last six months, which is an element used in the estimation of loyalty to the mentioned company, an algorithmic procedure for reconstruction of number of visits within the last six months based on the invoice numbers had to be defined. After discovering the key indicators, the consultant and the chief information system architect created the documentation for the preprocessing of the data, encompassing all defined categories and their key indicators. Documentation pertaining to the profitability category is shown in Table 3.

Using the documentation in such a form, the chief information system architect developed detailed algorithms for each indicator. Based on these algorithms the team of programmers created the application for data preprocessing. The data preprocessing is much easier to perform when a data warehouse exists. In the described

Table 3. A process of key indicator calculation

Category: Client Profitability	
Indicators	**Calculation Process**
Total sales price difference in the last six months.	Market value – (purchase value + rebate + dependent costs) summed for all invoices within last six months per each customer. Unit – Croatian kuna.
Total promotion expenses based on the loyalty card program (gifts) within the last six months.	Total sum of distributed promotional materials and gifts obtained based on the loyalty card data for the period of last six months per each customer. Unit – Croatian kuna.
Total expenses based on the advertising campaigns within the last six months.	Total sum of expenses based on each campaign executed during the last six months estimated per each customer (global campaigns on regional level promoted in the press and on the television + targeted campaigns in the form of direct mailing to selected market segments containing product samples). Unit – Croatian kuna.

case, PL/SQL was used for the data preprocessing, which resulted in the creation of a table of key indicators for each customer.

11.2.4.4 Model Structure Development

After defining the key indicators and the categories and subcategories during the interview, the basis of a fuzzy scoring model was defined. Having defined the categories, it was necessary to unite them in the form of a model depicted in Figure 1.

The depicted model was developed using the FuzzyTech program package. The key indicators in the model comprise the input variables for rule blocks. Each rules block estimates the output value of a category based on the defined rules. These output category values enter the block of rules for final scoring, where the final scoring is estimated on the basis of a defined set of rules. The experts defined the rules, and the consultant entered the so defined rules into the fuzzy model. As it can be observed in the figure, the method used for the defuzzification is the so-called Mean-of-Maximum Method (MoM). The reason why it was used originates from the fact that the output results obtained using this defuzzification method are very easy to interpret, especially when such models are integrated in the form of an applicative solution.

11.2.4.5 Key Indicator Range Development

Classical logic, allowing only strict limits among classes, is much further from human perception mechanisms that it is the case with fuzzy logic. For example, if we define

Figure 1. Fuzzy scoring model

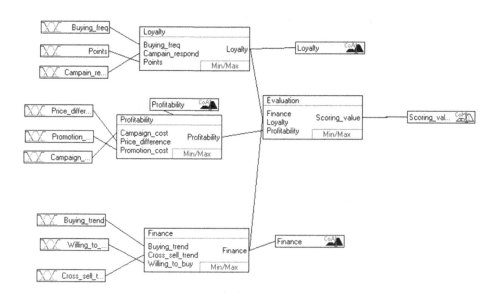

the key indicator 'number of visits' resorting to classical logic, we would categorize a small number of visits in the class of 0 to 20 visits during the last six months. Of course, we can ask ourselves what happens with a customer who visited the retail store 21 times during the last six months. If we apply the mechanisms of classical logic, he would be placed in the subsequent class. Human perception mechanisms function on significantly different premises, and are more liberal when it comes to such classification. The limit of a small number of visits observed through the eyes of human perception mechanisms is subject to tolerance and deviation which are often subjective in nature.

In order to make categorization systems (or scoring systems, as it is the case here) as similar to the human process of making decisions and having in mind the limitations arising from the classical logic and its application, fuzzy expert systems were used in the development of scoring models for the Trgovina. These systems enable defining the range of key indicators on the premise of fuzzy logic, which is very close to the human way of thinking and categorizing. Figure 2 illustrates a manner of defining the range of key indicator frequency of purchasing within the last six months calculated by counting the number of visits during the last six months.

The frequency of purchasing is defined as low, medium or high based on the input parameters. The calculated values are further processed using the defined expert rules. The expert team defined a number of fuzzy classes for each key indi-

Figure 2. Defining the range of key indicator frequency of purchasing

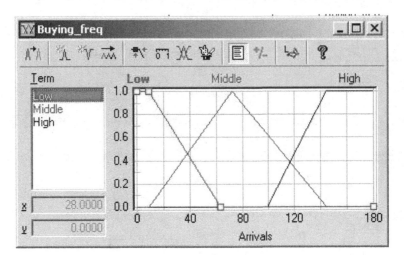

cator, as well as their titles and ranges. After that step, they were defined in Fuzzy-Tech as it is shown in the example of key indicator frequency of purchasing within the last six months. The key indicators were defined in such a manner as were the ranges of output variables in the model and became the basic elements for forming the rules.

11.2.4.6 Rule System Development

One common error present during the implementation of the scoring system using fuzzy expert systems is neglecting the role of the number of indicators describing a category and number of fuzzy classes defined by the expert team. The same happened during the development of such a system in the mentioned company. During the early phases of system development, in the interviewing process, the expert team often emphasized the importance of a large number of indicators for describing a certain category. The consultant played a key role here, since he had to limit the expert team to define a maximum of four or five key indicators best describing a category. Otherwise, a combinatory explosion of a number of rules may occur. The following formula is used for the prediction of total number of rules in a system Klepac (2006):

$$p_j = \prod_{i=1}^{n} r_j \, , \text{n>1}$$

where pj denotes a number of rules in block j, and is calculated as a product of a number of fuzzy categories of each i-th key indicator r.

Based on that, the total number of rules in a system is calculated using the following formula:

$$P = \sum_{i=1}^{n} p_j$$

where P denotes a total number of rules in a system, calculated as a sum of number of rules in all rules blocks of the system. Next table illustrates the relation of number of rules in a block, with four key indicators and different number of fuzzy categories defined within the key indicators.

In Table 4, we can observe a tendency towards growth in the number of rules in rule blocks with the increase in number of fuzzy categories. In addition to that, we can observe that the increase in number of rules is also influenced by the increase in number of key indicators. The control of the total number of rules in a fuzzy expert system may be exercised through reduction of the number of key indicators or reduction of the number of fuzzy categories within key indicators. Such methodology helped Trgovina to optimize the number of expert rules within their system. After reaching a consensus regarding the number of rules, the experts created the rules for the system, using the form shown in Table 5 depicting the key indicator loyalty.

In this manner, the experts defined the rules, for each category defined, as well as for the final scoring.

11.2.4.7 Scoring Transformation Matrix

Having created the model and performed the data preprocessing, as well as having defined the rules, the scoring of preprocessed data followed. The analysis was performed in three main stages. The first stage was characterized by conducting scoring using the created fuzzy expert system model, from which a sampling of

Table 4. Illustration of rule number growth

Number of Fuzzy Categories of the First Key Indicator	Number of Fuzzy Categories of the Second Key Indicator	Number of Fuzzy Categories of the Third Key Indicator	Number of Fuzzy Categories of the Fourth Key Indicator	Number of Rules in a Block
3	3	3	3	81
3	4	4	4	192
4	4	4	4	256

Table 5. Expert rules

IF			THEN	
No_points_card	Campaign_resp	Purchase_freq	DoS	Loyalty
Small	Low	Low	1.00	Low
Small	Low	Medium	1.00	Low
Small	Low	High	1.00	Medium
Small	Medium	Low	1.00	Low
Small	Medium	Medium	1.00	Medium
Small	Medium	High	1.00	Medium
Small	High	Low	1.00	Medium
Small	High	Medium	1.00	Medium

Table 6. Relation table containing the results of the performed analysis

Customer Code	Customer Loyalty	Customer Profitability	Customer Outlook	Scoring
28121998	High	High	High	Very high
34909332	High	High	Medium	High
67482875	Low	Medium	Medium	Low

obtained results was performed with the purpose of diagnosing the errors in the model. After several cycles of running the data through the model and controlling its reliability, the model has been declared reliable. The following stage, scoring and accepting the results obtained from the model, was performed.

Based on the scoring results for each region, a relation table as shown in Table 6 was created.

Further analysis at the level of each region was aimed at finding the relative structure of customer shares based on scoring. As a result within one of the regions, the data in Table 7 was obtained:

Table 7. Relative structure of customer shares based on the scoring categories

Scoring category	%
Very low	12
Low	16
Medium	23
High	30
Very high	19

The client structure shows that 49% of customers were classified in the high and very high scoring ranges. These customers are of great importance for the company. Further analyses established that 80% of the customers belonging to scoring category High obtained the value based on the high profitability and bright outlook, but their loyalty is Medium. This fact placed them in scoring category High instead of Very high. Speaking from the business point of view, this is a very important segment of clients and it is crucial to significantly increase their loyalty level in the future in order to successfully overcome the new situation on the market. Further analysis of the data using decision trees pointed out the fact that this category primarily consist of customers who rarely come to the store and rarely respond to campaigns that help them collect a large number of points on loyalty cards if they buy products advertised in the campaigns aimed at loyalty card holders. It was also noticed that this category of customers prefers a smaller number of visits to the store during one month, but the amounts on their invoices are higher than average for every purchase. Market basket analysis and clustering were performed using the data related to that group of customers. Based on the analyses, two main customer segments were defined:

- **"Healthy life" segment:** Customers who belong to this segment usually buy large amounts of fruit and vegetables, wines of better quality and ingredients related to specific cuisines (Chinese, Japanese, Indian). They rarely buy meat and meat products (even then in small quantities), but they buy more milk and milk products than usual. Based on the data from loyalty cards, this segment mostly consists of members of younger age groups and higher education.
- **"Cleanliness is next to godliness" segment:** Customers who belong to this segment usually buy home cleaning products and detergents. Some 70% of articles in their basket are related to the mentioned category and the remaining 30% is food. The representatives of this segment do not exhibit any regularity in buying foodstuffs. Based on the data from loyalty cards, this segment mostly consists of middle aged persons, who are married with children.

Further analyses showed that both segments mostly shop at the end of the week or during the weekends. All these data were used in planning of further promotional activities in the region. Based on the information, a certain number of promotional activities were directed towards the mentioned market segments. There were more promotional activities offering fruit and vegetables at reduced prices and an extra discount was given for buying certain wines with fruit and vegetables or milk. Such purchases were rewarded with more points on loyalty cards. Customers who took part in a certain number of promotional purchases of this type entered a competition for a vacation in an exotic destination. A number of promotional activities were directed to the second market segment, and these included buying home cleaning products and detergents at discount prices. This type of promotional purchase also included getting more points on loyalty cards. Customers who took part in a certain number of promotional purchases of this type entered a competition for complete child-size furniture for a nursery. After conducting the described promotional activities, 60% of clients who scored as High increased their loyalty level and scored as Very high during the following five months. Such analyses were conducted for each region. Each region exhibited its own specificities partially discovered after scoring and partially after additional analyses. The conducted analysis gains extra value if the results are observed in different time intervals. Based on that, we can obtain information on market differentiation and the success of past campaigns, the goal of which was to increase the number of customers with specified scoring values. This data may serve as basis for calculating the amount of resources invested per client in order to upgrade his scoring value from High to Very high. Monitoring of customers in this manner may also serve as a tool for monitoring customers' activities across different segments. It can yield very transparent information on a potential decrease in customers' activities on the market segment level. Monitoring the market segments over time provides us with a new dimension of analytical data overview. General trends of decreasing or increasing the volume of market structure provide us with guidelines for performing further analytical procedures. These analytical procedures should answer questions such as why these trends occur, what are their causes, how to prevent the trends if they are bad for business, or how to strengthen them if they are good for business. For example, if we observe a 30% increase in the number of customers who acquired scoring value "Very high" between two quarters, and if their scoring value was "High" during the previous period, it is necessary to discover the reason that lead to the change in their status. Besides that, it is necessary to conduct further analysis and discover potential regularities within the population of such customers. These insights can be used to motivate other customers from "High" scoring category who are the most similar to this population to achieve the scoring value "Very high" in a certain period of time. The insights regarding the regularities within a population, which can be recognized, using data mining techniques can be useful in developing a strategy for promotional activities with the aim of increasing the value of clients from the perspective of a sales-oriented company.

11.2.4.8 Scoring Models Integration

The implementation of a scoring model based on a fuzzy expert system is mostly performed in two main steps. The first step consists of scoring based on the basic model. In such a model there is no applicative solution based on the designed fuzzy expert system, but the analyst performs most of the scoring based on the created model. This step is also characterized by the procedures for evaluation of the model, so the model is subject to frequent changes in this phase.

The second step, characterized by stability of the created model is oriented towards finding and developing a more permanent applicative solution, which is based on the created model. The same happened during the implementation of the model to Trgovina. After a period of intensive testing and analysis of the scoring, an applicative solution, which should be integrated into the existing information system, was needed. Such a solution had to meet some basic criteria in its final phase:

- The possibility of viewing scoring results for each client with explanation why of the client was allocated to a certain scoring category
- The possibility of running an automated scoring procedure over the entire customer database, with the possibility of saving the scoring values
- The possibility of retrieving historical scoring results for each customer.

Besides monitoring the individual categories, the scoring problem is also solved in a manner that encompasses the values of all categories, together with the score value. The applicative solution with such a concept provides the end user with the derived information that resulted from the estimation made by the expert system. Applicative solutions designed in this manner may be a part of a CRM system, or even a central module of a CRM system.

11.2.5 Customer Churn Analysis Model Development

11.2.5.1 Churn Analysis Strategy Definition

Having performed the scoring of its customers with respect to the expected activities of its competition, Trgovina has to establish a system for permanent monitoring of customer churn and a decrease in the purchase activities of existing customers. Since the market was stable prior to the arrival of the competition when it comes to the intensity and volume of purchase, the first step of evaluation of possible customer churn encompassed market research performed before the competition started its business on the representative sample of customers using telephone interviewing method. This research roughly indicated that the existing Trgovina customers would be strongly motivated to defect to the competition if the competition offered significantly lower prices. The results of the research suggest that more than 60% of Trgovina customers in almost all regions had the intent to make at least one purchase in competitor store once it opened. Although troublesome, this information was expected and it was used in developing a strategy for retaining the existing population of customers. After they perform the initial purchase in the competitor's store, the customers must stay loyal to Trgovina. During the last eight years the market was stable and the customer churn in Trgovina was negligible. Based on the data available from the company it is very difficult, almost impossible, to build a transparent prediction model of customer churn, especially if the expected market turbulences are taken into account. One segment of the strategy aimed at retaining the existing customers was to add extra points to loyalty cards in accordance with their scoring category and to inform the customers of the number of points based on which they can buy products at cheaper prices. The points were added based on the scoring category. For example, the customers labeled "Very high" were given more points than the customers with the "High" scoring category. The final goal is to keep as many existing customers, especially those labeled as desirable for the company.

As opposed to e.g. the telecommunication sector, where customer churn is clearly defined through the moment of breaking a contract, the moment of ending cooperation in retail is not clearly defined. Thus the expert team had to define the moment of customer churn in retail. Based on the market research results the management expected a decrease in turnover and number of customers in stores during the first month after opening the competition retail stores in regions where they were opened. This was partially due to the curiosity of customers and partially to the aggressive campaign of the competition. The customer churn in Trgovina was defined for each region as the absence of an existing customer from the store within two months after competitor retail store was opened in the region or if an existing customer decreased the amount of monthly purchase by an average 60% within two months in comparison to the previous three months. It was decided that the customer churn analysis will be conducted on a monthly basis even before the end of the two month period with the aim of predicting the customer churn in future period. After two months, a comprehensive analysis of customer churn will be conducted, which should provide the guidelines for further strategic planning. Based on the mentioned analyses and competition's moves, precise actions aimed at retaining customers will be defined. In order to achieve market advantage over the competition even before they enter the market, the plan is to increase the loyalty of existing customers by adding points to their loyalty cards so that they can buy products at discount prices. As a measure of precaution, a couple of weeks before the competition opens the stores promotional campaigns based on the reduction of prices of some products will be intensified as well as advertising in local media. From the perspective of Trgovina, the fact that the competition will not open stores in all regions simultaneously, but within intervals of several months is good news. This will make the development of the strategy for retaining customers in regions where the competition will open stores later on easier, based on the strategic patterns discovered in other regions.

11.2.5.2 Survival Models Data Pre-Processing

In order to analyze customer churn in Trgovina, Cox regression was used Berry (2003). The advantage of this method is the possibility to include predictive variables (covariance) into the model. The goal of the analysis was to discover not only the trend of the customer churn curve, but also to estimate the probability of customer churn with regard to different customer characteristics, which is possible using this model. It is important to notice that customers can begin and end their cooperation lifecycle with Trgovina during different periods of time, as it is illustrated in Figure 3.

For the purpose of the evaluation of customer churn, it is necessary to define discrete time intervals (days, months, years...). The basic idea of a survival model boils down to the estimation of probability that someone who has "survived" as a Trgovina customer during a certain period of time will either stop or continue purchasing during the following period. Cox regression answered the question regarding the probability of customer churn with respect to their different attributes. For the purpose of creating the model, it is important to define the notion of customer churn as absence of an existing customer during the last two months after the competition opened a retail store in the region or if an existing customer decreased the amount of monthly purchase by an average of 60% within two months in comparison to the previous three months. Based on the definition, a preprocessing of the data for the status variable was performed. A status designation of 1 denotes a churned customer, while a status designation of 0 denotes an existing customer.

Another important variable important for the model is the number of months of continuous purchase. This variable is defined as the number of months since the date of customer churn minus number of months since the date of issuing the loyalty card. Having in mind the nature of the Cox regression, the model includes

Figure 3. Different periods of beginning and ending the business cooperation

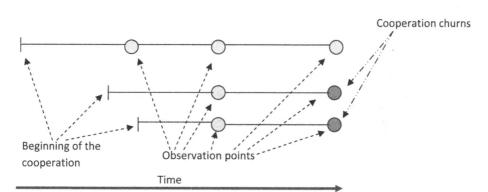

other attributes (predictive variables). Continuous variables, such as age variable are made discrete. Data pre-processing resulted in next table.

Based on Table 8, it is possible to perform the analysis using Cox regression.

11.2.5.3 Churn Analysis

Unlike businesses such as telecommunications, a range of specificities, which guide the data adjustment in order to build a customer churn model, characterizes retail business. Besides the specificities related to the definition of the moment of customer churn, retail business does not have the privilege of receiving transparent information on a daily basis regarding the relationship of a customer and the company defined by a contract. Due to that reason, it is much easier to monitor the client structure in telecommunications with regard to breaking the contracts. If we observe the situation from the competition's point of view for a moment, we can notice that they lack usable data for performing a deeper analysis of the structure of clients who decided to make a purchase in their store during the first month, since they will not issue loyalty cards during the first couple of months and having in mind the specificities of retail business.

At the moment of closing the contract, the telecommunication companies obtain much more information from the client, which may be used for analysis. At the same time, client of a retail company provides only the data on past transactions, so he can not be uniquely identified. From this point of view, Trgovina has a certain analytical advantage, because they own data more suitable for analysis acquired from loyalty cards, which is important for analyzing the customer churn. At the moment of entering the market, telecommunication companies and similar businesses that base their operation on contracts closed with clients count on a certain percentage of customer churn, which is manifested in the form of breaking the contracts. Such companies do not have a problem with conducting the analysis of reasons and profiles of clients who churn based on the collected data.

From the point of view of a competition retail company, the analogy of customer churn can be compared with the arrival of a customer who makes a purchase during

Table 8. Structure of the data for performing Cox regression

Customer code	Number of purchasing months	Status	Age	Gender	No of complaints
23345342	18	1	<25	M	1
54336564	20	0	46+	Z	1
34566334	19	0	36-45	M	3

the first month after acquisition motivated by an aggressive advertising campaign, and gives up purchasing in the competition store after that. It is very difficult to uniquely identify a group of such customers. This fact almost disables the competition company to perform the analytical procedures in order to influence those trends with the purpose of motivating this group of customers to further purchasing. In such cases, the competition company has to rely on market research results obtained through performing surveys on samples of customers, which are a rather big investment. Trgovina performed the analysis of customer churn based on pre-processed data using Cox regression. In regards to market stability during the previous period, the focus of the analysis was on the last twenty months of operations. The competition started its operation in the region since the sixteenth month observed within the model. After the analysis was performed, the survival curve for Trgovina customers was obtained, as illustrated in next figure.

Figure 4 clearly indicates that with regard to the population of customer after the sixteenth observed month, in the relatively stable market, there is a decrease in Trgovina customer population. Translated to model jargon, the probability of survival of the customer population is decreasing. The curve shows that the decrease in promotional activities of the competition had influence on the decrease of customer churn in Trgovina (seventeenth and eighteenth month in the model on figure 7). With the intensification of promotional activities, the trend again started to shift in favor of the competition. After the twentieth week, using the defined notion of customer churn, Trgovina lost 15% of existing customer population who were loyalty card holders in the region observed. The results of the analysis provide us with guidelines regarding the structure and dynamic of the churn, but the results are not sufficient for reaching firm conclusions which might be used in the process of decision making. For that purpose, predictive variables which will provide us with a clearer picture of customer churn in Trgovina need to be included in the model. Predictive variables are included in the table made on the basis of data pre-processing. These variables were selected based on the attribute relevance analysis. A certain number of variables for which it was proved that they best describe the variable end of churning status based on the calculated Gini index were included in the data model which was further analyzed. After the analysis was performed on the pre-processed data using Cox regression, it was found that certain categories of age structure and customers with a defined number of complaints filed through the call center have the biggest influence on churn trends. It was also noticed that there are no significant differences in churn trends among customers classified in different scoring categories.

The results of the analysis are shown in Figure 5 and Figure 6.

If we pay closer attention to the graphs and compare the intensities of competition advertising campaigns that were less intense during the seventeenth and eigh-

Figure 4. Survival curve for the Trgovina company customers

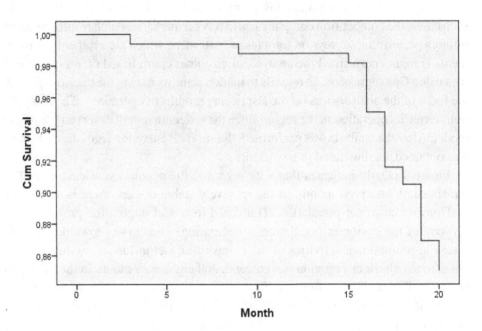

Survival Function at mean of covariates

teenth month observed, we can notice that during this period customer churn decreased in comparison to the following periods and that it increased in the following months observed. It can also be noticed that the highest probability of churn is connected with younger customers, as well as customers who filed more than four complaints through the call center. Based on the analysis, it was concluded that the risk of customer churn grows with younger age groups as well as with the number of complaints via the call center. The probable reason of more frequent churn when it comes to younger population stems from the fact that the competition advertising campaign targets that exact group – their strategic market segment. Regarding the more frequent customer churn related to clients who filed more than four complaints through the call center, further analysis was conducted on that customer population with the aim of finding common attributes of customers belonging to that population. The analysis did not yield results that would enable recognizing the dominant significant attributes in that population.

Figure 5. Survival function with regard to "complaints" variable

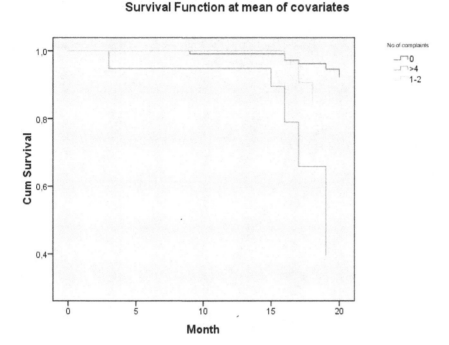

Survival Function at mean of covariates

11.2.6 Churn Analysis Based Business Decisions

Diagnosed risky categories for the observed region exhibiting a greater tendency towards customer churn are younger customers and customers who had more that four filed complaints in the call center. Generally speaking, the risk of customer churn grows with the diminishing age of customer and with the increase in number of complaints. Regarding the competition campaign aimed at younger customers, Trgovina decided to pay special attention to that market segment through the advertising campaigns in order to prevent as much churn related to younger customers. Special attention will be paid to younger customers who were categorized based on the performed scoring in the "High" and "Very high" scoring categories. These groups will be targeted by special promotional activities in order to additionally motivate them to continue purchasing in Trgovina stores. Regarding the discovered regularities related to customer complaints, the decision was made to further analyze the reasons of dissatisfaction and contact each client who had filed more than two complaints through the call center with the intent of solving them. This is another

Figure 6. Survival function with regard to "age" variable

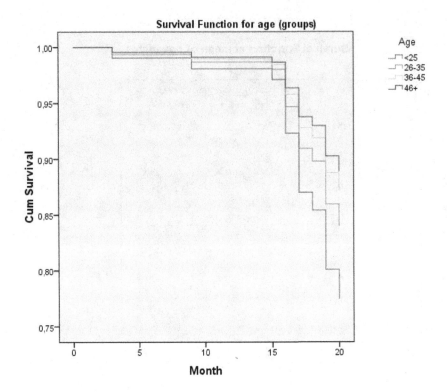

Figure 7. Portfolio structure calculated through concentrations within four major abstract terms

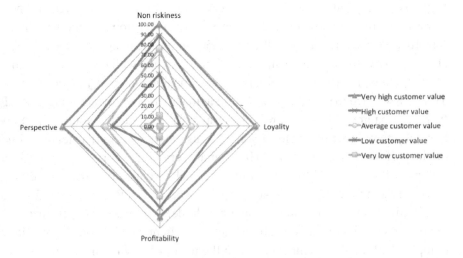

strategy for increasing client loyalty which will also influence the reduction of customer churns.

11.2.7 Case Conclusion

A relatively stable market takes on a significantly different character after the arrival of competition to certain regions. Trgovina discovered the structure of its customers according to their value to the company using scoring techniques. This knowledge resulted in focusing on the most valuable customers from the perspective of the company, with the purpose of retention and increasing their loyalty. Based on the scoring results, an even more flexible policy of discount prices was developed for purchasing products from recognized categories obtained during the scoring procedure. The period immediately before the arrival of the competition was used for conducting activities for increasing client loyalty with the aim of their long-term retention. Trgovina was aware of the fact that they will inevitably lose a portion of their customers, so their goal was to diminish those trends as much as possible. Although their final goal was to keep as many of existing customers as possible, the main emphasis was on the customers who were most valuable for the company. A further step was aimed at the creation of an early warning system in the shape of a customer churn analysis model, based on which it is possible to recognize basic regularities within the population of customers who either churn or decrease the intensity of purchase according to the specified criteria. The analyses conducted and business decisions made based on that analyses resulted in a significant reduction of customer churn, especially in the younger customers segment, which was targeted by the competition. Trends of customer churn related to customers with higher number of complaints were also diminished with the help of call center operators who contacted customers who had filed complaints trying to solve their problems and alleviate the consequences related to the complaints. In the long run, this approach resulted in an increase in customer satisfaction and consequently in growth of sales revenue.

Trgovina managed to keep a satisfactory number of customers who were ranked high in the scoring procedure, which was one of the goals. Regarding the new market conditions of fierce competition, Trgovina had to constantly monitor the development of the market and analyze market trends on a global and regional level, especially the population of its customers. Mandatory scoring on a monthly basis initiated the analysis of market segments differentiation and its causes on the level of the Croatian market and on regional levels. Such an approach enabled establishing an early warning system which is of vital importance in conditions where the competition continually undertakes targeted promotional actions with the aim of winning clients. The system of conducted analyses proved to be very effective concerning the situation on the market and it served as a basis for the development of further analytical systems that contributed to the success of Trgovina decision support at all management levels. The presented case represents one of the possible solutions in given circumstances. The developed model shows good performance in practice. Churn is specific to a given area and there is no cookbook data mining solution which could be applied in each case (Berry, 2000; Berry, 2003; Giudici, 2003; Namid, 2004). The existing model could be extended with an early warning system, and segmentation model which takes into consideration the customer prospective value as a part of customer relationship model. Churn analyzes will certainly use more than several common data mining models. As the market condition becomes complicated, and that fact leads us to combine a variety of data mining techniques to achieve better results. Customer relationship management systems will play a more important role in churn prediction, as churn prevention system. Recognizing customer needs and behavior is first and most important step in churn prevention.

11.3 CASE STUDY 2: CHURN REDUCTION AND CUSTOM PRODUCT DEVELOPMENT IN TELECOMMUNICATION COMPANY

Case study represents business case in telecommunication Company called Veza, in domain of churn prediction and churn mitigation. Churn project was divided in few stages. Due to fact of limited budget, and cost optimization, first stage was concentrated on prospective customer value calculation model based on fuzzy expert system. This stage helps Veza company to find most valuable telecom subscribers. It also helped company to better understand subscriber portfolio structure. Developed fuzzy expert system also helped Veza company in detection of soft churn (subscriber did not cancel contract, but he decrease usage of services). Profiling and customer segmentation based on time series analysis was next important part of the project, and it provided potential predictors for predictive churn model. Central stage was concentrated on developing traditional predictive churn model based on logistic regression. This model calculated probability that subscriber will make churn in next few months.

Final stage was dedicated to SNA (Social Network Analysis) model development. SNA model find out most valuable customers from the perspective of existing subscriber network. In other words, this model gave us the answer which subscribers has greatest influence on other subscribers, in way what is danger if they leave Veza company that they will motivate other subscribers to do the same thing. All three steps made complete churn detection/mitigation solution which take in consider past behavior of subscribers, their prospective value, and their strength of influence on other subscribers. This project on the one hand, helped Veza company to decrease churn rate, and on the other hand it gave directions for better understanding of customer needs and behavior, which were base for new product development (Klepac, 2014).

11.3.1 Project Goals

Veza company is telecommunication company in Croatian market which started to operate in 1998. In the beginning of lifetime, Veza company operated at relatively peacefully market with few competitors, with which it shared market without much unpredictable market situations.

During period of time, more and more competitors entered into the market, and a condition has changed. Veza company has been faced with increasing problem of subscriber churn, and company also realized need for developing telecommunication products more related to customer needs. One of the major problems was limited budget, and company should recognize most valuable subscribers, to spend budget on them. Important part of the project was data sources (databases), and there were several major difficulties during final solution development.

Veza's top management wanted to find out long-term churn solution. They did not want to recognize clients with high churn probability only, they wanted complete solution which will show complete picture on client portfolio, and which will have long-term value. Regarding that, following four functionalities in future solution were recognized as important:

Prospective customer value calculation engine for recognizing most valuable subscribers periodical evaluation. Churn probability calculation on subscriber level with possibility of model monitoring and redevelopment in line with changes in subscriber portfolio structure. Testing adequacy of existing telecommunication services packages taking in consider subscriber portfolio segments. Recognizing potentially dangerous subscribers from perspective of social network leadership influence. This subscriber does not need to have highly calculated churn probability, but in case of churn, they could cause serious damage to Veza's company because they have great influence on other subscribers. They might not be conscious of their position, but it is important to recognize them and to try to keep them into subscriber's portfolio. Some of the mentioned aims are common goals in churn prediction data mining projects (Dresner 2008) (Berry 2000) (Berry 1997) (Faulkner 2003).

11.3.2 Solutions from Data Mining Methods Perspective

It is evident that requested solution given by top management was very complex, and it is not possible to finish whole project using single data mining method. On the other hand, using only data mining methods does not guarantee successful solution. It is much more important to find optimal analytical strategy considering existing data sources and to connect it with appropriate data mining methods/ methodology. Regarding first request, which was focused on prospective customer value calculation for recognizing most valuable subscribers and to evaluate their value periodically, it was decided to use fuzzy expert system. Fuzzy expert systems are based on expert knowledge, and they are intuitive and easy understandable for management. Prospective value calculations are focused on loyalty evaluation, profitability calculation, perceptivity evaluation and evaluation of similar categories. As a final result, developed solution should provide single category for each subscriber, and that category should point on subscriber value from perspective of Veza company. Given results could be easily explainable by triggered rules within expert system. When we talk about periodically evaluation of each subscriber from perspective of customer value, expert systems provides solution, because it can be run periodically, and it can measure customer value trends.

For fulfilling second request related to churn probability calculation on subscriber level with possibility of model monitoring and redevelopment in line with changes in subscriber portfolio structure, traditional modeling based on predictive models was used. As it will be shown, after attribute relevance analysis and model predictive power evaluation, neural networks and logistic regression was used. This methodology is commonly used, and it is expected that developed model should be monitored and redeveloped periodically to be in line with market/subscriber structure changes. Third request was generally most doubtful from perspective of data mining model usage. Main reason for that lies in fact that there were unclear adequacy of existing data sources. *Veza* company offers various service packages which includes fixed phone lines, mobile phone lines, internet connection, IP TV in many different ways. General idea was to recognize adequacy of created service packages for existing subscribers. For customer profile recognition, we need a lot of specific data, which on first sight was not visible from existing data sources. First idea was usage of data mining models like Self Organizing Maps, segmentation methods or decision trees. Problem was in data adequacy for this kind of purpose. Data, which were recognized as potentially valuable, was socio demographic data from contracts, and behavioral data collected during service usage, and derived behavioral attributes as well.

Fourth request aimed on subscriber recognition which has strong influence on other subscribes (influencer) was planned to be solved using Social Network Analysis. Proposed solution takes into consideration specifics, which are related to specific company, and takes into consideration not only traditional approach with stress on predictive model development. Proposed solution takes into consideration fact of limited budget, which means that we should recognize most valuable customers, it takes into consideration fact that we should recognize subscribers which are risky in way of breaking contract. On the other hand knowledge about who is most valuable and risky subscribers will not stop them in intention to break contract. To stop them, we have to understand their behavior, motivators and lifestyle. For this kind of purpose we should use adequate methods, which will help us in creating services and meet their needs and mitigate churn rate. Final step in holistic solution was SNA analysis, which gives us an answer who is greatest influencer within portfolio, and who can damage portfolio as a leader in case that he or she makes churn.

Whole analytical process is described with following steps:

- Fuzzy expert system creation for prospective customer value.
- Apply Fuzzy expert system on subscribers portfolio and categorize all subscribers within following categories (Very high customer value, High customer value, Average customer value, Low customer value, Very low customer value).
- Exclude subscribers with Low customer value and Very low customer value for further analytical process.
- Find subscriber behavior and segments on reduced data set (Low customer value and Very low customer value categories are excluded from the sample)
- Create predictive (probabilistic) churn model on reduced data set. Also use recognized patterns from step 4. as potential predictors for churn model (Low customer value and Very low customer value categories are excluded from the sample).
- Apply SNA analysis on whole portfolio (Very high customer value, High customer value, Average customer value, Low customer value, Very low customer value).
- Make decisions based on given results.

Fuzzy expert system in first step recognized most valuable subscribers, and company can put focus on that population for future marketing activities regarding churn reduction. For most valuable subscribers understanding their needs, behavior, and wishes is important element in intention to stop churn rate. Next activity was concentrated in predictive model development, and in this process reduced samples were used (most valuable subscribers) and recognized patterns from previous step were also used as predictors into model. SNA analysis was applied on whole population, because subscribers with low values potentially could have great influence on other subscribers and they are potentially dangerous in way that they can motivate other valuable subscribers on churn. It is important to recognize all the subscribers, which has great influence on other subscribers in way to stop potential churn, which could be caused, by social network relations.

At the end, company makes strategy with focus on most valuable subscribers, which has high probability of churn, and subscribers, which were recognized as influencers. Strategy should be in line with recognized customer behavior, needs and motivators. If somebody (or specific segment) has intention to break contract company should offer some conditions or benefits, which will be attractive to them.

11.3.3 Data Preparation

Key factor creditable for project success is appropriate data, which enters into data mining models. *Veza* company has mostly unconnected data sources, for which base existed in core systems. They started to develop data warehouse, but at the moment when churn-solving project started, it was far away from adequate solution. They had several main data sources like contracting transaction system which also had information about services in use, billing system, call center system which was semi connected with other existing systems, and IP TV system which was not transactional oriented, but was recognized as valuable data source. Socio demographic data, which mainly existed in contracting transaction system, was not good choice for model development as single source of data. It is well known fact that best predictors in churn models are behavioral attributes. First step in data cleansing and preparation was finding ways to connect all disposable data sources on subscriber level. That includes establishing connection between all existing data sources (contracts, used services, call center, IP TV system, mobile phone data center, fixed phone data center). Basic idea was to use hidden data potential from existing data sources with stress on derived data attributes, which has behavioral character and consolidate all existing business segments. This approach in data integration was base for holistic view on subscribers. It gets an opportunity to find out specifics derived from usage of specific services as IP TV in combination with mobile phone services and sight on subscribers potential activities in call center.

11.3.4 Modeling Variations Based on Prospective Value Calculation

11.3.4.1 Importance of Prospective Value Calculation

As it was already mentioned, main reason why *Veza* company has started churn detection/mitigation project was to observe increasing churn rate. Due to fact of limited budget, which could be, spend with intention to hold subscribers; the most important thing is to recognize most valuable customers for the company. Contrary to conviction that profitability is only criteria for customer value evaluation, aim was to build system, which could be able to calculate other factors like loyalty, perspective, long-term perspective, and riskiness as elements for customer value evaluation. This model had task to recognize most valuable subscribers, which are worth for spending budget on them, because there are most valuable customers for *Veza* company. Problematic of customer value calculation is often neglected in two ways. First way neglects fact that in portfolio exists clients with different degree of worthiness. Second one trivializes way how to calculate customer value. Often ambitious projects in first step for customer value calculation became trivial in latest phases, after system designer realize that there are to many rules, which should be incorporated into SQL statements. After that conclusion customer value calculation often became profitability value calculation, and other aspect of customer worthiness like loyalty, perspective, and potentials as elements for customer value calculation are neglected.

Practice often shows Parreto effect within subscriber portfolio, and we can say that we have less number of customers, which generates most of the profit. To generate profit often does not mean to be profitable only, because profitability in one point of time does not mean that customer/subscriber will be profitable also in the near future period. The reason for that can be soft churn trends, less buying potential in future, seasonal oscillation or other reasons. Because of all mentioned facts, for the precise customer value evaluation we should use in consideration different subscriber characteristics. To achieve this aim we should operate with numerous amount of data and numerous business rules. That means that we need powerful tool, which can operate with huge databases and big numbers of rules. A fuzzy expert system shows good performance for solving these types of problems (Klepac, 2010).

11.3.4.2 Model Development

First task in model development process was aimed on knowledge elicitation from the experts. There are numerous knowledge elicitation techniques (Pedricz, 1998; Siler, 2005), but for this project, *typical case method* was used.

Model development process contained following steps:

- Knowledge elicitation (interviews with experts).
- Recognising main meta categories in model based on interviews (like profitability… loyalty…).
- Linguistic variable definition and their connection to meta categories.
- Model structure development.
- Data pre-processing from database
- Rule definition
- Model testing
- Model applying

Typical case method, gives task to experts to describe characteristics of most valuable customer. This task has several iterations in correlation with level of abstraction. First iteration was concentrated on highest level of abstraction, and experts defined which terms best describes most valuable customer. After brainstorming, it was clear that we could operate with four major abstract terms:

- Profitability
- Loyalty
- Perspective
- Riskiness

First level of abstraction was used as base for the further development of fuzzy expert system structure. Next iteration was concentrated on deeper definition of recognized terms. For example perspective was defined through campaign responding ratio in one year period, trend of product usage in one year period, number of calls in call center for questioning about new products and services, paying bills on time, and some other behavioral characteristic. Forthcoming iteration comes closer to data definition in database, what was the final aim. The idea was, to find path from terms in highest level of abstraction to database attributes, and to connect them through rule blocks within fuzzy expert system. After process of knowledge elicitation, basic relations from the high level abstract terms to database attributes were presented with mind map. It was solid basic point for fuzzy expert system shell construction.

Next task in expert system development was to concentrate on linguistic variable definition, and rules definition. Next figure shows structure of developed fuzzy expert system for customer value calculation.

11.3.4.3 Using Fuzzy Expert System for Prospective Customer Value Calculation

Additional benefit from the model was ability to find out reason why each of subscribers was categorized into one of the defined category. For example customer can have average customer value, because he or she is average profitable for the company but not perspective, and medium risky. He or she is not perspective, because campaign responding ratio is low, trend of product usage in one year period is low, number of calls in call center for questioning about new products and services are low, and he or she does not have habit to pay bills on time.

From the other hand fuzzy expert system gives us opportunity to look at customer structure on very high level, and to make judgment, what is our weakest or strongest characteristic of portfolio structure. Next figure shows main portfolio structure calculated through concentrations within four major abstract terms presented in next figure.

It is visible that the major factors, which cause downgrade into lower category, was loyalty and perspective. Subscriber value downgrading is in correlation with loyalty and subscriber perspective. This fact leads us to conclusion that loyalty and perspective are the weakest factors into subscriber population. Main hypothesis was that subscribers during their lifecycle migrate from better to worst level of loyalty and perspective. To prove that hypothesis, Cox regression model was developed. Model shows that average of 25% of all subscribers migrate from zone of very high customer value to high customer value in period of one year. Model also shows that in average 18% of all subscribers migrate in zone of high customer value to average customer value in period of one year. Same model shows that key driven factors for those migrations are loyalty and perceptiveness, which became weaker and weaker as period of existence in portfolio are closeness to one year. Main influences which were recognized, like influencers on loyalty and perceptiveness are intensity of usage contracted services, responding on campaigns, and stopping usage of some contracted services. Recognized trend were mainly responsible for downgrades in zone of most valuable subscribers. Most valuable customers were in scope of analyze with intention to find out the reasons for migrations to less valuable categories. Data, which were used for, analyze, had limits regarding information about subscriber profiles. Except basic socio demographic data from the contract, product usage data, and billing information, there were no additional data which can be useful for profiling and deeper investigation why subscribes has decreased trend in usage of contracted services, why do they do not respond on campaigns, and why do they stop in usage of some contracted services.

11.3.4.4 Using REFII Model for In-Depth Investigation

Due to the limited information insufficient for profiling, additional data sources were investigated. Regarding fact that about 82% of all subscribers use IP TV as service, IP TV was recognized as potentially valuable data source for profiling purposes. Mitigating circumstance was fact that around 92% customers which were recognized as most valuable use IP TV. The idea was to analyze their behavior in IP TV usage through watched channel and period of time when they watch those channels with intention to find out more information about their profiles. This step was crucial for customer behavior recognition, and recognizing important patterns important for making customer segments. Basis for such conclusion was time series from IP TV data sources on which was applied REFII model. Analysis was done only on most valuable customer segments recognized by Fuzzy expert system.

If we take in consider that most of the subscribers lives with their families, it would be mistake to neglect time component of the analysis. Some of the family members could watch some of the channels during the week at same period of time, and other family members could watch some other channels during the week at other period of time. Watching specific channels, or group of specific channel, in correlation with days and specific day of the week, give us opportunity for profile recognition. Challenge was to make segmentation based on watching habits taking in account temporal factors. For this purpose REFII model was used (Klepac, 2013). Basic functionality of REFII model is time series transformation into form adequate for temporal data mining with conventional (clustering, decision trees, self-organizing maps ..) and unconventional data mining techniques. Transformation process of time series into REFII model is given by following algorithm (Klepac, 2013).:

Time series can be expressed as a sequences of values S(s1,..,sn), where S represents the time series and (s1,..,sn) represent the elements in the S series.

Step 1- Time Interpolation: Creation of auxiliary time series Vi(vi1,..,vin) on interval <1..n> (days, weeks, months, quarters, years) with the value 0. Based on the created sequence, interpolation of the missing values in S(s1,..,sn) with the value 0 based on the created sequence Vi is carried out. The result of processing is the series S(s1,..,sn) with interpolated missing values from the series Vi(vi1,..,vin).

Step 2- Time Granulation: In this step the degree of compression of time series S(s1,..,sn) in the elementary time unit (day, week, month…) is defined. In the second step, the elements of the existing time series are compressed by using statistical functions such as sum, average and mode on the level of the granulated segment. In that way, the time series can be converted to a higher degree of granulation (days into weeks, weeks into months…), resulting in the time series S(s1,..,sn) with a higher degree of granulation. Depending on the objectives we can return to this step during the process of analysis, which means that the processes described in the following steps must also be repeated.

Step 3- Standardization: The standardization procedure consists of transformation of the time series S(s1,..,sn) into the time series T(t1,..,tn), in which each element in the series is subjected to min-max standardization on interval <0,1>, where

  a. Time series T consists of the elements (t1,.., tn), where t_i is calculated as $t_i=((s_i- \min(S))/(\max(S)-\min(S))$, in which $\min(S)$ and $\max(S)$ represent the minimum and maximum value of time series S.

  b. The time variation between elementary patterns (time complexity measure) of the segment on the X axis is defined as $d(t_i,t_{i+1})=a$

Step 4– Transformation to REF Notation: According to the formula $Tr=t_{i+1}- t_i$ $Tr > 0 =>R; Tr< 0 =>F; Tr=0 =>E$, where Y_i are elements of series Ns

Step 5– Calculation of Angle Coefficient:

Angle coefficient=>

Tr > 0 (R) Coefficient = t i+1-t i

Tr < 0 (F) Coefficient = t i -t i+1

Tr = 0 (E) Coefficient = 0

Step 6 – Calculation of area beneath the curve: Method of numeric integration based on the rectangle

p= ((t i*a)+(t i+1*a))/2

Step 7– Creation of Time Indices: Building of a hierarchical index tree depending on the characteristics of the analysis, in which an element of the structured index can also be an attribute, such as the client code.

Step 8– Creating Categories: Derived attribute values creation based on area beneath the curve and the angle coefficient. It is possible to create categories by application of standard *crisp* logic or by application of *fuzzy* logic.

Step 9: Connecting the REFII model transformation tables with relational tables containing attributes which do not have a temporal dimension.

As a final result of transformation into REFII model each subscriber (account) was represent as it is shown in Table 9.

Basis for time series creation was minutes within one day when IP TV was switched on. Granularity level was day as elemental time span, and each subscriber was represented by time series, which were two years long. This REFII representation gives us opportunity for temporal data mining, and profiling because additional attributes on daily level were ratio of watching specific group of channels. Channel grouping was done by channel thematic like sport, documentary, movies, local tv channels, national channels, cartoon channels, comedy channel etc.

Each record within table represents data for the one subscriber and his behavior within one specific day determined with time segment index. Time segment index was constructed that it represents specific day within two years. Index contains information about day, month, and specific day of the year with stress on the day in week. This index structure is suitable for deeper analysis about subscriber habits on daily level and trends regarding usage of IP TV.

Table 9. Subscriber habits in REFII notation

Subscriber Number	Time Segment Index	REF Mark	Angle Coefficient	Area of Time Segment	Channel A	Channel B	Channel N
1	I1	REF1	Angle coefficient 1	P1	%	%	%
1	I3	REF2	Angle coefficient 2	P2	%	%	%
1	I3	REF3	Angle coefficient 3	P3	%	%	%
n	In	REFn	Angle coefficient n	Pn	%	%	%

REF mark, angle coefficient and area beneath time segments derived from minutes of watching IP TV are core elements of REFII model. Additional attributes represented as "Channel A", "Channel B",... "Channel n", represents ratio in watching some specific channel within one day and period within one day when IP TV was switched on. Area beneath the curve was used as tool for calculation intensity of watching channels.

During analysis process one unusual segment was discovered. This segment represents undecided watchers, or a watcher, which continuously changes program channels. This segment was assigned to channel grouping as an additional attribute.

REFII transformation and assignation of channel groups gave good foundation for deeper data investigation. First analysis was aimed on finding out expected combination of watching channels in global (during whole observation period), and on daily basis for each subscriber.

Next step was concentrated on creating clusters based on previous findings.

A final result shows few interesting patterns:

- 18% subscribers mostly looks movies only.
- 9% subscribers mostly look movies in combination with cartoons, and remain period they acts as undecided watchers.
- 7% subscribers mostly looks sport channels, and in remain period they acts as undecided watchers.
- 3% subscribers mostly looks comedy channel, documentary channels, and cartoon channels.
- 14% subscribers mostly looks cartoon channels only, and in remain period they acts as undecided watchers.
- 5% subscribers mostly looks documentary channels only, and in remain period they acts as undecided watchers.

Next question was, if there is any temporal relation between observed patterns? For this purpose REFII notation was also used in combination with OLAP reports. That combination revealed some new facts:

- Subscribers, which mostly look movies, only, watch TV very rare during week, and they watch TV mostly during weekend. Intensity of watching IP TV grows during period of weekend, and it falls during rest of the week.
- Subscribers, which mostly look movies in combination with cartoons, and remain period they acts as undecided watchers, watch movies mostly during week, and they watch cartoons mostly during weekend. Intensity of watching IP TV is during week is much higher than during weekend.
- Subscribers, which mostly look sport channels, and in remain period, act as undecided watchers watches TV mainly in second part of the day. Their intensity of watching IP TV is mostly the same during whole week.
- Subscribers, which mostly look, cartoon channels only, and in remain period acts as undecided watchers acts as undecided watchers during whole week, and they watch cartoon channels during weekend. For those subscribers it is evident that they much intensive use IP TV during weekend.

Revealed knowledge gives us some idea about profiles and needs among subscribers. Term "mostly" in analysis means "watching some specific channel group more than 20% into observed time span". Regarding watching cartoon channels we can assume existence of children and families, and regarding watching some specific channel group we can roughly set up hypothesis about subscriber profiles. Recognized segments were used in next analytical stage for churn probability measurement. Undecided watchers were extracted as additional segment, and all subscribes which showed those characteristic within some recognized segment were assigned to additional stand-alone group. OLAP analysis on REFII transformation gave additional relations and patterns, including details about watching preferences of subscribers, which prefer some specific group of channel, within those groups. This analysis finds out for example that subscribers which are mostly looking movies in combination with cartoons, and remain period they act as undecided watchers, watches movies mostly during week, and they watch cartoons mostly during weekend, prefer to watch channels with old movies. Also, subscribers, which mostly look documentary channels only, and in remain period they act as undecided watchers, prefer to watch documentary channels dedicated to history and UFO related themes. After analytical activities related to IP TV, similar models were developed for fix telephone line users, and mobile telephone users. Recognized segments were compared with discovered segments within IP TV users which already use mobile phone or fix line.

Most interesting finding was:

- Subscribers, which mostly look sport channels, and in remain period, act as undecided watchers watches TV mainly in second part of the day. Their intensity of watching IP TV is mostly the same during whole week. They intensive use mobile phones in first part of the day, and during weekend they raise in mobile phone usage during whole day.
- Subscribers which mostly looking cartoon channels only, and in remain period acts as undecided watchers acts as undecided watchers during whole week, and they watch cartoon channels during weekend. For those subscribers it is evident that they much intensive use IP TV during weekend. These subscribers prefer fix line, mostly at the evening during whole week, and their activities regarding using fix line drops during period of weekend.

Reveled information gives a general overview about existence of subscriber segments, and it could be useful for setting important hypothesis for finding main churn triggers. Presented analysis does not provide answers on question why, and who will break contract, but it was valuable for understanding existing subscriber behavior.

As shown in Figure 9, fuzzy expert system at the end gives unique value, which represents customer value. This value is represented through five linguistic categories:

- Very high customer value
- High customer value
- Average customer value
- Low customer value
- Very low customer value

Whole system had 597 rules, 46 input variables, 26 output variables, 26 rule blocks, and 200 linguistic terms. For the purpose of data entry into the model, Extract Transform Load process was developed on existing databases. After applying model on extracted data, all subscribers were categorized into one of the final linguistic categories, which represent subscriber value from the perspective of *Veza* company.

11.3.5 Churn Prediction Model Development

When we are talking about classical churn predictive models, major task is to build model, which should be able to calculate probability of churn for each subscriber, which already signed contract. For this purpose logistic regression and neural network were used.

Figure 8. Structure of developed fuzzy expert system

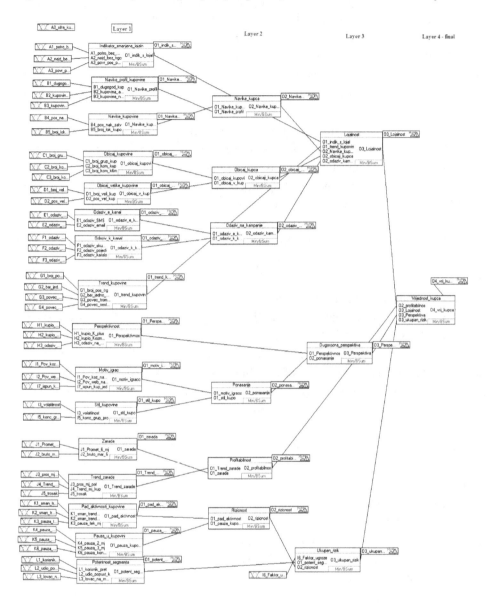

Churn prediction modeling was divided in following steps:

- Data sample creation (most valuable customers included only).
- Splitting basic sample in two samples (development and test sample).
- Attribute relevance analyses.
- Creating dummy variables.

- Correlation calculation on created dummy variables.
- Model development using logistic regression and neural network.
- Predictive power measuring using ROC curve and KS test.
- Selecting most appropriate model regarding ROC and KS.
- Calculation churn probability for most valuable customers and expressing probabilities as score.

Before modeling it is important to construct appropriate development sample, and to recognize attributes which is most relevant for model development. During the process of model development it is most important thing to understand reasons of churn. On the one hand in modeling process existing variables from data sources could be used, but variables, which shows most predictive characteristic, are behavioral variables. They describe subscriber behavior in service usage. This kind of variables is mostly derived from existing ones. In their construction analyst should consult business owner, because they can suggest additional variable construction based on experience.

It is not unusual, that in the first phase after cooperation with the experts, numerous derived variables are generated. In this phase huge number of potential predictors (variables) exists in initial sample. During the process of attribute relevance analysis, for each variable predictive power is measured, and in that way we also test hypothesis about importance of variables derived by experts, or variables which been selected from the databases. After attribute relevance assessment, it is possible to make rough expertise about churner profile, based on most predictive variables.

11.3.5.1 Data Preparation and Data Sampling

Important thing in building predictive models is appropriate sample construction. Predictive models should reflects business reality and expectance, which means that constructed sample should represent holistic picture of the subscriber portfolio, with adequate number of churner population which is sufficient for model building. As shown in Figure 9, sample for model developing should be constructed taking in consideration three main parts:

- Outcome period
- Observation point
- Observation period

Outcome period is used for churn recognition. If subscriber brakes contract in this period, it is marked as churner. In model development sample attribute *churn* in that case has value *churn="Yes"*, otherwise *churn="No"*. Observation point has

Figure 9. Data sample

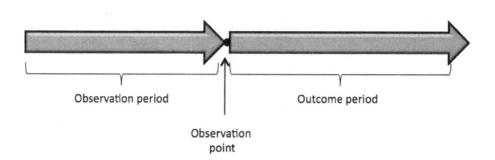

orientation role during sample construction, it defines border, which splits observation period from outcome period. If we take in account subscriber's socio demographic and other static characteristic like for example "number of services used", this is time point from which we take those characteristic. Observation period was used for calculating characteristics of derived variables such as: average minutes in the evening when IP TV was turned on during observation period or average number of late night calls from mobile phone during observation period, average number of calls in call center during observation period. Presented technique is known as fixed window sample creation technique, and it is convenient for situations when we do not have significant number on newcomers during observed period. *Veza* company in their portfolio had contractors which mostly signed contracts few years ago, and those contractors shows bad performance regarding churn in period of last observed year. Sample of part time contractors, which entered into portfolio 4 months before observation point, as a result of one specific campaign, was removed from the sample. It was evident that most of the contracts were stopped 7 months from observation point. Churn rate was 6.9%. In case of *Veza* company outcome period was 9 months long (9 months from observation point), and observation period was 12 months long. This sample had relatively statistically sufficient number of churners for the purpose of predictive model development. In case when it became problem, one of the possible solution is to extend outcome period. With this technique, we can extend outcome period too much in way that we can capture historically irrelevant period. It has implication also on observation period, because we are doing calculation of behavioral characteristic on old data. Those activities could result with unrealistic and unstable models. *Veza* company had good performance from statistical point of view, regarding ratio between number of churners, and data freshness.

11.3.5.2 Attribute Relevance Analysis

Main task of attribute relevance analysis is reducing number of predictors, which entered into the model by predictive power criteria.

In situation when aim variable has two states (it is common situation in churn modeling), as attribute relevance analysis method information value calculation could be used. First step in information value calculation is calculating weight of evidence. Weight of evidence gives a detailed insight to variable distribution and their partial impact on aim variable. This stage is crucial for understanding relations within predictors and aim variable. With this information it is possible to find out patterns, which has strongest impact aim variable (churn flag). For prediction model development in specific area like in finance, logical weight of evidence trend could be also another selection beside predictive power criteria for model building (Thomas, 2002). In churn modeling, logical weight of evidence trend is welcome, but variable with strong predictive power could be removed from the building sample only if weight of evidence trend is extremely illogical. Information value calculation uses weight of evidence calculation for predictive power calculation. Final calculation should provide list of most predictive variables due to aim variable. Strong predictive models in average contain 6-10 predictors, which is selected through attribute relevance analysis process. Formulas for weight of evidence calculation and information value calculation are shown below:

$$WoE = \ln\left(\frac{D_{nc}}{D_c}\right)$$

$$IV = \left(D_{nc_i} - D_{c_i}\right) * \ln\left(\frac{D_{nc_i}}{D_{c_i}}\right)$$

Weight of evidence is calculated as a natural logarithm of ratio between distribution of non-churners (Dnc) and churners (Dc) in distribution spans. Information value is calculated as sum of differences between distribution of non-churners and churners in distribution spans and product of corresponding weight of evidence. Regarding task for the churn predictive model development for *Veza* company, weight of evidence and information value were calculated. As a base for calculation 183 variables (potential predictors) were used. Those 183 variables were socio-demographic variables, behavior variables, variables derived by expert (mostly ratio oriented), segments reveled after applying fuzzy expert system described in first part of the chapter.

After calculation some variables with highest predictive power in sample were:

- Undecided watchers (yes/no).
- Segment of subscribers which mostly looking cartoon channels only, and in remain period acts as undecided watchers acts as undecided watchers during whole week, and they watch cartoon channels during weekend (member of the segment: yes/no).
- Number of used services.
- Number of long distance calls.
- County
- Age
- Average number of rejected calls (mobile phone) by operator within month.
- Number of calls to Veza's call center in last observed quarter.
- Usage trend of contracted services.

There were also more variables with average significant predictive power, but enumerated variables had highest predictive power in the sample. Those variables after dummy variable creation based on weight of evidence calculation and correlation calculation were used for model development.

11.3.5.3 Model Development Using Logistic Regression, Survival Analysis, and SNA

After recognition of most predictive variables, and correlation calculation between them, logistic regression and neural network were used for building predictive churn models on development sample. Initial sample has been split on development sample and test sample in ratio 80%: 20%.

Idea of building traditional predictive churn models is to develop tool for calculation churn probability. Model based on logistic regression showed better performance on test sample with area under ROC curve 78,4%, versus model based on neural network with area under ROC curve 71,8%.

Model was applied on recent sample, with result presented in Figure 10.

Subscribers with lower score given from the model has higher probability of churn, and there are mostly concentrated on scale from 0-200, other subscribers with higher probability of churn are spread on scale from 200-600, but their concentration in given bins are not so high like in zone from 0-200. It is important to mention that we are talking about most valuable subscribers, recognized through fuzzy expert system. Decision was to set up the cut off for churn observation on 300 points, because this scale contains about 80% of all potentially recognized churners. Model recognized 21% potential churners in future period. Subscriber, which has more than 300 points, is not so risky in relation with subscriber, which has less than 300 points.

Figure 10. Churner concentration by model score

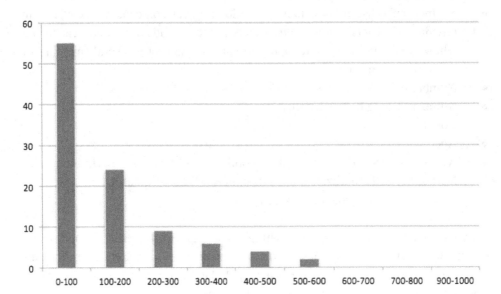

After predictive model development, survival analysis (Cox's regression) was used on each variable recognized as relevant for churn prediction. Survival analysis was done for period of 12 months. Survival analysis discovered some new fact from the data:

- Segment of subscribers which mostly look cartoon channels only, and in remain period acts as undecided watchers acts as undecided watchers during whole week, and they watch cartoon channels during weekend have worst survival rate than other segments. This segment from initial 100% dropped to 70% after 12 months.
- Subscribers with more services has better survival rate than subscribers with less services.
- Subscribers with more long distance calls have worst survival rate than subscribers without or few long distance calls.
- Younger and middle aged subscribers has worst survival rate than older subscribers.
- Subscribers with more rejected calls (mobile phone) by operator within month has worst survival rate than subscribers without rejected calls or few rejected calls.

- Subscribers with more number of calls to Veza's call center in last observed quarter has worst survival rate than subscribers without calls to call center or few calls.

Most surprising discovered fact was evident difference about survival rate between Undecided watchers segment, and other segments, which does not belong to this category.

Results are presented in Figure 11.

As it is visible from figure 92, if subscribes belongs to undecided watcher segment after 12 months only 20% of population will survive. This segment was defined through results of REFII model and represent subscribes in any other segment, which additionally has characteristic of undecided watchers. Finally, Social Network Analysis was applied on whole subscriber population, not only on most valuable ones. Reason for that laid in fact those subscribers which could have strong influence on other subscribers, does not have to be valuable for the *Veza* company or with high probability of churn. Problem is, if they will sometime in the future commit churn, it could cause serious damage from churn perspective on significant part of portfolio. Social Network Analysis has task to recognize those influencers.

For this purpose following Social Network Analysis metrics was used:

Figure 11. Survival rate undecided watchers vs. watchers within this category

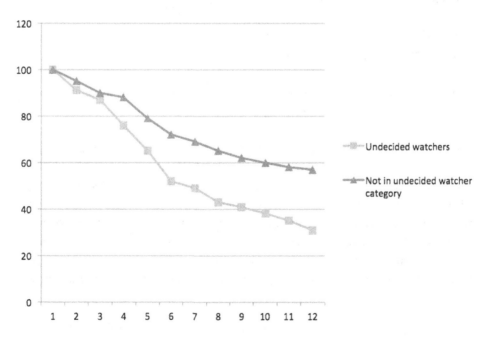

- Closeness
- Eigenvector
- Degree
- Betweenness

Using mentioned metrics 3% of influencers within subscriber population have been recognized. Most interesting thing was that:

- 34% of them was not recognized as valuable subscribers.
- 28% of them belongs to undecided watchers segment.
- 14% of them has churn score less than 300 which imply on high churn probability.

Regarding to the given results, it has been potentially high danger within recognized influencers. Recognized subscribers had great influence on other subscribers, and if they churn it could cause uncontrolled churn of other subscribers. If we take in consider influencer's structure, 34% of them are not valuable subscribers, which means that regarding on focus at most valuable subscriber we could neglect it in case that we did not apply Social Network Analysis on whole population . On the other hand, *undecided watchers* segment (28%) has bad survival rate, which means that 80% of them will probably churn of and it could have a consequence on great part of the other subscribers. Similar situation is with 14% of influencers with calculated high churn probability.

11.3.6 Discovered Knowledge as a Base for Churn Mitigation Strategies and New Products Development

Every analysis from business perspective does not have sense, if it cannot be used for making business decision. Regarding that, all given results have been consolidated, and observed as one big picture. First step has been focused on most valuable customer recognition. This step helped in budget saving and precise sample creation for further model development as well. As a result *Veza* company realized that it has problem with subscriber's loyalty, and perspective of existing subscribers. After REFII model was applied on reduced sample of existing subscribers (most valuable), several subscriber segments and their characteristics have been discovered.

Developed logistic regression model was used for churn probability calculation. After calculating churn probability, as a most important segments with highest probability which highly contribute in churn, following segment were recognized:

- Subscribers, which mostly look sport channels, and in remain period, act as undecided watchers, intensive use mobile phones in the first part of the day, and during weekend they raise in mobile phone usage during whole day.
- Subscribers which mostly watches cartoons, and in remain period, act as undecided watchers and act as undecided watchers during whole week, watches cartoons during whole weekend, use fixed line at the evening during whole week, except weekend.
- Subscribers which mostly looks documentary channels only, and in remain period, act as undecided watchers, prefer to watch channels dedicated to history and UFO related themes.

Common characteristic for the all recognized segments are fact that all of them has subscribers, which acts as undecided watchers. Undecided watchers characteristic has been recognized as strong predictor at attribute relevance analysis stage. Same characteristic showed strong negative influence on survival rate. Hypothesis about more than one users of IP TV behind one subscriber should not be neglected, and following hypothesis is that offered channel packages should adapt to recognized segments. Other visible fact has been that characteristic of "to use IP TV" has highest influence in segmentation and churn analysis then characteristic of "use land line" or "to use mobile phone". For the first segment, additional analysis was done, and there were no additional useful information after analysis about reasons why do they behave as undecided watchers. Decision was to offer them option with lower prices on fix line with few new cartoon channels in existing IP TV service package.

Members of the second segment were obviously families with small kids. Decision was to offer them option with lower prices on mobile services with few new cartoon channels in existing IP TV service package. Members of the third segment got new sport channels dedicated to history and UFO related themes within existing IP TV service package.

During model development process two interesting facts have been noticed:

- Subscribers with more rejected calls (mobile phone) by operator within month has worst survival rate than subscribers without rejected calls or few rejected calls.
- Subscribers with more number of calls to Veza's call center in last observed quarter has worst survival rate than subscribers without calls to call center or few calls.

Calls can be rejected in existing service packages if subscriber does not have enough additional money on account for establishment of call. Existing package offers some amount of data transfer in MB, number of minutes for calls and SMS for fixed price, which should be paid at the beginning of the month, but each establishment of call should be paid additionally. That means if subscriber can have unused minutes for calls, but it could not be used if does not have money on account (or he/she already spend it) for establishment of call. Surprisingly this finding was in connection with other one- number of calls to *Veza's* call center in last observed quarter. There were significant percentage of customers who has many short calls by mobile phones and they have problems with additional payments. They made complaints to *Veza's* call center regarding that situation. As it became evident, that situation has serious impact on churn. Management of *Veza's* company decided to decrease for 50% establishment of call fees, regarding discovered pattern.

Finally, it was decided that all influencer recognized by Social Network Analysis should get additional benefits and discounts, regarding to segment to which they have been recognized. For the non-valuable customers recognized as influencers *Veza* company will give additional discounts on used services. Regarding changes in prices and services adoption, as well as other measures, *Veza* company mitigated in following next 12 month period. Created models are still in use and quarterly reviewed as a tool for churn detection.

11.3.7 Case Discussion

Real data-mining projects requests usage of several data mining methods for achieving defined goals. Churn projects in telecom industry is no exception. Presented case study is description of one real data-mining project for east European telecommunication company which had problem with increasing churn trends. Traditional solutions for churn prediction are mostly based on developing predictive models, which calculates probabilities that customer will break contract.

Advantage of presented solution was holistic approach, which takes in consider fact that every subscriber does not have the same value for the company, and company should concentrate on spending budget on most valuable clients, instead of spending budget for churn mitigation to whole client portfolio. After realizing who is worth for further marketing activities, next movement is concentrated on finding behavioral patterns and churn probabilities for the most valuable clients. That approach leads us to the fact that we could spend more of the budget on valuable customers. Client evaluation, presented through soft aspects as loyalty or riskiness, instead of client evaluation based on profitability is much more objective, but also much more complicated. Thanks to Fuzzy expert systems chapter shows how it was done for this case study. This step was crucial for following activities, revealing customer habits and creation traditional probabilistic churn model on most valuable customer data sample. Project would be insufficient without SNA analytics on whole portfolio, because less valuable customers can cause problems in case that they commit churn as a network leaders.

Presented approach showed good results for the specific company taking in consider their market position, data sources and market conditions. Case does not have intention for introducing some new churn method. It shows how real world problem in domain of churn could be solved by chaining different data mining methods, and how the given results could be used for better decision making in domain of churn mitigation. Presented solution shoved good performance in presented case, but success of presented methodological approach on some other telecom company depend on portfolio structure, data sources and many other factors. In general, idea that predictive models and behavioral characteristics models should be developed on most valuable customer sample is universal, as a fact that SNA analytics should be done on whole population.

11.3.8 Case Conclusion

Case study does not have intention for introducing some new churn method. It shows how real world problem in domain of churn could be solved by chaining different data mining methods, and how the given results could be used for better decision making in domain of churn mitigation. Taking in consider that fact, it is possible to introduce some new elements and analysis into churn detection/mitigation solution as using clustering methods for customer segments recognition.

Revealed segments could be used as input variables for survival analysis, and also could be investigated with methods like decision trees for segment profiling. It could be much alternative ways for reaching similar information usable in decision support for presented case study. There is no cookbook for churn detection. Same company at same time with same data sources, with same problem, but in different market conditions probably needs some different solution for successful decision-making. Introducing new data mining methods into presented solution as potentially useful elements could discover some new dimensions and ideas for better decision-making process. Real world data mining solutions are always complex in way of chaining and usage more than one data mining methods. Presented churn project in telecommunication industry is not exception in complexity. Usage of numerous data mining methods is not guarantee of project success. Even more important is cooperation between analyst and business insider within company, which initiate project, and creativity of all project members. Traditional assurance, that churn modeling is developing predictive model, which calculates probabilities, is not correct. It is more than that. We should understand why churn has begun, who are the churners, do we concentrate on most valuable customers because of limited budget and how to stop them in the future. Simple predictive models calculate probabilities, and in process of developing we can get rough picture about churn reasons without deeper expertise. For deeper expertise usage of various data mining methods is must. Unfortunately there is no cookbook for the churn modeling, each business case is unique story, and each step forward in analysis can change initial analysis direction. Most important of all things is to derive useful information for decision support, because main aim of business modeling with data mining methods is knowledge recognition, which can be applied in decision-making. Presented case study shows business cooperation synergy of all team members and data mining method usage regarding recognized business problem.

REFERENCES

Aracil, J., & Gordillo, F. (Eds.). (2000). *Stability Issues in Fuzzy Control*. Heidelberg, Germany: Physica-Verlag.

Berry, J. A. M., & Linoff, G. (1997). Data mining techniques for marketing sales and customer support. New York: John Wiley & Sons Inc.

Berry, J. A., & Linoff, G. (2000). *Mastering data mining*. New York: John Wiley &Sons Inc.

Berry, J. A., & Linoff, G. (2003). *Mining the web*. New York: John Wiley &Sons Inc.

Dresner, H. (2008). *Performance management revolution*. New York: John Wiley &Sons Inc.

Faulkner, M. (2003). *Customer management excellence*. New York: John Wiley &Sons Inc.

Giudici, P. (2003). *Applied Data Mining: Statistical Methods for Business and Industry*. New York: John Wiley &Sons Inc.

Klepac, G. (2010). Preparing for New Competition in the Retail Industry. In A. Syvajarvi, & J. Stenvall (Eds.), *Data Mining in Public and Private Sectors: Organizational and Government Applications* (pp. 245–266). Hershey, PA: Information Science Reference. doi:10.4018/978-1-60566-906-9.ch013

Klepac, G. (2014). Data Mining Models as a Tool for Churn Reduction and Custom Product Development in Telecommunication Industries. In P. M. Vasant (Ed.), *Handbook of Research on Novel Soft Computing Intelligent Algorithms: Theory and Practical Applications*. Hershey, PA: IGI Global.

Pedrycz, W., & Gomide, F. (1998). *An Introduction to Fuzzy Sets: Analysis and Design of Complex Adaptive Systems*. Cambridge, MA: MIT Press.

Siler, W., & Buckley, J. J. (2005). *Fuzzy expert sytems and fuzzy reasoning*. New York: John Wiley &Sons Inc.

KEY TERMS AND DEFINITIONS

Cox Regression: Survival analysis method.

Fuzzy Logic: Logic which presumes possible membership to more than one category with degree of membership, and which is opposite to (exact) crisp logic.

Fuzzy Expert System: Expert system based on fuzzy logic.

Scoring: Process of assignation of some usually numeric value as grade which show as performance of observed case/object.

Survival Analysis: Analysis that shows survival rate (example: from population of customers) in defined period of time.

Conclusion

In 1930s professor Rosenbleuth, medicine doctor and professor in Harvard Medical School, organized scientific meetings with different young scientists where they discussed different topics and problems and share experience of method they are using. They found areas which were not covered with researches inside traditional scientific fields. One of reasons for that is that those areas cannot be explored with traditional approaches. Those, "areas outside known borders" Mr. Norbert Wiener father of cybernetics called "nobody's land" and he focused mostly on those areas founding discipline later known as cybernetics.

Looking at usage of analytic method in business as a scientific field, it is obvious that it is needed to combine different areas (mathematics, information theory, system theory, game theory, chaos theory, economics etc.) to achieve synergic effect similar to one earlier seen in cybernetics. Competitive analytics is very open discipline, which is absorbing scientific achievements from other fields but in different way. It mostly deals with problems out of standard focus, which can't be solved with widely known patterns and methodologies. Therefore, methods have to be innovative or they simply won't work. By knowing this, it is important for researcher to be able to manage, explore and combine many methods to be able to solve complex business problems. Furthermore, to be able to manage different methods is one of the essential assumptions for efficient usage of business intelligence. Researcher needs to step out of mechanical step-by-step approach and try to do thing in different way over and over again, with every new step in iteration process. Even final goal is important, we can say that art of combining methods and focus on path have to be key drivers for performance. To be able to find answers with satisfying level of accuracy is crucial.

This kind of approach for usage of analytic methods in business can be best illustrated through practical business cases where methods are essential for every analysis and where goals are targeted in very precise way. Analysis goals were defined based on real business problems or with intention to improve business efficiency while every new step in iteration process is subordinated in order to reach targets. Of course, we can reach goals in many ways and that is where analyst should unlock its knowledge and skills in order to choose and combine methods and analytic instruments from different sciences. If researcher is over impressed with specific method or methods, it can be limitation factor and can affect results.

Having in mind complexity and analyst-centric environment, person able to provide high quality research have to fulfill many skills required like:

- Ability to understand large number of methods, tools and different methodologies,
- Has to be concise in analysis covering all relevant business facts and able to separate important from less important,
- Has to always consider several different methods and approaches while structuring problem area towards methods and not towards problems,
- Has to try to solve problem with every efficient method with same chance with outcome relevance ratio as major driver for method selection,
- Has to be able to combine different methods to reach higher efficiency level which can be crucial for business performance and adequate accuracy level.

Let us imagine a hypothetic situation from person A perspective. Person A has certain number of close friends. Person A knows what kind of reaction to simple situations can expect from every of his friends based on previous experience. If Person B was always late for meetings in average of 10 minutes, person A can estimate that he will be late again. Person C likes movies and he doesn't miss any of their meetings with overview of movies that are currently showing. Because of that, person A expects that their today's meeting will be enriched with Person's C comments to latest blockbuster. By knowing that Person C prefer classic instead of modern titles, Person A can expect very critical comments from Person C because new blockbuster is science-fiction based. Person D collect old books. Person D introduce his friend, Person E and also old book collector, into their group. Person A knows that next week antique fair will take place in their neighborhood and he can find Person D and Person E there.

Variety of patterns, behavior, interests and relations helps Person A to come to different conclusions. Let us imagine situation in with Person A did not have any contact or cognitive information about Persons B, C, D and E. We can easy assume that Person A won't be able to predict specific situations and behavior patterns of other persons. How is this related to our business?

In business, we are in daily pursuit of achievements aiming efficiency and profit. Even some of us may not like it, we always need to take a look from "the bottom" and understand our market segment and our customers to be able to create and develop our products and services. There is no use in creating service not needed by anybody.

There are many good reasons for development and management of churn models beyonf to impress executive management. One of most obvious is to provide lists to the marketing department giving them ability to be very precise both in targeting campaigns but also masuring campaing effects. Another application is customer lifetime value and potential by using calculations of length of time that customer are estimated to remain loyal. Another different application is prioritizing customer segments where SNA provide powerful improvement to traditional approach.

It is important to remember three most important churn modelling goals (among many others) (Berry & Linoff 2001):

- **Near-Term Goal:** Identifiy a list of probable churners
- **Mid-Term Goal:** Buil a churn management application
- **Long-Term Goal:** Create complete CRM (customer relationship management)

This book is covering certainly one of the most important topics that business people need to face today, how to better understand our customers and how to manage their experience with all pros and cons which are coming their way. We need to understand how to deal with strong rising trends but also with "bad days" managing whole perspective and being able to travel through time towards efficiency even with some setbacks which are normal.

After explaining key points of churn and churn management, this book is going step further in explaining most efficient techniques and field best practice approach combining author's 20+ years of experience pushing churn topic to higher level. Practical experience and "real life" approach so needed in these turbulent times is shown on examples from real projects making churn perspective completely covered for researcher, student or individual interested for this book. We should not let our experience mislead us neither we should think that future is already written. But, we need to face causes and consequences and accept that most things really are happening for a reason.

REFERENCES

Berry, M., & Linoff, G. (2001). *Mastering data mining*. New York: Wiley.

Appendix

SOFTWARE TOOLS AND APPLICATIONS FOR DATA MINING AND CHURN MANAGEMENT

Authors' Selection

Data mining and churn management software is generally used to identify, represent, analyze, visualize data. Especially for SNA analysis to simulate nodes (e.g. agents, organizations, or knowledge) and edges (relationships) from various types of input data (relational and non-relational), including mathematical models of social networks. The output data can be saved in external files. Various input and output file formats exist.

Various tools provide mathematical and statistical routines that can be applied to the research while ability to visually represent data is important to better understand data, network data and convey the result of the analysis. Visualization is often used as an additional or standalone data analysis method.

Our selection of tools with brief explanation and links is alphabetically summarized as follows.

IBM I2[1]

IBM i2 provides intelligence analysis, law enforcement and fraud investigation solutions. i2 offerings deliver flexible capabilities that help combat crime, terrorism and fraudulent activity. Consisting of several tools IBM I2 provide powerful family for intellignece, SNA and text analysis.

IBM SPSS Software[2]

Powerful software family for statistical analysis. IBM SPSS Statistics is one of the world's leading statistical software used to solve business and research problems by means of ad-hoc analysis, hypothesis testing, and predictive analytics. Organizations use IBM SPSS Statistics to understand data, analyze trends, forecast and plan to validate assumptions and drive accurate conclusions.

Microsoft Excel[3]

Part of Microsoft Office software family one of most popular spreadsheet tool with more features in every new version.

Network Overview Discovery Exploration for Excel (NodeXL)[4]

Tool for network overview, discovery and exploration. NodeXL is a free and open Excel 2007Add-in and C#/.Net library for network analysis and visualization. Itintegrates into Excel 2007 and 2010 and add directed graph as a chart type to the spreadsheet and calculates a core set of network metrics and scores. Supports extracting email, Twitter, YouTube, WWW and flickr social networks.

NetworkX[5]

Python package for the creation, manipulation, and study of the structure, dynamics, and functions of complex networks. NetworkX (NX) is a rich integrated toolset for graph creation, manipulation, analysis, and visualization. User interface is through scripting/command-line provided by python. NX includes a large set of key algorithms, metrics and graph generators. Visualization is provided through pylab and graphviz.

Orange for Python[6]

Open source data visualization and analysis for novice and experts. Data mining through visual programming or Python scripting. Components for machine learning. Add-ons for bioinformatics and text mining. Packed with features for data analytics.

Parc ACH[7]

Analysis of Competing Hypotheses (ACH) is a simple model for how to think about a complex problem when the available information is incomplete or ambiguous, as typically happens in intelligence analysis. ACH is grounded in basic insights from cognitive psychology, decision analysis, and the scientific method. It helps analysts protect themselves from avoidable error, and improves their chances of making a correct judgment.

Pajek[8]

Tool for analysis and visualization of large scale networks. A widely used program for drawing networks, Pajek also has significant analytical capabilities, and can be used to calculate most centrality measures, identify structural holes, block-model, and so on. Capable of combining data with R.

R[9]

R environment contains several packages relevant for social network analysis: igraph is a generic network analysis package; SNA performs sociometric analysis of networks; network manipulates and displays network objects; tnet performs analysis of weighted networks, two-mode networks, and longitudinal networks; ERGM implements exponential random graph models for networks; latentnet has functions for network latent position and cluster models; degreenet provides tools for statistical modeling of network degree distributions; and etworksis provide tools for simulating bipartite networks with fixed marginals.

SQL (Structured Query Language)

Structured Query Language, special-purpose programming language designed for managing data held in a relational database management system (RDBMS), together with Python and R standard for database data manipulation

Tableau[0]

Tableau is business intelligence software that allows anyone to connect to data in a few clicks, then visualize and create interactive, sharable dashboards with a few more. It's easy enough that any Excel user can learn it, but powerful enough to satisfy even the most complex analytical problems. Securely sharing your findings with others only takes seconds.

Xanalys Link Explorer[11]

Visual analytics tool combining link analysis with temporal and spatial analysis. Interactive visual analytics tool combining data acquisition and querying with link analysis, temporal analysis and spatial analysis (GIS) techniques. Integrates with other desktop applications and services such as Excel and Bing mapping

ENDNOTES

[1]   http://www-01.ibm.com/software/info/i2software/

[2]   http://www-01.ibm.com/software/analytics/spss/
      3 http://office.microsoft.com/en-us/excel/

[4]   http://nodexl.codeplex.com/

[5]   http://networkx.github.io/

[6]   http://orange.biolab.si/

[7]   http://www2.parc.com/istl/projects/ach/ach.html

[8]   http://vlado.fmf.uni-lj.si/pub/networks/pajek/

[9]   http://www.r-project.org/

[10] http://www.tableausoftware.com/

[11] http://www.xanalys.com/products/link-explorer/

Compilation of References

Ahn, J. H., Han, S. P., & Lee, Y. S. (2006). Customer churn analysis: Churn determinants and mediation effects of partial defection in the Korean mobile telecommunications service industry, Science direct. *Telecommunications Policy*, *30*(10-11), 552–568. doi:10.1016/j.telpol.2006.09.006

Ants Analytics. (2013) *The Executive's Guide to Reducing Customer Churn with Predictive Analytics*. Retrieved from www.11antsanalytics.com

Aracil, J., & Gordillo, F. (Eds.). (2000). *Stability Issues in Fuzzy Control*. Heidelberg, Germany: Physica-Verlag.

Barabási, A. L. (2002). Linked: The New Science of Networks. Cambridge, MA: Perseus. Available at http:\\barabasilab.com\networksciencebook

Berry, M., & Linhoff, G. (2004). Data Mining Techniques for Marketing Sales and Customer Support. Wiley.

Berry, J. A., & Linoff, G. (2000). *Mastering data mining*. New York: John Wiley & Sons Inc.

Berry, J. A., & Linoff, G. (2003). *Mining the web*. New York: John Wiley & Sons Inc.

Berry, M., & Linoff, G. (2004). *Data Mining Technique for marketing Sales and CRM*. Wiley.

Berson, Smith, & Therling. (1999). *Building data mining applications for CRM*. New York: McGraw-Hill.

Blass, T. (2004). *The Man Who Shocked the World: the life and legacy of Stanley Milgram*. New York, NY: Basic Books.

Bollobás, B. (2001). *Random Graphs* (2nd ed.). Cambridge, UK: Cambridge University Press. doi:10.1017/CBO9780511814068

Buckinx, & Van den Poel. (2005). Customer base analysis: Partial defection of behaviourally loyal clients in a noncontractual. *Europeaz Journal of Operational Research*, *164*, 252-268, 296.

Carpenter, H. (2009). *Foursquare + Square = Killer Small Business CRM*. Retrieved from http://bhc3.com/2009/12/14/

Carrington, P. J., Scott, J., & Wasserman, S. (Eds.). (2005). *Models and Methods in Social Network Analysis*. Cambridge, UK: Cambridge University Press. doi:10.1017/CBO9780511811395

Chandar, L. K. (2006). Modeling churn behavior of bank customers using predictive data mining techniques. Institute for Development and Research in Banking Technology(IDRBT).

Chu, B., Tsai, M., & Ho, T. (2007). Toward a hybrid data mining model for customer retention. *Knowledge-Based Systems*, *20*, 703–718. doi:10.1016/j.knosys.2006.10.003

Coleman, J. S. (1964). *Introduction to Mathematical Sociology*. Glencoe, IL: Free Press.

Cooper, C. (2011). *10 Tips for Retaining Loyal Guests*. Retrieved from http://www.hotelnewsnow.com/Articles.aspx/6068/10-tips-for-retaining-loyal-guests

Corr, J. (2008). *Why could 'frustration churn' be costing you over 15% of the potential value of your business?* London, UK: Close Quarter Limited.

Coser, L. A. (1977). Masters of Sociological Thought: Ideas in Historical and Social Context (2nd ed.). New York, NY: Harcourt.

Coser, L. A. (1977). *Masters of Sociological Thought: Ideas in Historical and Social Context* (2nd ed.). New York, NY: Harcourt.

Coussement, B., Benoit, D. F., & Van den Poel, D. (2010). Improved marketing decision making in a customer churn prediction context using generalized additive models. *Expert Systems with Applications*, *37*(3), 2132–2143. doi:10.1016/j.eswa.2009.07.029

CSBSJU. (n.d.). Retrieved from http://www.physics.csbsju.edu/stats/KS-test.html

Davis, G. F., Yoo, M., & Baker, W.E. (2003). The small world of the American corporate elite, 1982–2001. *Strategic Organization, 1*(3).

Davis, G. F., & Greve, H. R. (1997). Corporate Elite Networks and Governance Changes in the 1980s. *American Journal of Sociology, 103*(1), 1–37. doi:10.1086/231170

De Bock, K., & Van den Poel, D. (2010). Ensembles of Probability Estimation Trees for Customer Churn Prediction, Trends In Applied Intelligent Systems, Pt Ii. *Lecture Notes in Artificial Intelligence, 6097*, 57–66.

De Sola Pool, I., & Kochen, M. (1978). *Contacts and Influence. In Social Networks*. Amsterdam: Elsevier.

Dnevnik, P. (2008). *Marketing: Važne rodne razlike*. Author.

Dresner, H. (2008). *Performance management revolution*. New York: John Wiley &Sons Inc.

Engel, F. J., Blackwell, D. R., & Miniard, W. P. (1995). *Consumer Behavior*. The Dryden Press.

Erdös, P., & Rényi, A. (1960). *On the Evolution of Random Graphs*. Mathematical Institute of the Hungarian Academy of Sciences.

Erdös, P., & Rényi, A. (1961). On the strength of connectedness of a random graph. *Acta Math. Acad. Sci. Hungar., 12*.

Erdös, P., & Rényi, A. (1959). *On random graphs*. Debrecen: Math.

Faulkner, M. (2003). *Customer management excellence*. New York: John Wiley &Sons Inc.

Feller, W. (1971). *An Introduction to Probability Theory and Its Applications* (Vol. 2). Wiley.

Filip, A. (2012). *Best Practice: Requirements of CRM Processes*. Retrieved from http://www.ec4u.de/en/2012-09-24/best-practice-requirements-of-crm-processes

Freeman, L. C. (2004). The Development of Social Network Analysis: A Study in The Sociology of Science. Vancouver, Canada: Empirical Press.

Fullen, A. (2013). *Live from Mobile World Congress: How to Enhance the Customer Experience in the "First 90 Days"*. Retrieved from http://info.sundaysky.com/blog/bid/271910/Live-from-Mobile-World-Congress-How-to-Enhance-the-Customer-Experience-in-the-First-90-Days

GFK. (n.d.). *Stats report Croatia 1995-2010*. Retreived from http://www.gfk.hr/public_relations/press/press_articles/006398/index.hr.html

Giudici, P. (2003). *Applied Data Mining: Statistical Methods for Business and Industry*. New York: John Wiley &Sons Inc.

Gladwell, M. (2002). *The Tipping Point: How Little Things Can Make a Big Difference*. New York, NY: Back Bay Books.

Godin, S. (2008, June 26). Loš stol. *Livingstone Magazine Croatia*, 72-73.

Granovetter, M. S. (1973). The strength of weak ties. *American Journal of Sociology*, 78(6), 1360. doi:10.1086/225469

Guare, J. (1990). *Six Degrees of Separation: A Play*. New York, NY: Vintage Books.

Hadden, J., Ashtoush, T., Rajkumar, R., & Ruta, D. (2006). Churn Prediction: Does Technology Matter? *International Journal of Electrical and Computer Engineering*, 1, 6.

Hale, A. E. (1981). *Conducting Clinical Sociometric Explorations: A Manual for Psychodramatists and Sociometrists*. Roanoke, VA: Royal.

Haunschild, P. R. (1993). Interorganizational Imitation: The Impact of Interlocks on Corporate Acquisition Activity. *Administrative Science Quarterly*, 38(4), 564. doi:10.2307/2393337

Heuer, R. J., & Pherson, R. H. (2010). *Structured Analytic Techniques for Intelligence Analysis*. Washington, DC: CW Press College.

Hwang, T., & Suh, E. (2004). An LTV model and customer segmentation based on customer value: A case study on the wireless telecommunication industry. *Expert Systems with Applications*, 26(2), 181–188. doi:10.1016/S0957-4174(03)00133-7

Jackson, M. O. (2010). *Social and Economic Networks*. Princeton, NJ: Princeton University Press.

Karinthy, F. (1929). *Láncszemek: Minden másképpen van (Ötvenkét vasárnap)*. Budapest: Athenaeum, Irodalmi és Nyomdai Rt.

Kimball, R. (1996). *Data Warehouse Toolkit*. Wiley.

Kim, P., Park, M.-C., & Jeong, D.-H. (2004). The effects of customer satisfaction and switching barriers on customer loyalty in Korean mobile telecommunication services. *Telecommunications Policy*, 28(2), 145–159. doi:10.1016/j.telpol.2003.12.003

Kirkman, T. W. (1996). *Statistics to Use*. Retrieved from http://www.physics.csbsju.edu/stats/KS-test.html

Klepac, G. (2010). Preparing for New Competition in the Retail Industry. In A. Syvajarvi, & J. Stenvall (Eds.), *Data Mining in Public and Private Sectors: Organizational and Government Applications* (pp. 245–266). Hershey, PA: Information Science Reference. doi:10.4018/978-1-60566-906-9.ch013

Klepac, G. (2013). Risk Evaluation in the Insurance Company Using REFII Model. In S. Dehuri, M. Patra, B. Misra, & A. Jagadev (Eds.), *Intelligent Techniques in Recommendation Systems: Contextual Advancements and New Methods* (pp. 84–104). Hershey, PA: Information Science Reference.

Klepac, G. (2014). Data Mining Models as a Tool for Churn Reduction and Custom Product Development in Telecommunication Industries. In P. M. Vasant (Ed.), *Handbook of Research on Novel Soft Computing Intelligent Algorithms: Theory and Practical Applications*. Hershey, PA: IGI Global.

Klepac, G., & Panian, Ž. (2005). *Poslovna inteligencija*. Masmedia Zagreb.

Konno, T. (2008). *Network Structure of Japanese Firms: Analysis from 800,000 Companies*. Academic Press.

Kumar, S. (2005). *Understanding the Relationship Between Loyalty and Churn*. Retrieved from http://www.information-management.com/specialreports/20051018/1039409-1.html

Larose, D. T. (2005). *Discovering Knowledge in Data: An Introduction to Data Mining*. New York: John Wiley & Sons Inc. doi:10.1002/0471687545

Larose, D. T. (2006). *Data mining methods and models*. New York: John Wiley & Sons Inc.

Lazarov, V., & Capota, M. (2010). *Churn Prediction*. Retrieved from http://home.in.tum.de/~lazarov/files/research/papers/churn-prediction.pdf

Madden, Savage, & Coble-Neal. (1999). Subscriber churn in the Australian ISP market. *Information Economics and Policy, 11*(2), 195–207.

Majer, A. (2009). *The Selling Process*. Institut prodaje/Seles Institute. Retreived from http://kakoprodavati.com

Maletta, H. (2006). *Weighting*. Retreived from Rayland Levesque's website: http://www.spsstools.net/Tutorials/weighting.pdf

Mannila, H., & Hand, D. (2001). *Principles of Data Mining*. The MIT press.

Marconi, G. (1967). Wireless telegraphic communication. In *Nobel Lectures, Physics 1901-1921*. Amsterdam: Elsevier Publishing Company. Available at http://www.nobelprize.org/nobel_prizes/physics/laureates/1909/marconi-lecture.html

Markets and Markets. (2014). *Internet of Things (IoT) & Machine-To-Machine (M2M) Communication Market by Technologies & Platforms (RFID, Sensor Nodes, Gateways, Cloud Management, NFC, CEP, SCADA, ZigBee), M2M Connections, IoT Components - Worldwide Market Forecasts (2014 - 2019)*. Retrieved from http://www.marketsandmarkets.com/Market-Reports/internet-of-things-market-573.html

Masse, D. (2010). Cellular M2M Connections Will Show Steady. *Growth*. Retrieved from http://www.microwavejournal.com/articles/10376-cellular-m2m-connections-will-show-steady-growth-to-2015

Milgram, S. (1967). The Small-World Problem. *Psychology Today, 1*(1), 61–67.

Moreno, J. L. (1951). *Sociometry, Experimental Method, and the Science of Society*. Ambler, PA: Beacon House.

Compilation of References

Morik, K., & Opcke, H. (2004). Analyzing Customer Churn in Insurance Data. In *Proceedings of Knowledge Discovery in Databases* (LNCS) (vol. 3202, pp. 325-336). Berlin: Springer. doi: 10.1007/978-3-540-30116-5_31

Mršić, L. (2005). *Appliance of data mining methods in textile retail*. (Master of Science Thesis). Faculty of Economic and Business, Zagreb, Croatia.

Mršić, L. (2012). *Decision support model in retail based on unique time transformation method (REFII) and Bayesian logic*. (Doctoral Thesis). Faculty of Humanities and Social Sciences, Zagreb, Croatia.

Noize, V. (2015). *Financial. The Pro & Con of Groupon*. Retrieved from http://www.evancarmichael.com/Marketing/3973/The-Pro--Con-of-Groupon.html

Nolan, J. (2000). *Information on Stable Distributrions*. Retrieved from http://academic2.american.edu/~jpnolan/stable/stable.html

Osei-Bryson, K. (2004). Evaluation of decision trees: A multi-criteria approach. *Computers & Operations Research*, *31*(11), 1933–1945. doi:10.1016/S0305-0548(03)00156-4

Parks Associates. (2003). *US Mobile Market Intelligence August*. Author.

Pavlek, Z. (2008). *Marketing: Važne rodne razlike*. Poslovni dnevnik/Business daily.

Pedrycz, W., & Gomide, F. (1998). *An Introduction to Fuzzy Sets: Analysis and Design of Complex Adaptive Systems*. Cambridge, MA: MIT Press.

Peppers, R. (2008). *Rules to Break and Laws to Follow* example taken from *"Customer centricity int he telecommunications industry"*. Pitney Bowes Business Insight.

Pinheiro, C. A. R. (2011). *Social Network Analysis in Telecommunications*. Hoboken, NJ: John Wiley and Sons Inc.

Pitney Bowes Business Insight. (2011). *Customer centricity in the telecommunications industry*. Author.

Popović, D. (2009). Churn Prediction Model in Retail Banking Using Fuzzy C-Means Algorithm. *Faculty of Electrical Engineering and Computing*, *33*, 243–247.

Popović, D., & Dalbelo Bašić, B. (2009). Churn Prediction Model in Retail Banking Using Fuzzy C-Means Algorithm. *Faculty of Electrical Engineering and Computing*, *33*, 243–247.

Price Waterhouse Coopers. (2011). *Curing customer churn*. Author.

Rao, H., Davis, G. F., & Ward, A. (2000). Embeddedness, Social Identity and Mobility: Why Firms Leave the NASDAQ and Join the New York Stock Exchange. *Administrative Science Quarterly*, 45.

Rao, H., & Sivakumar, K. (1999). Institutional Sources of Boundary-spanning Structures: The Establishment of Investor Relations Departments in the Fortune 500 Industrials. *Organization Science*, 10.

Rapoport, A., & Horvath, W. J. (1961). A Study of a large sociogram. *Behavioral Science*, *6*(4), 279–291. doi:10.1002/bs.3830060402 PMID:14490358

Rashid, T. (2010). Classification of Churn and non-Churn Customers for Telecommunication Companies. *International Journal of Biometrics and Bioinformatics, 3*(5).

Ravasz, E., & Barabási, A. L. (2003). Hierarchical organization in complex networks. *Physical Review E: Statistical, Nonlinear, and Soft Matter Physics, 67*(2), 026112. doi:10.1103/PhysRevE.67.026112 PMID:12636753

Remer, R. (2006). Chaos Theory Links to Morenean Theory: A Synergistic Relationship. *Journal of Group Psychotherapy, Psychodrama, and Sociometry, 59*.

Remer, R. (2008). Sociometry. In W. A. Darity (Ed.), *International Encyclopedia of the Social Sciences* (2nd ed.). Detroit, MI: Macmillan Reference.

Retention Science. (n.d.). Retrieved from http://retentionscience.com/products/Pitney Bowes Business Insight. (2011). *Customer centricity in the telecommunications industry.* Author.

Reza, A., & Keyvan, R. (2012). Applying Data Mining to Insurance Customer Churn Management. In *Proceedings of 2012 IACSIT Hong Kong Conferences.* IACSIT Press.

Sarraf, S., & Chen, D. (2007). *Creating weights to improve survey population estimates.* Paper presented at the INAIR 21st Annual Conference. Bloomington, IN.

Sayad, S. (2014). *Model Evaluation – Classification.* Retrieved from http://www.saedsayad.com/model_evaluation_c.htm

Scott, J. (1987). *Social Network Analysis: A Handbook.* London: Sage Publications.

Silber. (1997). Combating the churn phenomenon. *Telecommunications, 31*(10), 77–81.

Siler, W., & Buckley, J. J. (2005). *Fuzzy expert sytems and fuzzy reasoning.* New York: John Wiley &Sons Inc.

Simmel, G. (1971). How is Society Possible?. In *On Individuality and Social Forms.* Chicago, IL: University of Chicago Press.

Simmel, G. (1971). How is Society Possible? In *On Individuality and Social Forms.* Chicago, IL: University of Chicago Press.

Soeini, R., & Rodpysh, K. (2012). Evaluations of Data Mining Methods in Order to Provide the Optimum Method for Customer Churn Prediction: Case Study Insurance Industry. In *Proceedings of 2012 International Conference on Information and Computer Applications* (ICICA 2012). ICICA.

SPSS Inc. (2007). *Clementine 12.0 Algorithms Guide.* Author.

Taper, T. G. (1999). *Interpreting Diagnostic Tests.* University of Nebraska Medical Center. Retrieved from http://gim.unmc.edu/dxtests/roc3.htm

Travers, J., & Milgram, S. (1969). An experimental study of the small world problem. *Sociometry, 32*.

Tsai, C., & Lu, Y. (2010). Data Mining Techniques in Customer Churn Prediction. Taiwan: Department of Information Management, National Central University.

Tsai, C., & Chen, M. (2010). Variable selection by association rules for customer churn prediction of multimedia on demand. *Expert Systems with Applications, 37*(3), 2006–2015. doi:10.1016/j.eswa.2009.06.076

Tsai, C., & Lu, Y. (2009). Customer churn prediction by hybrid neural networks. *Expert Systems with Applications, 36*(10), 12547–12553. doi:10.1016/j.eswa.2009.05.032

Compilation of References

Tsiptsis, K., & Chorianopoulos, A. (2010). *Data Mining Techniquies in CRM: Inside Customer Segmentation.* Wiley. doi:10.1002/9780470685815

UNMC. (n.d.). Retrieved from http://gim.unmc.edu/dxtests/Default.htm

Wang, Z. J. (2014). *Research On Customer Churn Early-warning Based On Neural Network.* Retrieved from http://www.economics-papers.com/research-on-customer-churn-early-warning-based-on-ig_nn-double-attribute-selection.html

Watts, D. J. (1999). *Small Worlds: The Dynamics of Networks between Order and Randomness.* Princeton, NJ: Princeton University Press.

Watts, D. J. (2004). The "New" Science Of Networks. *Annual Review of Sociology, 30*(1), 243–270. doi:10.1146/annurev.soc.30.020404.104342

Watts, D. J., & Strogatz, S. H. (1998). Collective dynamics of "small-world" networks. *Nature, 393*(6684), 440–442. doi:10.1038/30918 PMID:9623998

Whitten, I. H., & Frank, T. (2005). Data Mining. Elsevier.

Zhang, M. (2010). Social Network Analysis: History, Concepts, and Research. In *Handbook of Social Network Technologies and Applications.* New York, NY: Springer. doi:10.1007/978-1-4419-7142-5_1

About the Authors

Goran Klepac works as the head of the Strategic unit in the Sector of credit risk in Raiffeisenbank Austria Inc, Croatia, Europe. In several universities in Croatia, he lectures on subjects in domain of data mining, predictive analytics, decision support system, banking risk, risk evaluation models, expert system, database marketing and business intelligence. As a team leader, he successfully finished many data mining projects in different domains like retail, finance, insurance, hospitality, telecommunications, and productions. He is an author/coauthor of several books published in Croatian and English in the domain of data mining. (www.goranklepac. com).

Robert Kopal is a lecturer at several university colleges in Croatia, and at CROMA (Croatian Managers' and Entrepreneurs' Association) EduCare Program. He is an author and co-author of six books (on competitive intelligence analysis, game theory, etc.), numerous chapters in books of various authors, and more than 40 scientific and professional papers. He is a workshop manager and teacher at more than hundred business and intelligence analysis workshops, a designer of several specialized IT systems, and a certified trainer in the area of structured intelligence analysis techniques and SW. He is a SCIP and IALEIA member, has held presentations at various national and international conferences, and participated in and led a number of national and international intelligence analysis projects.

Leo Mršić graduated with a major in insurance, earned an MSc degree with a major in business statistics, and earned a PhD degree in data science all at the University of Zagreb, Croatia, Europe. Combining the business and technology approach, he has had great field experience related to many industries like retail, insurance, finance, ICT, business law, and project management. He has relevant top management and consulting experience participating in many projects across the supply chain with a focus on retail. He is active in conferences and is a guest lecturer on several university programs related to various aspects of business like management, consumer behavior, data science/data mining, and managing business risks. He is a Co-author on several books in the area of data science and it's appliance in business. He is a member of the board at Croatian Oracle Users Group, member and mentor in the Young Executives Society in Croatia, and a member of the Croatian Association of Court Expert Witnesses in Croatia.

Index

T

U

W